Personal Relationships. 2:

Developing Personal Relationships

Personal Relationships. 2:

Developing Personal Relationships

Editors

STEVE DUCK and
ROBIN GILMOUR

Department of Psychology,
University of Lancaster, England

1981

ACADEMIC PRESS
A subsidiary of Harcourt Brace Jovanovich, Publishers
London New York Toronto Sydney San Francisco

ACADEMIC PRESS INC. (LONDON) LTD.
24/28 Oval Road,
London NW1

United States Edition published by
ACADEMIC PRESS INC.
111 Fifth Avenue
New York, New York 10003

British Library Cataloguing in Publication Data

Personal relationships.
  2

  1. Interpersonal relationships
  I. Duck, Steven W.
  II. Gilmour, Robin
  301.11   HM132   80-41360

  ISBN 0-12-222802-2

Filmset by
Colset Private Ltd, Singapore

Printed in Great Britain by
Whitstable Litho Ltd, Whitstable, Kent

Contributors

JOHN K. ANTILL, School of Behavioural Sciences, Macquarie University, North Ryde, New South Wales 2113, Australia.

RODNEY M. CATE, Department of Family Life, School of Home Economics, Oregon State University, Corvallis, Oregon 97331, USA.

SHEILA M. CHOWN, Department of Psychology, Bedford College, University of London, Regents Park, London NW1 4NS, UK.

JOHN D. CUNNINGHAM, School of Behavioural Sciences, Macquarie University, North Ryde, New South Wales 2113, Australia.

WENDA J. DICKENS, Department of Psychology, University of Manitoba, Winnipeg, Manitoba, Canada R3T 2N2.

MARY ANN DOUGLAS, Department of Psychology, Nova University, Fort Lauderdale, Florida 33314, USA.

NANCY M. FITZGERALD, Department of Psychology, Northwestern University, Evanston, Illinois 60201, USA.

TED. L. HUSTON, College of Human Development, The Pennsylvania State University, University Park, Pennsylvania 16802, USA.

IGOR S. KON, Institute of Ethnography, USSR Academy of Sciences, Leningrad Branch, Leningrad, USSR.

JOHN J. LA GAIPA, Department of Psychology, University of Windsor, Windsor, Ontario, Canada N9B 3P4.

TERU L. MORTON, Department of Psychology, 2430 Campus Road, University of Hawaii, Honolulu, Hawaii 96822, USA.

SUSAN J. PAWLBY, Family Research Unit, The London Hospital Medical College, 16 Walden Street, London, UK.

DANIEL PERLMAN, Department of Psychology, University of Manitoba, Winnipeg, Manitoba, Canada R3T 2N2.

JOHN M. REISMAN, Department of Psychology, De Paul University, 233 North Seminary Avenue, Chicago, Illinois 60614, USA.

M. M. SHIELDS, University of London Institute of Education, 24-27 Woburn Square, London WC1H 0AA, UK.

CATHERINE A. SURRA, Department of Family and Human Development, Utah State University, Logan, Utah 84322, USA.

Preface

Development of personal relationships is only barely understood in either of the two senses (namely, relationship growth during acquaintance on the one hand, and relationships in different developmental age groups on the other hand). Despite the vigour of research by developmental psychologists into mother–infant relationships, this has not extended into later points of childhood and it is significant that the publication of books on children's friendships developed only very recently (e.g. Foot *et al.*, 1980a; Rubin, 1980; Asher and Gottman, 1981). At the other end of the life-cycle also, almost nothing is known about the significant features of relationships in the elderly and very little is clear about the changes in personal relationships that occur in adulthood. Equally, theoretical views on the development of relationships from strangers to close friends were rare until the early 1970s and even the ones put forward then have had only infrequent and unsystematic testing — and that usually by their authors alone.

It can only be a matter for considerable surprise that such crucial features of social development and adult social life have been so poorly researched until so recently, given also their practical and social importance. Many issues of child rearing and social policy hang upon the growth in understanding of children's friendships and the development of the understandings and behaviours necessary to relate satisfactorily to other people. Similarly, our treatment of adolescents ought to depend on a fuller understanding of the significance to youth of its place in society and its dealings with others via friendship and personal relationships. Despite the frequency of common observations that youth is a time of turbulence and experimentation in relationships, social psychology has to its discredit a notable and outstanding failure to do adequate research on these issues, such that when society asks us for advice about the treatment of adolescents, we have little that we can offer. Neither can we offer useful comments on the housing, treatment and social care of the elderly except on the basis of systematic research which remains to be done. Thus many tasks with specific populations await the personal relationships researcher as we attempt to build a more useful understanding of friendship over the life cycle. Equally, a fuller understanding of relationship development in general can only be valuable to society — it can never be wasted when psychiatric clinics, hospitals, divorce courts and other administrative casualty departments of society are filled by the products and consequences of poor relationship-building.

Since the necessary work into such topics has recently begun to grow, coalesce and establish itself scientifically, it is clearly time for the representations of the work to be collected into one source for those working on the problems. Accordingly, when we began to plan a set of books on personal relationships, it was clear that one of them would have to be the present volume on "Developing Personal Relationships."

Many general issues surrounding the growth and significance of the new research area of Personal Relationships have been covered in our Preface to the first companion volume: "Personal Relationships. 1: Studying Personal Relationships" (Eds. S. W. Duck and R. Gilmour, Academic Press, 1981). However, it is worth reiterating here those parts which concern the general conceptualization of the set of volumes on personal relationships. When we first began to plan a text on personal relationships we originally envisaged one that would be generally focused on the important research into disturbances in relationships—but as we began to work out this conception we began to see that it was inevitable that we cover a range of conceptual issues first, and also then to map out what was known about the development of relationships, before the reader was pointed towards disturbances in them and to their decline. Accordingly, we proceeded to prepare lists of topics for four separate but cognate volumes, each dealing with its own particular set of related issues but yet having a clear place in relation to the other volumes of the set. Each was intended to stand on its own but to gain strength from its association with the others; thus there is a family relationship among the four volumes: separate but complementary. Each one covers a wide range of work into personal relationships by writers with a variety of academic backgrounds and so reflects the variety of perspectives that exist in the area. The four volumes in the set are: "Personal Relationships. 1: Studying Personal Relationships" which deals with conceptual, methodological and topographical issues in the study of relationships; the present volume, "Personal Relationships. 2: Developing Personal Relationships" which deals with issues in the explanation of development of intimacy in relationships as well as with relationships developmentally through the life span; "Personal Relationships. 3: Relationships in Disorder", which will deal with breakdown of relationships, disorders of certain types of relationships, and the relationships of disordered people; and "Personal Relationships. 4: Dissolving Personal Relationships" which will deal with the ending of relationships.

Despite the advantages of such a set, the volumes are not claimed to offer an exhaustive coverage of the field of personal relationship research. What we hoped to do through them was to accelerate the emergence of personal relationships as an interdisciplinary research perspective; to show its coherence as a body of knowledge; to map out the kind of terrain that the subject holds — and to encourage the fullest possible exploration and creative practical development of that territory. In the context of the present volume, these large but important objectives take the form of presentation of some available conceptions of developing relationships along with some indications of underexplored areas of study. Together, the combination and application of these different approaches will, we hope, promote the successful achievement of the larger aims, which will eventually help to determine the extent to which ensuing research will ultimately produce noticeable improvements in understanding in the field of human relationships.

The present volume, "Developing Personal Relationships", is thus concerned with two broad sorts of issues, one, arguably, less coherent than the other, for theoretical overviews of relationship development and change in the life-cycle are only just beginning to emerge. However, the two strands (development or growth of relationships' depth or extent; and development of relationships in populations of different ages) are both important, and yield for this book the bipartite structure that it now contains.

The first strand is reflected in thought-provoking chapters by Morton and Douglas (on growth of relationships), by Cunningham and Antill (on love in developing romantic relationships) and by Huston *et al.* (on the interpersonal processes in courtship development). Together these present new approaches to complex and underworked topics along with simulating new methods of charting the progress and dynamics of relationship growth.

As an introduction to the second strand, the chapter by Dickens and Perlman invites us to extend the range of our conception of relationship development to the more global one which considers the whole life-cycle and, in so doing, gives considerable attention to the integrative problems that arise, since such syntheses are only just beginning to be thought through by other workers. Indeed, in common with attempts in other areas of developmental psychology to propose a view which encompasses the complete life-span as the appropriate developmental framework for investigating human behaviour, it shows that serious questions about the meaning of integration must precede the development of a global view of lifespan processes. We strove to cover the full developmental range of relationships in selecting authors for the rest of this Section where we asked contributors each to take a view of relationships at different segments of the developmental sequence. The book presents these careful attempts as a chart for the stages along the full range of human growth from very early childhood to old age. The numerical balance of chapters concentrating on earlier rather than later periods of development reflects, as we note elsewhere, the past (and existing) bias towards work on children and indeed, within that, towards work on younger rather than older children. Thus Pawlby provides an excellent summary of the area where most work has been done (mother–infant interaction) though even here, as she points out, important questions still need to be answered; for instance, researchers are not yet able to define satisfactory criteria for assessing the success of a mother–infant relationship, a point which clearly has significant theoretical and practical implications. Moreover, once we move on from the *relatively* well-covered ground of infancy, similar problems are pointed out in their respective areas by the other authors. Shields, La Gaipa, Kon, Reisman and Chown all have occasion to observe that their areas are characterized as much by a paucity of adequate research and by methodological difficulties as by anything else.

Readers will note the frequency with which our contributors point to the inadequacy of definitions or taxonomies of relationships as a fundamental weakness of research in this area. We reiterate this observation both in general (cf. Vol. 1, "Studying Personal Relationships") and again in the present context. Here, however, it assumes a special significance since the "growth during friendship" sense of development implies different sorts of qualitative changes in relationships, and the "friendship of growing people" sense suggests that there are different ways of achieving or developing what are essentially similar relationships. It is therefore of *crucial* significance for theory and subsequent empirical work that we define different sorts of relationships and get clear whether any observed changes are actually changes in quality or type or quantity or depth or . . . what? Do any apparent changes have real significance or are they merely terminological artefacts of different workers' background theories? Until such questions are clearly answered, it will be impossible to answer other questions concerning the functions of relationships at different ages and hence to begin to understand the significance of the failure to satisfy those functions (but see Vol. 3, "Personal Relationships in Disorder" and Vol. 4, "Dissolving Personal Relationships") — one of the ultimate aims of the research, as noted above, and one which gives it both social justification and social validity.

Readers will also note that several of the contributors point out reasons or excuses for the inadequacy of previous research. Most of these come down to advanced methodological cowardice or lack of resourcefulness, and hence we were particularly glad to include chapters here and in Volume 1 which demonstrate that several scholars in this field are beginning to take the necessary corrective steps. The field can develop properly, however, only if others follow such leads and, as we have continually stressed, such development is socially necessary. We judge, on the other hand, that a certain amount of academic iconoclasm is also needed. Our initial view in planning this book was that unreasonable claims had been made for many areas, but we had hoped to be disabused of this. On the contrary, our contributors provided ever more detailed and scholarly confirmation of our initial view and pointed out the actual neglect of areas of research in developing personal relationships for which great claims had been made by previous writers. Our contributors show not only *that* but *how* many parts of research have been unduly overlooked, under-researched or allowed to form the basis of unsupported and unwarranted assumptions or generalizations. In short, our contributors had reached the same conclusions as we had, but on better evidence and after a fuller conversance with the relevant parts of the literature. We conclude that the reasons for a development that has been slow and ponderous lie in the neglect of certain areas at the expense of others that have been, perhaps, too thoroughly mined. Unfortunately, the nuggets so obtained cannot properly be assayed until the above questions about "development" have been addressed, and this book is an attempt to begin this task.

In constructing the volume we have had considerable amounts of friendly advice from our colleague Andy Lock and we benefited from useful discussions with Ceri Roderick, Dot and Dave Miell, Martin Lea and Colin Brydon. As usual, however, the burden of our unceasing toil and limitless editorial vigour actually fell most often upon our capable secretarial assistants: Jane Dickinson, Margaret Gill, Anne Parker, Hazel Satterthwaite and Sylvia Sumner, all of whom fully deserve our thanks and this we happily and gratefully acknowledge. Whether or not they believe us when we say we will stop at four books in this series is up to them.

University of Lancaster   Steve Duck
July, 1980   Robin Gilmour

Contents

Section II

Relationships
Across the Lifespan

To H.C.G. and L.K.R.

for their valued friendship

Section I

Relationship Growth During Acquaintance

CHAPTER 1
Growth of Relationships

Teru L. Morton and Mary Ann Douglas

The *Zeitgeist* emerging in the wake of the "me decade" seems to be characterized by a fascination with intimacy, communication, and "meaningful relationships". The proliferation of popular paperbacked books and magazine articles devoted to such topics in recent times is striking, although there may be those who think the subject an improper domain for serious scholars. While clergy and clinicians may be struggling with such issues as how to have open communication with one's children and how to keep a marriage growing, academic scholars have been wary of entering the arena, and for some good reasons. The domain of relationship development is awesomely vast and incompletely charted, and our present array of instruments and maps may not prove sufficient to navigate it. Certain regions of the terrain are beginning to be illuminated, however, and a growing number of scholars are addressing themselves to establishing what fits where, and what elements might still be missing.

This chapter will begin by describing some of the more apparent difficulties in conceptualizing relationship growth, where "growth" is distinguished from "change", the latter also subsuming decline or deterioration of the relationship (but see Duck, 1981). As will be discussed in a later section, development involves quantitative increases in intimacy and attraction, as well as attendant qualitative changes in these dimensions. Next, the domain of the endeavour will be sketched in light and broad strokes, suggesting what might

3

be involved in the movement from new to advanced relationship levels or phases. Discussion will then turn to a review of areas which have received varying amounts of attention from researchers and theorists. Loosely ordered in terms of developmental sequence in the acquaintance tradition, they are: (1) attraction and person perception; (2) information and attraction in the acquaintance process; (3) social penetration theory as a molar exchange paradigm; and (4) relationship definition and its features — resources, rules of distributive justice, and nature of interdependence.

We make no claim to an exhaustive review of any one of these areas, choosing, as much as possible, generality and breadth rather than specificity and depth as a perspective for this chapter. Furthermore, our interest was in drawing attention to the kinds of constructs that might be promising in integrating the thinking in various disconnected areas of study in a broad enough way to apply to development of a wide variety of relationships. The faithful reader who processes the thoughts contained in this volume as well as the three accompanying ones will, we hope, be able to advance more usefully towards the ultimate goal — the development of a conceptual paradigm for relationship development applicable to all classes of relationship.

Problems in Characterizing Relationship Growth

Inevitably, the study of any complex and multifaceted phenomenon is fraught with problems of conceptualization and measurement. Hinde (1979; 1981) has reviewed problems in characterizing relationships *per se*. The attempt to characterize relationship growth includes these and others, most particularly the movement from individual to relational levels of analysis and the difficulties in establishing change dynamics over a long period of time. Some of the more salient issues for the task at hand will be addressed categorically.

Unit of analysis

The development and growth of interpersonal relationships is an exceedingly complex social phenomenon. As Duck (1973a) has pointed out, many of the problems inherent in the study of personal relationships are a function of reductionistic efforts to fit the phenomena into existing scientific paradigms. The following are some examples of dimensions along which these reductionistic efforts might progress in order to manage the complexity of relationship growth.

Individual versus relational versus situational levels

The level of analytic abstraction of the phenomenon under study dictates what is available for observation and description. The conceptual focus that one adopts must ultimately be selected as a function of the questions to be asked, but the study of relationship growth and function has begun to shift from the individual to the relationship level (Gottman *et al.*, 1976; Millar and Rogers, 1976; Morton *et al.*, 1976). Whereas psychological processes and behaviours of the individual are important, they fail to capture the unique system functions of the social relationships which are considered qualitatively greater than the collection of individuals within them (Watzlawick *et al.*, 1967). A relational level of analysis focuses on events which are a product of the social relationships, thus incorporating the metacommunication as well as the content levels of information (cf. Hinde's, 1981, "emergent properties of relationships"). Thus, exchanges within relationships contain not only information that is inherent in the content of the words, but also information that has special meaning for the unique relationship dyad. Relational level of analysis focuses on (1) relational control, not content, of messages; (2) sequencing of messages, not on individual message units; and (3) patterns of sequential interaction over time (Millar and Rogers, 1976).

The larger situational context within which the relationship operates must also come to bear on the analysis of relationship development. For example, variables like others' knowledge of the relationship, what they know about it, and how they evaluate it can be used, for instance, to distinguish the development of a secret "affair" from a public romance (Duck, 1977b). Behaviour, individual or relational, is beginning to be recognized in relation to the larger ecological systems within which it operates (Altman, 1975; Argyle, 1979; Lamb, 1979).

Cognitive versus affective versus behavioural domains

Interpersonal relationships entail cognitive, affective, and behavioural aspects (Hinde, 1981), and more integrated research into these response modalities seems desirable. Cognitive/affective responses have often been the focus in studies of initial attraction and acquaintance (Byrne, 1971; Duck, 1977a, b). On the other hand, studies of overt behavioural exchange between partners are more commonly found in investigations of advanced relationships such as marriage (Gottman, 1979; Morton, 1978; Raush *et al.*, 1974).

The selection process which has led investigators to study different response modalities at various stages of relationship development may reflect the relative importance of those processes at different stages. However, a comprehensive understanding of relationship growth would be greatly facilitated by careful theoretical integration of these three modalities of functioning within research on relationships.

Verbal versus non-verbal versus environmental channels

Analysis of multimodal processes of communication in relationships implies the importance of verbal, non-verbal, and environmental channels of exchange (Morton *et al.*, 1976). Processes of growth in relationships, primarily via regulation of intimacy, are managed by the systemic functioning of these three communication channels.

The regulation of relationship growth via the verbal modality occurs primarily through self-disclosure, whether it be superficial and primarily informational, as is characteristic during early acquaintance, or selectively intimate and affect laden, as is more typical of relationships at advanced stages (Altman and Taylor, 1973). Non-verbal channels of body language (e.g. posture, facial behaviour) and environmental channels of territorial behaviour (e.g. use of space, furnishings, proximity) must also be considered as an alternative means of facilitating and regulating the processes of relationship growth.

Static versus dynamic perspective

Difficulties inherent in studying change in personal relationships across time have led researchers to select manageable "bits" of growth as targets of investigation. These increments, albeit important in themselves, are part of a continuous process of relationship development. Research efforts should begin to focus on these continuous processes in studying relationship growth.

The investigation of "bits" of relationship growth in isolation, while problematic in itself, has led to a second but perhaps more important problem. Those attraction and acquaintance processes that are studied in relatively new relationships (Byrne, 1971; Duck, 1977a, b; Berscheid and Walster, 1978) are not those usually studied for relationships which have progressed further along the developmental continuum, where the focus has been on processes of calibration or recalibration of relationship definition (Morton *et al.*, 1976; Watzlawick *et al.*, 1967) and the regulation of conflict and intimacy (Douglas, 1980; Haley, 1963, 1971).

Various interpersonal processes may indeed be differentially salient at various points along the continuum of relationship growth. However, the processes of attraction, attribution, exchange, and relationship definition no doubt function in interaction, one with the others, throughout the entire course of relationships. Focusing on the ways in which partners integrate these various functions — within a model of continuous and dynamic relationship functioning — would prove useful to our understanding of relationship growth as well as deterioration.

As a final point, a dynamic perspective on relationships focuses attention on the continually fluctuating and evolutionary processes of relationship development (or deterioration) as partners attempt to develop (or give up) their relational status. A dynamic model of relationship functioning maintains focus on these continuous changes, thus allowing for the detection of change within established relationship units as well as accounting for the development of newly formed relationships.

Methods of assessment

The assessment of relationship growth implies two things: assessment of change across time and assessment of the relationship unit, the social system involving two or more individuals. In order to determine growth across time, it is necessary to know both *whether* change occurred and to know the *direction* in which it occurred: increases in self-disclosure and liking, social control, complexity and mutuality of relationship definition, and increased commitment to this mutually defined relationship, are central changes which define relationship growth. Finally, the *desirability* of relationship growth for the individuals within the relationship needs to be assessed as independent of the growth process itself.

Self-report and direct observations are categorical methods of assessment which provide unique information important to the understanding of relationship growth. To the extent that assessment of relationship growth incorporates cognitive, affective, and behavioural response modalities, the use of both self-report and observational techniques becomes imperative. Advances in observational methodology (Ginsburg, 1979a; Kendon, 1979; Patterson and Moore, 1979; Yarrow and Waxler, 1979) have enabled researchers to incorporate information about the *behavioural relationship* between two people with self-report of cognitive and affective processes of the individuals within the relationship.

In summary, there are major problems yet to be overcome before an overarching framework for understanding relationship growth will emerge. In addition, the increasing interest in analysis across time, and the development of new conceptual and measurement tools are greatly facilitating the necessary explorations. Discussion turns next to the domain of exploration.

Describing the Space: from Non-relationship to Personal Relationship

The challenge here is to identify central phenomena regarding relationship growth construed at the broadest and most universal level, so as to permit application to the range of relationship forms possible, e.g. doctor-patient, mother-child, and dating couple. Three characterizations of the sequential levels of developing relationships are briefly reviewed here, so as to highlight common elements. It is also worth noting, perhaps, that these characterizations originate from and reflect three different disciplinary approaches to the topic: namely, the sociological, the communicational and the social-psychological. While other workers have suggested alternative terms, they are not included here because they are partly synonymous with these, or too specific and narrow in the choice of response mode, relationship type, developmental period, or measurement operation for present purposes.

Levinger and Snoek (1972) have suggested three levels of relationship — awareness, surface contact, and mutuality. First, person X is simply aware of person Y; only if there is attraction or external situational pressures to interact will the second level of relationship follow. Here, in surface contact, X and Y are in interaction, but in relatively superficial format — often ritualized behaviour governed by sociocultural norms and X and Y's respective assessments of one another and their relationship. There is a qualitative jump between the surface contact level and the third level of mutuality, in which the relationship emerges as personal (vs impersonal), uniquely tailored (vs normative and role-bound), and intimate in the kinds of personal exchange and emotional investment of both parties.

Miller (1976), in a similar vein, has noted that relationships begin non-interpersonally, and given preliminary contacts, may proceed in one of three ways: (1) towards termination if either party finds future interaction unpromising; (2) persisting at a friendly but impersonal level as a casual acquaintanceship; or (3) proceeding, if certain conditions obtain, towards intense personal intimacy, e.g. close friendship or romantic involvement. Miller suggests that the qualitative shift from non-personal normative relating to a personal relationship is paralleled by a qualitative shift in the communication processes. The increasingly personal relationship is characterized by greater differentiation of presentations of self and the perceptions of the other, so that persons X and Y increasingly perceive one another as individuals rather than occupants of social roles. Further, the content and control strategies of communication shift so that increasingly more private and personal self-disclosures are made, and exchange governance shifts from sociocultural norms to shared idiosyncratic rules or predictions based on individual differentiation. Miller underscores the importance of uncertainty reduction in this evolution, as the two parties operate to make increasingly more accurate predictions in coming to know one another better.

Walster *et al.* (1978) have suggested that as relationships increase in intimacy, there are typically increases in: (1) intensity of liking or loving; (2) depth and breadth of information exchanged, so that intimates know much about one another's idiosyncracies, personal histories, and vulnerabilities; (3) actual and expected length of relationship; (4) value of resources exchanged, with partners increasingly willing to invest more of their resources, but also able to punish more keenly, particularly through termination of the relationship; (5) interchangeability of resources, such that a husband may repay a wife's ironing his shirts with expression of love and appreciation, flowers, or repairing the roof; (7) "we-ness" (p. 153), the tendency for partners to define themselves as one unit in interaction with the external social world. The features of a highly intimate relationship between "loving people whose lives are deeply entwined" (Walster *et al.*, 1978, p. 154) may not all characterize other less intimate, yet personal, relationships. There is clearly much to be gained, however, in conceptualizing relationship growth from initial awareness between two people all the way to the functioning of an advanced unit relationship.

These descriptions suggest by their common elements that an overall framework in which to conceptualize relationship development must ultimately account for the movement from the processes of two individual entities, possibly operating via role dynamics, towards the intimate interdependence of a prototypic pair bond, e.g. marriage. Two major dimensions of change appear to present themselves in this process — increasing familiarity or personal knowledge of the other person, and increasing attraction and connectedness.

Intimacy is generally construed as high familiarity, and knowledge of private, highly unique and personalistic information about the other. This first dimension of relationship development, where two people come to "know" each other, is a salient feature of acquaintance.

The second dimension of relationship is an affective or motivational component — that which draws two people together and causes their increasing connectedness or engagement with one another. This second aspect appears to change qualitatively from initial attraction between two unengaged strangers to engaged and highly interdependent mutuality in advanced relationships. It suggests a move from positive attraction towards one another to an acceptance or assumption of the interdependence of the unit relationship, a shift from individualistic processes to dyadic processes of engagement.

Finally, relationship development entails interaction and exchange, so there must be some synchronization, cooperation, or mutuality of control, since "it takes two to tango". If, at any point, one person in the dyad disengages, or refuses further engagement with the other (at least in the way the other wishes to engage), development is halted or retarded. If, however, the conjoint regulation can be re-established, then the relationship can continue to grow.

In short, an ultimate overall framework for conceptualizing general relationship growth will have to incorporate principles concerned with increasing understanding or knowledge of one another and of the relationship, and one or more motivational constructs incorporating notions of attraction and interdependence. In addition, the regulatory aspect of the relationship at all points in time must be considered by such a framework, such that the members operate in a synchronized, orderly, and organized fashion. It is this system of regulation, more than the two persons involved, which may be salient for understanding relationship development at more advanced stages.

In the following sections, areas of theory and research focusing on specific aspects of a developing relationship will be reviewed. It will be seen that different areas of inquiry have highlighted differing constructions of the information and attraction dynamics, such that regulatory aspects of relationships at various points in time may shift, although this last regulation or mutuality of control feature has been least attended to.

Attraction in Person Perception

Personal relationships require some degree of attraction, or liking, on the part of at least one person if they are to develop. Considerable research has been done on this construct although such findings are primarily useful only for describing the phenomena that precipitate interaction, or "approach motivations" — phenomena which precede but certainly do not ensure the other, subsequent, processes necessary for relationship growth. Such work indicates that some personal qualities such as physical attractiveness (Dion *et al.*, 1972) and sincerity, loyalty, and trustworthiness (Anderson, 1968) are qualities making their possessor highly attractive to others. In turn, an attractive person elicits more approach behaviour and globally positive attributions from others, and also provokes more conformity, imitation, and acquiescence (Lott and Lott, 1971). Other determinants of liking include proximity (Festinger *et al.*, 1950), familiarity or mere exposure (Zajonc, 1968), and the rewardingness of the other, including his or her liking for the person (Backman and Secord, 1959). Perhaps the most ubiquitous findings have been the "reciprocity-of-liking" phenomenon and the positive relationship between attitudinal similarity and attraction (cf. Berscheid and Walster, 1978).

Theoretical divisiveness has characterized this area, with reinforcement and cognitive consistency theories vying for dominance initially, and then an expanded derivative set of attribution theories entering to explain phenomena as well.

The reinforcement models (e.g. Byrne, 1971; Byrne and Clore, 1970; Lott and Lott, 1974) employ stimulus–response pairings as the unit of analysis, stress that rewarding stimuli arouse positive feelings and punishing stimuli arouse negative feelings, and suggest that neutral stimuli associated with an already conditioned positive or negative stimulus will acquire the corresponding positive or negative affect.

The cognitive-consistency models, particularly the balance theories of Heider (1958) and Newcomb (1968), take as the unit of analysis the cognition (idea, attitude, or belief) as well as the configuration of simultaneous cognitions. These theories propose that man prefers balance or consistency in cognitions, that imbalance/inconsistency leads to a negative psychological state, and that this will be remedied by changing a cognition in the direction of achieving balance. Thus, for example, Heider (1958) suggested that an individual in a unit relationship (in which partners see themselves as "belonging to" the relationship) will attempt to make sentiment relationship harmonious with unit relationship.

Attribution theories began with Heider's (1958) interest in the inferences that an observer makes from an actor's overt behaviour to that person's stable, underlying disposition. These theories address the way in which the observer assigns meaning or cause to an action — particularly the degree to which that action is attributed to external, environmental forces versus stable, internal personality traits or dispositions. Numerous extensions have emerged since Heider's original work (e.g. Bem, 1972; Jones and Davis, 1965; Jones and Nisbett, 1972; Kelley, 1972), all entailing the basic assumption that people are logical and rationalistic, needing to view the world as stable and coherent so that they can understand, predict, and control the events around them. Certain recent findings suggest, however, that systematic motivational biases may distort perceptual or attributional processes to support the invididual's self-esteem (Fontaine, 1975; Luginbuhl and Crowe, 1975; Stevens and Jones, 1976; Taylor and Koivumaki, 1976).

The two main sets of findings relevant to relationship growth (viz. the liking–liking and similarity–liking relationships) have been addressed by all of these theoretical perspectives. That X, learning that Y likes him/her should then like B can be explained by reinforcement theory, since Y's liking for X constitutes a reward and attraction is a function of rewardingness. Cognitive consistency theory would predict that X, liking Y, would presume that Y returns the liking. Here is is not the other's rewardingness but X's attraction to Y which distorts X's perception of B's regard. Indeed, there may be a tendency to overestimate this reciprocated liking (Tagiuri, 1958). Finally, attribution theory has drawn attention to the special case of ingratiation, such that if X attributes Y's expression of liking to an ulterior motive, e.g., dishonest manipulation, X's liking for Y is decreased (Jones, 1964; Jones and Davis, 1965; Jones and Wortman, 1973).

All perspectives likewise address the similarity–attraction phenomenon. The reinforcement formulation is that attitudinal similarity *is* a powerful reinforcer, since validation of one's attitudes through congruence with another's attitudes represents a reward (Byrne, 1971). A second school of thought suggests that if X likes himself/herself, then he/she is cognitively consistent in liking others with similar attitudes (Heider, 1958). An attributional approach proposes that attitudinal similarity enables X to make a better prediction about other (rewarding) similarities to be discovered in future interactions (Jones and Davis, 1965).

In summary, attraction would appear to represent a multifaceted phenomenon. It would seem that these theoretical positions can account equally well for many of the empirical relationships established by prior research, and each accounts particularly well for certain attraction phenomena in person perception. Thus, reinforcement theory addresses the way in which affective responses are conditioned in the early internalizing of cultural norms and values concerning what is attractive. Cognitive consistency formulations draw attention to the cognitive/affective distortions made in attempting to impose coherence and consistency in perceptions of the world. Attribution theory underscores the importance of an observer's inferences made about the actor's underlying personality dispositions and intentions in determining attraction.

Most of the theory-based research on attraction has focused on a subject's expressed attraction to a "bogus stranger", where isolated information about that stranger is presented, and the relationship between information and attraction is assessed. Such research and theory have only a specific and limited place in explanations of relationship growth, as noted earlier, most particularly in regard to the initial, pre-interaction cognitive and affective phenomena. Yet until relatively recently, such research and theory were often treated as if they represented a comprehensive framework for examining relationships. Once initial attraction has occurred and leads to interactive engagement the dynamics between information and attraction must inevitably become more complex. Hence they should be conceptualized and examined accordingly.

In the actual person-to-person interactive sequence, people are exchanging certain information over time, so that changes in information and in the relationship of attraction to information must be assessed over a long time-span. The next section discusses theory and research concerning information and attraction in the acquaintance process, assuming a more temporal perspective.

Information and Attraction in the Acquaintance Process

During acquaintance, people come to know one another and to evaluate one another on the basis of this information. In most cases, acquaintance will not proceed very far, but in other cases, it proceeds toward friendship and even mate selection. Some approaches have examined the importance of evaluating certain kinds of information at the molar level of analysis, the "filtering" approach to friendship and mate selection, while others have adopted a more molecular approach to examining how information and attraction operate in the evaluation of self-disclosure, the most salient information exchanged in acquaintance.

Filter theories

Theories of friendship and mate selection have been largely dominated by cognitive perspectives focusing on the ways in which individuals sift through a "field of eligibles" to select a desirable mate or small pool of close friends to support their personality structure. Winch (1958) hypothesized that the choice of a mate is determined on the basis of need complementarity, and presented findings to this effect. Kerckhoff and Davis (1962) postulated that value consensus is important early in the filtering process, while need complementarity emerges as a selection criterion later in relationship development, and also reported supporting results. A large number of studies have been conducted to replicate these findings concerning need complementarity, with disappointing results, however (cf. Tharp, 1963). With few exceptions (e.g. Rychlak, 1965; Bermann and Miller, 1967) research findings point to similar rather than complementary personality features among members of well-established personal relationships (Burgess and Locke, 1960).

Circumventing the problems associated with need, Murstein (1971, 1976) has postulated a three-stage filtering process through which a couple progresses before deciding to marry; (1) a stimulus stage in which people are attracted on the basis of what can be seen; (2) a value stage, wherein the couple is concerned with evolving compatible values, and (3) a role stage, in which partners establish the adequacy of the "fit" between themselves. He has provided some promising but indirect evidence to support the proposition that what draws people together varies as a function of relationship stage.

Filter theories are valuable for molar level analysis of the different evaluations important at different stages of relationship development. They call attention to the fact that not all of one's friends become close friends, and not all of these become a mate. Much more inquiry is desirable, however, concerning what kinds of information are evaluated to establish role "fit". A much more molecular analysis quite compatible with the filter theories examines information and attraction in the context of self-disclosure.

Self-disclosure and attraction

Self-disclosure has been defined as "the act of making yourself manifest, showing yourself so others can perceive you" (Jourard, 1971), as "any information exchange that refers to the self, including personal states, dispositions, events in the past, and plans for the future" (Derlega and Grzelak, 1979), and as "intentional verbal disclosure of self-referent material to another" (Cozby, 1973). Although communication in non-verbal and environmental modes is surely important, researchers in this area have largely focused on the narrower definition of self-disclosure as verbal and intentional. Chelune's volume (1979) reviews the considerable amount of research on this construct.

Duck (1976, 1977a), in theorizing about friendship formation, has argued that the relationship between information and acquaintance is analogous to that between a hierarchy of knowledge and a sequence of attraction behaviour. His model relies on Festinger's (1954) social comparison motive, stating that the individual seeks out similar others to attain validation of his/her own attitudes and values. He employs an information processing model to describe how information about the other's personality is assessed for similarity to one's own, both at the present level of disclosure and the next. Since similarity is reinforcing, attraction occurs to the extent that the other is assessed as providing a good (similar) model for social comparison. This theory is promising in suggesting that different kinds of information are differentially attractive at different times in relationship growth, and recent findings are supportive (Duck, 1977a; Miell *et al.*, 1979; Wortman *et al.* 1976). Duck's analysis employs both reinforcement and information as variables and is thus extremely useful in reconciling two apparently disparate motives of a person in a relationship — to attain reward, and to better understand and predict the other.

In a congruent vein, Jones and Archer (1976) have offered an attributional analysis of personalistic self-disclosure, or disclosures which are privately geared to the recipient and not shared with others. These theorists propose that recipients of self-disclosure infer positive dispositions to the discloser (e.g. discriminating taste and trusting/trustworthy person), which lead the receiver to trust and therefore like the discloser. Gould, Brounstein, and Taylor (1978) offered strong support for this. An attributional explanation for disclosure reciprocity is promising and both suggests why different aspects of another person are rewarding at different times in relationship development, and also appears to account for the disclosure–liking–disclosure findings, which will be discussed in the next section.

In summary, the work on acquaintance and the early stages of relationships is exciting, and suggests that different levels of information are important at different times. More specifically, it suggests that active cognitive processes are occurring as the two individuals evaluate one another, and also as they evaluate their *relationship* in terms of its known past and its future potential. Attribution and information models of acquaintance will quite likely assume an increasingly more central position in the eventual framework for conceptualizing relationship development, for they help to relate attraction at any given time to information concerning the other's interests and intentions for relationship growth.

Discussion thus far has examined the way in which one person's increasing disclosure might be rewarding to another person, and therefore encouraged. This interactional aspect of self-disclosure, and the general phenomenon of disclosure reciprocity is taken up in the next section, which examines self-disclosure and other acquaintance phenomena from an exchange theory perspective.

Social Penetration Theory: A Molar Exchange Paradigm

Social penetration theory (Altman, 1973; Altman and Taylor, 1973) proposes that relationship formation proceeds, gradually and in an orderly fashion, through reciprocal exchange from non-intimate, relatively unemotional aspects of the selves to intimate, private, and vulnerable central core aspects of the selves. Thus, it hypothesizes that disclosure depth and breadth increase as relationships grow. Altman and Taylor employed a kind of exchange model, which incorporates principles from reinforcement, attribution, and economic exchange theories, to explain what propels relationships forward. Thus, individuals evaluate the rewards and costs of an interaction, and then forecast, or project, both the relative rewardingness of future interactions at the same and at higher levels of intimacy, and also a cognitive structuring of the other, or subjective model of the other person. If either projection is unsatisfactory, the relationship development is terminated, or at least proceeds more slowly. A favourable forecasting signals the desirability of future interaction, with each new series of exchange accompanied by an assessment and revision of the two-fold forecast.

This theory extends Thibaut and Kelley's (1959) concepts of rewards and costs in distinguishing between interpersonal, personal, and situation. Interpersonal rewards and costs are intrinsic to the social relationship itself, e.g. liking, power, or status, and reflect the amount of mutual response facilitation and the appropriateness of behavioural sequencing. Personal factors are those concerning gratification associated with personality, e.g. values, needs, or skills, whose rewards or costs depend upon mutual satisfaction through some "fit" such as complementarity or congruency. Situational factors are aspects of the psychological environment, e.g. satisfactory accomplishment of a task by the cooperating dyad.

Thibaut and Kelley's (1959) Comparison Level and Comparison Level of Alternatives are also incorporated in this theory. The former represents the standard for assessing satisfaction with the relationship — the average value of outcomes an individual has known directly or vicariously. The latter is the standard for evaluating commitment to the relationship — the lowest level of outcomes a person will accept in the light of available alternative opportunities, or relationships.

Jourard and his colleagues (Jourard, 1959; Jourard and Landsman, 1960) were early explorers of a now well-documented finding, reciprocity of self-disclosures. Altman (1973) expanded concepts of reciprocity as a norm within the exchange paradigm, hypothesizing that reciprocity depends upon the stage of the relationship, the intimacy of the topic, and the length and degree of commitment to the relationship. Thus, when a relationship is expected to be short-term, people may disclose in a highly intimate or non-reciprocal fashion. Commitment to maintaining the possibility of a long-term relationship, however, generates caution such that non-intimate disclosures are exchanged reciprocally (presumably via norm guidance), followed by increasingly intimate disclosures which are reciprocated (presumably now through exchange considerations), and the eventual waning of disclosure reciprocity as the relationship matures.

These authors (Altman, 1973; Altman and Taylor, 1973; Taylor, 1979) have amassed a considerable amount of research evidence providing general corroboration of various propositions within social penetration theory, specifically that intimacy of self-disclosures increases with acquaintance, and that reciprocity occurs in the ways hypothesized. It is important to note, at the same time, that other theoretical perspectives can account for many of these findings as well. Major issues not fully dealt with by social penetration or any other single theory to date concern the motivational aspects of self-disclosure and the dynamic of disclosure reciprocity.

Instrumentality of self-disclosure

In a recent review of research to date concerning appropriateness of self-disclosure, Derlega and Grzelak (1979) have suggested five functions of self-disclosure: (1) self-expression, or the cathartic release of pent-up feelings; (2) increased self-clarification, where anticipated self-presentation causes the speaker to attend to his or her own consistency and integration of ideas (Duval and Wicklund, 1972); (3) obtaining social validation through social comparison processes (Festinger, 1954); (4) acting as a vehicle for relationship development; (5) social control via impression management.

This perspective, which examines the actor's motives for self-disclosure, is a relatively new and important one which brings us closer to understanding relationship growth. The first three reasons are essentially individualistic, although the third does suggest that another's response is necessary. Thus, one shares personal information because it feels good, it helps one understand oneself, and it elicits validation from the social world.

The last two functions described by Derlega and Grzelak are particularly germane to relationship growth, for they are concerned with relational control. The work on the relationship between information and attraction was reviewed in an earlier section. Here it is pointed out that both aspects of self-disclosure, reward and information, serve to propel future interaction in a social exchange framework. Thus, there is reward value in the information that the discloser gives, especially to the extent that it is articulated with precision and clarity. The information that the recipient receives is also potentially rewarding, leading the receiver to infer that the other likes or trusts him/her, validating his/her own attitudes and beliefs, and providing valuable information about the discloser's own interests in developing the relationship.

The view of self-disclosure as a means of manipulating the other to like oneself, or to reciprocally disclose intentions or interests in the relationship, is also a valuable one. From an exchange perspective, one is attempting — even during acquaintance — to increase one's control over one's own and the other's outcomes. Viewing the individual as attempting to control the other's response as well as the direction and speed of relationship growth, and viewing this mutual regulation as a central feature of relationships, represents a valuable and relatively new perspective.

Self-disclosure reciprocity

The plentiful research documenting the dyadic effect has been described elsewhere (cf. Chelune, 1979). Various motives or mediating variables have been proposed to account for this effect. Some writers, stressing the widely held rules concerning disclosure appropriateness and the negative sanctions levied when such norms are violated, have argued that reciprocity is both a norm, and explicable in terms of cost-reward considerations (Altman, 1973; Altman and Taylor, 1973; Derlega and Grzelak, 1979; Jourard, 1971). Others argue that reciprocity is a function of both modelling and social exchange, with context determining which dynamic operates (Kleinke, 1979). Yet others suggest that the equitable exchange and personalism hypothesis from the attribution theory of Jones and Davis (1965) offers the most convincing account (Taylor, 1979). In all probability, different mediators are differentially salient at various points in a growing relationship, and in differing contexts.

Reciprocity has so puzzled workers in the area that some have questioned whether the construct is necessary, since exchange relationships are reciprocal by definition (La Gaipa, 1977b; Taylor, 1979). Yet, as predicted by social penetration theory, reciprocity of intimacy is higher among strangers than spouses (Morton, 1978) or friends (Derlega *et al.*, 1976). Rather than dispose of reciprocity, perhaps it would be useful to conceptualize it as a primitive mutual control strategy, functioning for relational control at certain stages and in certain types of relationships.

A relevant distinction here concerns the differences between non-contingency-based and contingency-based reciprocity (Gottman, 1979). One difference concerns rate matching vs a probability change approach to definition. A rate matching definition implies that the rates of some behaviour in dyadic interactions occur at comparable levels for both partners, e.g. rates of positive verbal behaviour may occur equally often for husbands as for wives. A probability change definition emphasizes that the occurrence of behaviour X in partner A affects the probability of the occurrence of behaviour X (or Y) in partner B, e.g. wife's positive verbal behaviour would alter the likelihood of husband subsequently emitting positive verbal behaviour. A second difference concerns the length of temporal interval: contingency-based reciprocity is grounded in moment-to-moment temporal intervals, whereas non-contingency-based reciprocity may refer to equivalence of behaviour over longer periods of time, from hours to years.

The literature on self-disclosure reciprocity reveals some confusion in usage of the term. Whereas the conceptual definitions often would imply contingency-based reciprocity, requiring careful scrutiny of moment-by-moment probability change, in fact much of the empirical work has involved rate matching operations over long periods of time. It would seem that more careful scrutiny of behavioural reciprocity, and congruence between conceptual and operational definitions, would be desirable in future research, particularly that concerned with relationship growth.

Advantages and limitations of the social penetration paradigm

Social penetration theory is given special attention here for several reasons. First, it has had a major influence on the current field of study concerned with self-disclosure and its reciprocation. Secondly, it has been the most detailed paradigm of acquaintance and relationship development employing a social exchange formulation of costs and rewards. Thirdly, it is a broad-reaching descriptive framework incorporating a wide range of variables, including standards for evaluating the other and overall satisfaction with the relationship, verbal, non-verbal, and environmental behaviour and their integration, and an emphasis on change across time. Because of this breadth, it seems generally compatible with other more molecular theories devoted to examining with greater rigour and sophistication the specific aspects of relationship development. Social penetration theory suggests that cognitive structuring of the other — the inferring of underlying dispositions (e.g. similarity, trustworthiness, etc.) is important, and that different information about the other is attended to at different points in acquaintance. It also points to other sources of attraction such as co-orientating successfully (e.g. playing tennis or raising children together), and rewards associated with external-to-the-dyad sources (e.g. being "seen" with an attractive other or receiving society's approval for being a "good" mother). Indeed, the social penetration framework guides us beyond verbal self-disclosure to other modes of relational development more salient in other relationship types, e.g. mother–child.

One limitation of the social penetration paradigm rests on the problems of operationalizing costs and rewards, problems for all of the exchange theories (cf. Hinde, 1981). It is difficult, though not impossible, to assess individuals' perceptions of costs and rewards outside of the laboratory, particularly if participants expect rewards to increase (Levinger and Snoek, 1972), or if expected reciprocity is more important than actual reciprocity in relationship growth (La Gaipa, 1977b). Contextual elements, e.g. degree of acquaintance, and trust in the other's sincerity, also influence costs and rewards differentially over time.

A more important limitation concerns a lack of theoretical attention to what might have been called a cognitive structuring of the *relationship*, as well as of the other person. Individuals have some idea of what their relationship to the other could be, or should be, and also what it appears to be, based on the observations of the other and of their interaction. Their definitions of the present relationship must coincide if they are to have orderly, stable exchange. It is this *mutual relationship definition*, and its manifestation in the interaction process, which is attended to insufficiently in the social penetration paradigm.

In an earlier section, it was suggested that a concept or concepts of control, synchronization, or mutual regulation appeared desirable to explain interdependence in relationships. These phenomena are truly relational and appropriate to the study of relationships, whereas concepts such as information, attribution, and attraction are individualistic, albeit often social. Theorists concerning themselves with relationships must begin to deal with such concepts if we are to understand social systems and not simply aspects of individual functioning.

If, from an attributional perspective, two people in a developing relationship come increasingly to understand, predict, and control one another, then as an increasingly well-tailored and synchronized system, their relationship too is characterized by mutuality of control. If, in the acquaintance process, two people reciprocally exchange increasingly personal information, they are continually agreeing, then, to define their relationship in a certain way. The growth of the personal relationship in this form of acquaintance is by consensus, and the mutuality of control is reflected in the reciprocity of disclosures. As more regulatory modes are learned through this process, reciprocity (a crude guiding system) fades and more efficient regulatory processes are manifest. Issues concerned with relationship definition are discussed in the next section.

Mutuality of Relationship Definition

Morton *et al.* (1976) have postulated that a viable relationship requires mutuality of relationship definition, or consensus about the nature of the relationship. Since, however, modes of exchange expand and diversify as the relationship develops, relationship crisis in the form of non-mutuality will occur and mutuality of relationship definition must be re-established if the relationship is to continue. As a relationship evolves from a relatively impersonal one to a highly personal one, mutuality of control appears to provide an increasingly useful means of predicting relationship status.

Three features of relationship definition will be discussed here: the resources exchanged, the rule for distributing these resources, and the nature of the interdependence structure. Two parties in a relationship must have some tacit agreement concerning all of these features. Thus, a hair stylist and her customer must agree on what they are exchanging, what the justice rule is, and what the nature of their interdependence structure is. A dating couple must likewise agree about the nature of their relationship, e.g. is it sexual or not, are they a "good match" by market place standards, how connected are they, and what will they become?

Resources

Foa and Foa (1971) have been credited with developing the most comprehensive taxomony of resource classes to describe a variety of relationship forms. These six resource classes — love, status, information, money, goods, and services — are identified along a two-dimensional model of particularism and concreteness. Particularism refers to the extent to which the resource is valued as a function of the particular individual who delivers it, whereas concreteness refers to the tangible versus symbolic characteristics of the resource.

To the extent that personal relationships are interdependent, the nature of the interdependence will involve mutual power (Kelley and Thibaut, 1978). Mutual power implies that each person has power over the partner to the extent that the partner is dependent on him/her. The nature of this power is a function of the basis of the partner's dependence.

Thus, bases of power identified by French and Raven (1959) provide another taxonomy of resources: (1) legitimate power based on given authority; (2) reference power based on another's attractiveness to the other; (3) expert power based on superior knowledge or skills; (4) informational power based on communication skills of explanation and persuasion; (5) reward power based on ability to provide reward to the other; and (6) coercive power, based on the ability to exert punishment.

Parallels between the resource classes of Foa and Foa and the power bases of French and Raven are striking. Both taxonomies identify classes of resources which an individual may possess and which can be "converted" to behaviour to be subsequently exchanged. It is overt behaviour which must eventually be of focus in order to observe the actual exchange structure and process in relationships, to quantify standard units of measurement (La Gaipa, 1977b), and probably even to confirm or verify the exchange for partners themselves. It is unlikely that simply knowing one's partner was giving love, for example, would be sufficient without identifying some concomitant behaviour as evidence for that exchange.

Partners in a developing relationship must agree on *what* they are exchanging, or have as exchange resources. They must also agree on the justice system employed to distribute available resources.

Distributive justice

Lerner *et al.* (1976) have categorized six forms of justice along two dimensions: (1) perceived relationship (identity, unit, and non-unit); and (2) object of perception (person and position). The identity relation, where there is minimal psychological separation between partners, and the unit relation, where partners see themselves "belonging to" a relationship, are both applicable to forms of personal relationship addressed here. The person-position distinction can equally apply to developing relationships, where a unique person is seen as trans-situational, and a position is a person-in-a-role, where the role could be filled by any number of persons (transpersonal).

Forms of justice within close relationships from the Lerner *et al.* (1976) framework are based on equity (position, unit relation), parity (person, unit relation), social obligation (position, identity), or need (person, identity). Theoretical concern with equity has been greater than with the other justice systems, and has been articulated elsewhere (Berkowitz and Walster, 1976; Walster *et al.*, 1978). According to equity theory, participants' outcome (positive and negative consequences) are gauged relative to their inputs (assets and liabilities). Relationship profits are equal only in so far as investments are also equal, but to the extent that one invests more, he/she is entitled to greater profits. Parity, on the other hand, implies equal outcomes, regardless of input. The other relevant justice forms imply distribution of resources as a function of relative need of the parties, or a grounding in social obligation to provide particular resources to the other.

Each of these justice forms may be important in a particular relationship definition. Further, it seems likely that the structure for ensuring just distribution of resources might change with advances in the relationship. As Walster *et al.* (1978) have noted, it is easier to calculate equity in casual, short-term relationships than in intimate, ongoing ones.

It might also be the case that different forms of justice are employed in different contexts or domains, especially in long-term relationships. Walster *et al.* (1978) have provided some empirical evidence for the existence of equity in mate selection and day-to-day interaction in intimate, long-term relationships. However, other forms of justice — including equity — may represent the rules by which partners "get what they deserve" in selected areas of the relationship. Thus, partners might agree that the benefits of their car be enjoyed more by the one making the car payments (equity rule over one resource), that the benefit of financial stability be offered based on social obligation to the role "wife", that the benefit of children be shared equally regardless of effort in caretaking (parity), and that the benefit of sexual pleasure be distributed according to need.

Equity, parity, need, and social obligation represent conceptually different methods of maintaining justice within relationships. It could be argued that the principles applying to equity (Walster *et al*, 1978) could apply as well to the more general concept of "just balance". That is, (a) individuals will attempt to maximize their outcomes; (b) when individuals find themselves involved in imbalanced relationships they will become distressed, with greater imbalance leading to greater distress; and (c) individuals will attempt to eliminate their distress by restoring balance. The key to viable relationships, it could be argued then, is not specifically equity but balance, a general principle of fairness based on whatever system(s) of justice might be adopted within the relationship.

Since the rule of justice is tied to the conjoint definition of the relationship and membership within it, unambiguous change in either will result in change in the other, and relationship development will be characterized by tentative attempts to change both the definition of the relationship and the operating rules. In most developing relationships, increasing resources are introduced and tentatively distributed, partners infer the justice rule from this distribution, and thereby infer the other's definition of the relationship/membership. The rule of distributive justice, then, is often established in retrospect and assists in cognitively structuring the relationship. Where there is disagreement about the degree to which the operating rule is being followed, or perceived incongruence between a desired relationship and the actual operating rules, a new rule will be tentatively explored. The more partners concur, by virtue of similar backgrounds and expectations, and/or skills of encoding and decoding, in their views and desires for (1) the operating rule, (2) the degree to which it is being followed, and (3) the implied relationship, the greater the chances of pursuing a course of relationship development maximally satisfying to both. It is also probable, as already noted, that in growing relationships there is an over-riding use of one characteristic distribution rule (often parity) with specific domains of the evolving relationship characterized by other rules, concomitant with an increasingly differentiated and conceptually sophisticated relationship structuring. These speculations, as well as others concerning change in rule usage in relationship growth are likely to prove fruitful areas for further inquiry in future research.

Rules of fairness of resource distribution represent one structural element of relationships about which partners must agree. Another agreement concerns interdependence, the manner in which partners fit together within the relationship.

Interdependence

Generally, interdependence in relationships refers to the dependence upon the partner for the occurrence of some action, outcome, or event. All social exchange theories imply some form of interdependence, but by far the most elaborated discussions of this topic have come from Kelley and Thibaut

(1978) and Kelley (1979). These writers present not only a theory of exchange, but one of coordination of exchange with outcome.

Major properties of interdependence patterns, according to the theory of interdependence, are: (1) mutuality of dependence, where dependence is shared (interdependence) or unilateral; (2) degree of dependence, the extent to which partners are dependent on each other; (3) correspondence of outcomes, the degree to which partners' outcomes represent a similar state for each; (4) basis of dependence, the patterns of action which define the dependence (Kelley and Thibaut, 1978).

The theory of interdependence applied to close personal relationships addresses structural interdependence, or the interdependence defined by how partners separately and jointly affect one another's outcomes (Kelley, 1979). According to Kelley, interdependence defined by outcomes facilitates: (1) the understanding and prediction of a variety of interactions within the relationship, (2) the analysis of affective as well as concrete consequences of interaction, and (3) the analysis of attributional process, or the inferring of personal disposition.

Interdependence theory offers quite elegant transformation of outcome matrices to account for the ways in which individuals in interaction might profitably and cooperatively shift from maximizing individual outcomes to maximizing shared, or interdependent outcomes. While these transformations might characterize the "exchange calculations" that two people go through in shifting from one relationship definition to another, the theory is still limited as it relates to relationship growth, in that it analyses relationships as a static, not dynamic, unit. As Kelley and Thibaut (1978, p. 317) have noted, "further elaboration of interdependence theory will profit, in our estimation, from the development of concepts that lend themselves not only to characterizing the patterns at any given point in time but also to determining their temporal trends and changes".

One direction towards describing change in relationships over time is to focus on the interaction processes between partners, since it is that interaction process which is the vehicle feeding the structuring and restructuring of interdependence at the outcome level. And, of course, true interdependence at the process level will be manifest in contingency-based interaction (Gottman, 1979).

Partners in developing relationships must engage in calibration of the relationship (Watzlawick et al., 1967), establishing rules, norms, or principles by which the relationship is to operate as a unique system. The developing relationship then becomes an interacting system governed by rules or a statement of redundancies observed at the relational level (Jackson, 1965). It is this conjoint agreement about the rules which govern relationship functioning that is required for viable social relationships. Mutuality of relationship definition requires that the two individuals agree about the redundancies characterizing their exchange, where the redundant configurations summarily define the relationship.

In summary, relationship definition, a structural aspect of relationships, must involve the definition of resources which are shared, the justice system which is employed to distribute those resources, and the nature of interdependence which characterizes the relationship. Developing relationships are confronted with the initial task of relationship definition, and ongoing relationships with redefinition. Relationship redefinition may be associated with a change in resources (or their value) within the relationship, non-mutuality of agreement regarding the justice system, or change in the nature of interdependence which binds the partners together. A better understanding of relationship growth and development, we would maintain, will follow a careful analysis of the structure and concomitant processes associated with relationship definition.

Implications

Much of the recent work on the ealier stages of acquaintance has focused on the examination of processes whereby two people come to define the other, and the reasons why different sorts of information concerning the other are attractive at different times in the growth of the relationship. Extending this, the processes whereby two people come to define their relationship are also important, as are the kinds of information that they use to assess it.

Much of the work on relationship development has stressed the properties of self-disclosures which are intentional and verbal. Certainly this is an important class of behaviour for the issue at hand. However, two people in a developing relationship typically do things together, and these shared activities need to be examined further. For example, two people might go on a weekened camping trip, during which they talk about their hopes and fears around the campfire, but they also may watch the sunset together in silence, and decide how the tasks of pitching the tent and preparing the food will be accomplished. These activities, too, may well prompt relationship growth, and will be experienced differently from the participants' perspective as well as from that of an outside scrutineer's, depending on the relationship definition.

People use definitions of relationships provided by society when they can make no better-fitting ones. Thus, "roles" are usually paired, e.g. doctor-patient, cashier-customer, parent-child, boy-girl, colleague-colleague. These socially established relationship forms are sufficient to provide a rudimentary mutual relationship definition, but dyads begin to evolve their own variations or new definitions quickly, given repeated interaction. In many acquainting pairs, the equal investment of both parties in any new redefinition of the relationship is ensured by reciprocal verbal self-disclosure, although redefinition will also be occurring in other non-verbal areas.

Examining similar and complementary patterns of exchange, particularly contingency-based responses, for their regulatory functions will aid in furthering understanding of exchange processes. Examining people as they make attributions and attempt to understand, predict, and control not only the other person but also their relationship, should help to integrate the presently still fragmented field of relationship development, and provide a better bridge from individual to relational processes than is currently available.

Social scientists concerned with relationships and their development must acknowledge, if conceptualizations are to advance, that attention to the *relationship per se* is necessary. Two people do not simply get fully acquainted using individualistic intrapsychic processes, and then suddenly enter a state of "we-ness". They are in relationship almost from the beginning, and relational constructs must be introduced at that point to explain their individual cognitive/affective/behavioural activity, and the synchronization of their relational behaviour.

In summary, the state of the field of relationship development is relatively new and certainly exciting. The numerous approaches which have already been overlaid onto the study of relationship growth reflect the richness of the many and varied issues involved.

The major themes reflected in Ginsburg's (1979b) volume may well be applied to the study of relationship growth. The first theme portrays individuals as active agents with expectations, intentions, and facilities for cognitive reasoning, all of which contribute to explaining individual behaviour in relationships. The second theme reflects another cognitive aspect, that of "meaning" which individuals attach to actions, events, and settings. These two major themes make the third even more compelling. The final of these themes reflects the notion of structural properties inherent in interactional processes, that is, the patterning of individual behaviours in relational interaction. The integration of these three basic themes in the study of relationship growth promises to take the development of the field in exciting and evolving directions.

CHAPTER 2

Love in Developing Romantic Relationships

John D. Cunningham and John K. Antill

A psychologist foolish enough to embark on the vast topic of love has to present several inevitable but important observations at the outset:

1. There are at least as many kinds of love as there are kinds of human relationships. Without considering how these differ, we shall concentrate our attentions on romantic relationships between peers.
2. There are at least as many definitions of love as there are thinkers and writers on the topic, each presenting a different theoretical approach to the same phenomena, or else definitions of different phenomena given the same name. We shall distinguish love as the ideology of romanticism, love as the characterization of a state of relationship, and the development of love.
3. Almost anything that can be said about love will be true for at least some people in some circumstances.
4. The romantic ideal of medieval courtly love is recognized as the cornerstone of Western attitudes on the topic, but its resemblance to modern practices surrounding love is quite tenuous.
5. Basing marriage upon love is nearly unique to modern Western societies, both historically and cross-culturally, and is associated primarily

with freedom to choose one's own spouse.

6. The study of love, to paraphrase someone, has had a long past but a short history. That is, psychological study of love in a systematic manner has begun only quite recently. In particular, we know almost nothing about the development of love.

7. Scientific knowledge about love, its antecedents, and its consequents, is as yet so meagre that novelists, poets, and playwrights are still the experts on this topic and likely to remain so. But we know much more now than we did a decade or so ago.

In this chapter we shall (a) explore very briefly the historical and cultural context of romantic love, (b) present a rough conception of the development of love, (c) review the accumulating but diverse empirical research on love and romanticism, and (d) report a few early findings on the course and correlates of love from a recent study of our own.

A Brief Historical Sketch

The origins of modern ideas on love can be traced back through Western intellectual history to the Platonic dialogue *Symposium* (see Murstein, 1974a, for a thorough review). At a banquet several views are aired before the playwright Aristophanes presents the myth of the androgynes, those half-male, half-female creatures who, along with male–male and female–female beings, were split asunder by Zeus and have been longing ever since for their other half to restore that primordial unity. After Aristophanes, Socrates describes the transition from loving with the body and senses to loving with the soul, progressing from contemplation of the loved one to contemplation of the ideal — from *eros* or lust to *agape* or service to the ideal. *Agape* became the basis of the Christian love of God, together with the misinterpreted Platonic idea that it was better to love with the soul, heart, or mind than with the body.

Many writers have cited traces of Platonism in Christianity as the intellectual predecessors of the medieval practice of courtly love. Here, young knights pledged their devotion to the wife of the lord of the castle in the apparent absence of any hope that their love would be consummated or that they could ever marry. Controversy rages over the precise origin of the practice and the functions that it served in court life (de Rougemont, 1940). An elaborate etiquette developed to guide the behaviour of lovers and was codified by Countess Marie de France in the twelfth century. Elements which are still identifiable today as part of the "romantic complex" are that love strikes at first sight, conquers all, accepts no substitutes, and is a consuming passion of both agony and ecstasy that knows no bounds of age, class, or propriety. The path of love is strewn with obstacles which the intrepid lover must manage to surmount. Counterpoint to the joy of love is provided by stories of tragic affairs which doom the lovers, from Tristan and Iseult, and Romeo and Juliet, to Elvira Madigan. Such love tragedies are universal; it is only in the modern West that love stories have happy endings, usually in marriage.

It is difficult to trace the transformation of this game of love, played by aristocrats, into present-day concepts of love and marriage as an expectation by and for the vast majority of society. For centuries before and after courtly love, marriage was arranged by parents and based on sober considerations of social class, health, and wealth. Love became a consideration in marriage to the degree that eligible young people were allowed a choice among potential partners. Greenfield (1965) hypothesized that romanticism maintained a high motivation to marry when traditional sources of motivation declined. Where class lines were not so rigid, as in America, this process proceeded further and faster. In a similar sociological vein Turner (1970) argues that love translates the social regulation of familial roles into a spontaneous individual desire.

Cross-culturally, the association of marriage with romantic love is accompanied by a particular configuration of circumstances, some of which are characteristic of modern industrial societies. In the US, Singapore, Burma, and India, personal motivation to marry was associated with a romantic view of marriage incorporating the importance of physical attraction, trust, equality of sacrifice, and companionship — aspects not always found in arranged marriages (Theodorson, 1965). Across 43 societies romantic love as a basis for marriage was linked to freedom of choice of spouse, which in turn was related to greater male–female contact, including marriage into the local community, dances, male–female antagonism in courtship, impractical grounds of spouse choice, and privacy for newly-weds (Cozby and Rosenblatt, 1971; Rosenblatt, 1967; Rosenblatt and Cozby, 1972).

The rising popularity of love as a reason for marriage in twentieth-century America was anathema to family sociologists and marriage educators. De Rougemont (1949) referred to it as a "pathological experiment", Burgess (1926) a "romantic impulse"; similar obloquies persist to recent times (Casler, 1969). The presumably irrational, arbitrary, and fleeting nature of a romantic choice of spouse was, in their view, diametrically opposed to the serious, prudent, responsible undertaking which it should be. Kolb (1950) refuted these criticisms by proving them to be an attack on democratic individualism based on outworn notions of romantic versus classical styles. Rubin (1973) and Udry (1971) reviewed numerous studies showing that, far from random and inexplicable, marriages are homogamous for residential or occupational proximity, familiarity, and similarity in age, religion, ethnic group, education, and physical attractiveness, among others. Rather than eloping with the first beau they fall in love with, most college students continually screen potential partners for about ten years (Kephart, 1970). Thus, in its role as a matchmaker, love is the frosting on a wedding cake of solid assets.

Development of Love

A basic antithesis: idealization versus exchange

A persistent perplexity in writings on love is whether the rules governing other human relationships also apply to romance. Exchange-theory, equity, and social reinforcement views on relationship development (e.g. Blau, 1964; Burgess and Huston, 1979; Walster and Walster, 1978) insist that the maintenance and intensification of close dyadic relations depend on the provision and/or promise of rewards sufficient to keep the partners together. This process points to an implicit or explicit assessment of the benefits obtained or forthcoming with the partner in comparison with those thought to be obtainable in alternative relationships.

Yet how can these exchange views be reconciled with the widely held notions that love is blind, that love is the "polar case of intrinsic attraction" (Blau, 1964, p. 76), and that the loved one is idealized rather than seen in a cold, objective light? Throughout world literature love is presented as striking without warning, driving lovers to heights of self-sacrifice in often hopeless quests to master social or physical impediments. Unrequited love is perhaps the most poignant instance of passion untempered by exchange considerations. It is this "irrational" feature of love which kept it out of scientific inquiry for so long and led to a number of typologies of love which have sought a reconciliation of these contradictions.

At the risk of oversimplification, this antithesis can be traced to a tension between *eros* and *agape*. Rubin (1973), translating *eros* as attachment and *agape* as caring, included both in his concept of love. As mentioned earlier, the Greek philosophy of love was based on *eros* — that through indulgence in sex and subsequent purification the lover could come to an appreciation of perfect love and perfect beauty. But the procedure required sex as a starting point, an activity which (at least for men) was pleasurable in itself. In contrast, Christian renunciation of the body in favour of communion between the soul and God brought *agape* to the foreground and cast *eros* as sinful. Deeds done for worldly gain could not serve the glory of God and ultimately were indicative of no more than self-love. Thus, self-sacrifice in asceticism or altruism was the most direct means of demonstrating love for God. It is in this sense that Karl Menninger argued that "the world's greatest lovers have not been Don Juans and Casanovas, but Schweitzers, Gandhis, Helen Kellers, and such saints as Francis of Assisi" (1963, p. 365). From this it is a small step to the ideal of courtly love where, instead of serving God, the lover served the lady of the castle with the same selfless dedication.

This tension between *eros* and *agape*, between profane and sacred love, is replicated in the contrasts between love as a sentiment and love as an emotion (Turner, 1970), between companionate and passionate love (Berscheid and Walster, 1978), between extrinsic and intrinsic attraction (Blau, 1964; Seligman, 1974), between conjugal and romantic love (Burgess, 1926), between reasonable and unreasonable love (Lilar, 1965), and between deficiency-love and being-love (Maslow, 1955; McGovern, 1975). Certainly, such a bold statement obscures the many important distinctions drawn by these theorists in the course of their work. But we contend that the central meaning of these typologies is captured in the contrast between, on the one hand, emotions felt and acts performed in gratitude for past rewards or in hope of future ones, and, on the other hand, emotions or acts with no such apparent implications. The development of love pivots on this tension between concern for self and concern for the partner.

Beyond exchange

The development of close relationships and friendships has been studied and analysed in depth (e.g. see Braiker and Kelley, 1979; Duck, 1977a; Huesmann and Levinger, 1976; Lewis, 1972; Murstein, 1976), but the development of love *per se* has been neglected. Possible explanations for this include a definition of love as simply an intense form of liking — different quantitatively but not qualitatively — or perhaps a reluctance to probe such a seemingly mysterious process. Huston and Burgess (1979, p. 8) have drawn up a succinct but comprehensive list of 12 characteristics of intimate relationships that distinguish them from superficial ones. All apply equally to love and to friendships. Beyond these, what else does love possess that friendship does not?

It is indisputable that most voluntary human relationships are based on considerations of equity and exchange. Barring the undoubtedly spurious notion of love at first sight (better termed infatuation), romantic couples usually begin as friends, where friendship is defined as contingent on the supply and/or expectation of sufficient rewards by both to maintain mutual interest over a period of time. At some point one partner may perceive that he/she is in love or has "fallen" in love. This is unlikely to occur simultaneously in both partners. One may require a higher threshold of commitment before acknowledging the existence of love. One may announce that he/she loves the other in order to induce the other to respond in kind. Because of the intricate tactics which may be involved, we shall not linger over factors governing the timing of the announcement but rather the inner perception of each as to whether they love the other.

It is effortful to "keep score" on an exchange-based relationship, to assess continually if one is under- or over-benefitted and to take steps to restore equity. Couples may use the term love as a criterion for no longer monitoring the state of equity in a relationship, at least not as closely as before. As Levinger (1979) suggests, if the "credit balance" of each is high, deposits and withdrawals involve less concern than when the balance is low. Thus, love may release people from this often necessary but stultifying weighing and sifting. A life filled with "Do I owe them, or do they owe me?" puts a crimp in spontaneity and free expression of one's wishes and impulses — whether prosocial or antisocial — and is costly in itself. If in love both share the same outcomes, then there is no need to keep separate tabs as to who gave and who took in any particular exchange.

Thus, we propose that ideal love differs from friendship in the identity of interests that the partners share. Love exists to the extent that the outcomes enjoyed or suffered by each are enjoyed or suffered by both, whether labelled empathy, communion, or whatever. As partners fall in love, the values in the equity equation (Hatfield and Traupmann, 1981) become transformed (Kelley and Thibaut, 1978, Chapter 7) by a rule which stipulates that the outcomes of all exchanges will have the same value for both partners. "Equality", undoubtedly a prerequisite for friendship, is not quite the proper term, as it implies that the pie is divided into halves and each partner takes his/her own half away. "Identity" is a preferable choice; love implies that the satisfaction of the pie-eater can be savoured just as much by the pieless partner. This contrasts sharply with the marketplace metaphor, where the tit-for-tat swap of one resource for another means that each trader loses what he had initially but acquires sole possession of the new resource. In love, both delight in one's gain, and both grieve at one's loss. The loved one's pleasure and pain become one's own, to borrow from Spinoza (Rubin, 1973, p. 85). Similarly, in an attempt to reconcile exchange with love, Blau (1964) discusses love as an instance of "reverse secondary reinforcement", in which the bestowal of reward enhances the bestower's love for the recipient as much as the reverse.

In terms of equity theory, identity translates into an equality of the outcomes experienced by both. For a balanced exchange the partners' inputs must also be deemed equal. Social relations based on equality are more likely to promote mutual respect and self-esteem than those based on equity, which when allowing for unequal inputs and unequal outcomes highlights the fact that the participants are of unequal worth (Deutsch, 1975). Thus, love can occur only between people who regard or treat one another as equals, despite any "objective" assessment of their inequality. But couples do not live in a vacuum; partners must recognize the actual or potential reactions of friends, parents and acquaintances to their liaison. That is, there must appear to others, as well as to the lovers, a rough comparability in their socially desirable characteristics. Much of their early interaction may be interpreted as an attempt to ascertain whether they are in fact equals in their inputs — that is, whether the equal outcomes of a prospective loving relationship represent a fair deal. As time goes by, and the relationship develops, the outcomes anticipated or enjoyed by each lover (1) are seen to exceed those thought to be available in alternative relationships and (2) become more highly correlated. This increasing correlation occurs through the increasingly knowledgeable selection of behaviours which yield maximum joint profit to the couple; this is often referred to as interdependence. As each person's rewards are obtained more and more in a given relationship, dependence on the partner grows.

Many observers have commented on the "we-feeling", solidarity, or identification that characterizes love. This likely reflects the high degree of common interest that develops across a wide range of behavioural possibilities. Because the partners in love typically react in similar ways to a given event — or have learned to do so — each will assume that the other's reaction will reflect his/her own in considering a potential behaviour or event. Hence we have the hackneyed joke of the wife who, thrilled by a new hat she has purchased, is dumbfounded at her husband's rage over what he sees as her profligacy; this is one exception to the rule that loving spouses are expected to share the same joys and sorrows.

The selflessness and altruism of ideal love are often cited as contradicting the exchange interpretation. But if there is a true merging of fates in love, the lovers themselves will not perceive such acts as selfless or altruistic. Acts benefitting the other, no matter how costly to the lover objectively, will be experienced by the lover as rewarding. In addition, as Hatfield and Traupmann (1981) note, it is unlikely that love will survive a chronic, complete moratorium of rewards received from the partner. More likely is the prospect that love can be self-sacrificing to a degree, or for a time, but that more will be expected in return the longer this continues.

The quality and quantity of love for a partner may change greatly over the developmental course of a relationship. Fantasy as a "mode" of love was found to be higher for adolescents and older adults than for young and middle-aged adults; while the physical aspect (sex) declined for older adults, no significant changes occurred for the affective, cognitive, behavioural, or verbal modes (Neiswender et al., 1975). Thus, both youth and the elderly may indulge in fantasy, since they are free of the heavy child-rearing responsibilities of those aged between. Feelings of love were shown to become more highly correlated with trust and acceptance as relationships develop through time (Driscoll *et al.*, 1972), though this was not replicated by Dion and Dion (1976a). Pam (1970) reported that the intensity of love feelings declines over a six-month period; those with the highest scores at the outset also had relationships which tended not to last. Finally, in couples married from zero to 15 years, longer-married couples exhibit lower love scores (Cimbalo *et al.*, 1976).

Braiker (Braiker-Stambul, 1975; Braiker and Kelley, 1979) investigated the developmental course of relationships from casual dating, serious dating, and engagement to marriage. She identified love as one of five factor themes that partners used retrospectively to describe change or growth in their relationships. The other themes were conflict/negativity, ambivalence, third-party influence, and unit relationship. Items loading on the love dimension dealt primarily with belonging, closeness, attachment, and love; endorsement of these as characteristic of the relationship rose linearly and significantly with successive stages. Combining these findings with those of Cimbalo *et al.*, it may be the case that love reaches its acme at marriage or shortly thereafter, declining gradually — like marital happiness (Pineo, 1961) — over the years. Interestingly, there was no relationship between responses to love items and conflict/negativity responses, suggesting that these reflect independent reward and cost processes, respectively.

When asked what qualities they sought in a spouse, engaged men and women both ranked someone "who believes strongly in love" first of ten descriptions (Baum, 1972). But investigators' definitions of love may differ from those of their respondents. Asked to define love and to indicate its most important component, these engaged people were much more likely to use companionate terms (sharing, understanding, companionship, mutual support and affection) than romantic or altruistic terms. Married couples viewed love as a form of relationship, rather than a feeling, attitude, or character trait, and regarded commitment to a life together as the most basic conception of love (Strauss, 1974).

The ideal of perfect identity in love — in which two become one — is only rarely achieved. Differences in pre-existing values and habits, commitments to third parties, and limited resources of time, energy, and money (among others) conspire to pit the partners against each other, to threaten their dream of unity and unanimity. Paradoxically, the more in love a couple may be, the more distress may result from conflicts of interest when they do arise.

In sum, developing love begins with *eros*, extrinsic attraction, or deficiency-love and blossoms into *agape*, intrinsic attraction, or being-love. Love begins with exchange and then attempts to transcend it. Increasing interdependence brings to light genuine conflicts of interest which must be resolved before further progress toward an identity of interests can be made.

Acceptance of the differences which inevitably appear may later dampen the flames of passionate or romantic love but leave a mature companionate love in its place.

Love and Romanticism

Theorists and researchers plumbing the mysteries of love have drawn abundant distinctions among the many phases, types, styles, expressions, and masks which love possesses. A simple distinction, slighted in the past, recognizes the difference between love as the ideology of romanticism and love as a characterization of an ongoing relationship. Nearly all adolescent and adult members of Western societies are familiar with the image of romance conveyed by the media of art and entertainment (cf. Kon's chapter in this volume). Equally, most have had some degree of experience with one or more romantic partners. Certainly, the extent to which one adheres to the romantic ideal of fiction as a paragon for one's own life may have little or nothing to do with the shape of one's own "love life" over the years. The mistake of family sociologists in debunking love as a basis for marriage earlier this century was the assumption that real life reflected romances on the silver screen — a highly dubious proposition. Thus, we distinguish between belief in love as adherence to the romantic ideal (romanticism) and as an attitude toward one's past or current partner in a close relationship.

Romanticism: the ideology of love

The first empirical study of romanticism as an ideology classified properties of the "romantic culture pattern" into four groups — characteristics of lovers, characteristics of the courtship process, marriage and its relation to other institutions, and philosophical implications (Gross, 1944). Forty statements suggestive of the romantic pattern (e.g. "lovers owe it to each other to marry against their parents' objections when necessary") were counterbalanced with 40 statements indicative of a "realist culture pattern" (e.g. "jealousy over a rival in love is uncalled for"). The fact that high-school students appeared more romantic than psychologists (age and sex composition unspecified for both) was used as a crude form of "known groups" validation.

Men evidence a significant increase in romanticism with deepening romantic involvement, from non-dating to dating to going-steady stages, on a 12-item subset from the Gross scale (Hobart, 1958). No such increase was apparent for women, who, contrary to the popular stereotype, also appear less romantic than males at every stage (no significance test reported). Similarly, men have greater "romantic idealism" than women when dating involvement is high — frequent dater or going steady (Rubin, 1973, p. 206). Men also outscore women on romanticism regardless of dating commitment (Knox and Sporakowski, 1968) or marital status (Oas, 1975). Moreover, male romanticism proved that "absence made the heart grow fonder" in terms of elevated scores for men separated from their "steady" or fiancee; the opposite was true (non-significantly) for women (Hobart, 1958).

It should be noted, however, that the predominance of student samples in such studies — composed mainly of single people — does not provide a fair test of sex differences. Wider samples of adults have shown that married subjects are more romantic than singles (Oas, 1975) and that married women are somewhat more romantic than married men (Reedy et al., 1976). Thus, though remaining hard-headed in the marriage market while single, married women may seek to justify their choice of spouse in romantic terms, just as loving women exaggerate their partner's physical attractiveness (Price et al., 1974, discussed below). Furthermore, engaged men were less romantic than non-engaged men, and romanticism declined steadily from freshman to senior year (Knox and Sporakowski, 1968), suggesting that men's early romantic fantasies become tempered in confrontations with reality. More analytically, women were both less idealistic and less cynical about romantic love than men but were more pragmatic, i.e. affirming the possibility of multiple romances (Dion and Dion, 1973).

The family sociologists' early attack on romantic love as a basis for marriage was refuted empirically by Dean (1961), whose 32-item romanticism scale showed negligible correlations with three of the four Bell Adjustment Inventory subscales but correlated positively (0.19) with emotional adjustment in freshman women. Further, the Dean romanticism scale had hardly any relationship (0.10) with scores on the Locke-Wallace Marital Adjustment Scale in married student couples (Spanier, 1972). Indeed, those above the median on an eight-item romanticism scale were more likely to report a happier-than-average marriage than those below, in a nation-wide sample of *Psychology Today* readers (Athanasiou et al., 1970). High-romantic respondents were more likely to regard their sex lives as "very satisfactory"; such women had a higher frequency of orgasm, and men a lower incidence of impotence. But high romantics also tended to prefer naive to sophisticated sex partners and were less likely to have swapped spouses or to have had extramarital sex. Likewise, romanticism was inversely related to attitudes towards premarital sexual permissiveness in adolescent and adult whites but unrelated to permissiveness in blacks (Reiss, 1964). In the *Psychology Today* sample romanticism, like marital satisfaction, declined somewhat with length of marriage (Glass and Wright, 1977). In conclusion, then, single men are generally more romantic than single women but this reverses in married samples. Single women cannot afford to be too romantic as their social status will depend to a large extent on their husband's; hence a cool, prudent choice is necessary. Even so, romantics do not plunge into subsequently unhappy marriages on the basis of momentary whims. As noted above, they are generally happy with their partners and their love lives.

Love: feelings, attitudes, and behaviour in couples

As we have seen, a number of investigators have developed scales of belief in romanticism as an ideology and related these to individual differences and personal history. An independent line of inquiry looks at love towards one's past or current partner as an index of the quality of the relationship. This approach takes the form either of *ad hoc* questions about love experiences or of scales with varying degrees of validation and support.

Some investigators have asked subjects to report on their love relationships retrospectively. College women reported a higher frequency and intensity of romantic experiences (infatuation and love) than men, even though both sexes began dating at the same age (Dion and Dion, 1973; Kephart, 1967). Curiously, the deeper their current relationship (not-in-love to married), the fewer romantic experiences women reported; the opposite was true for men. Kephart argued that women often redefine their past relationships as a means of rationalizing their current commitment. Reflecting greater romanticism, as discussed earlier, men find it easier to become attracted to the opposite sex (Kephart, 1970), fall in love more quickly (Kanin *et al.*, 1970), and rate the "desire to fall in love" as a more important reason for entering a relationship than their partners do (Hill *et al.*, 1976). The low romanticism of women is highlighted, finally, by the fact that fully 72% of women (but only 24% of men) were undecided when asked if they would marry a person who had all other qualities they desired but whom they did not love (Kephart, 1967). But such differences seem to be moderating; last year, 86% of men and 80% of women said they would not marry without love (Adler and Carey, 1980).

Once in love, though, women report more of the stereotypic emotions of love, e.g. euphoria, well-being, and difficulty concentrating (Dion and Dion, 1973; Kanin *et al.*, 1970). However, women are more ready to disclose feelings than men (Rubin, Hill, Peplau and Dunkel-Schetter, in press); the sexes may actually experience the symptoms of love to the same extent, but men may be more loath to reveal such experiences. As well as falling in love later, women may also fall out of love earlier; they saw the break-up coming sooner, indicated that more problems contributed to the break-up, and precipitated the break-up slightly more often than their partners (Rubin *et al.*,

1980). Thus, women may monitor the progress of their relationships more closely than men do. Though they may feel fewer emotions when in love, men reported more emotions — albeit negative ones — after the break-up than their previous partners did.

What sorts of people fall in love? Those with an external locus of control were more likely to have experienced romantic love or to see it as mysterious and volatile than internals — who feel that their outcomes are, for good or ill, their own doing (Dion and Dion, 1973). Internals also rejected an idealistic view of love more than externals. Similarly, internals were more conjugal and less romantic in their attitudes to love (Munro and Adams, 1978). Among low-defensive students, those with high self-esteem experienced romantic love more often than low self-esteem individuals (Dion and Dion, 1975); perhaps those who think highly of themselves are better able to attract love partners than those who do not. Among high self-esteem persons, those low in defensiveness were willing to admit more romantic- and unrequited-love experiences than those who were highly defensive (see Dion and Dion, 1979, for a review); low-defensive persons may disclose such personal or unflattering information more readily than the highly defensive. After a month's acquaintance, highest levels of love for a partner were found among high-extravert, low-neurotic subjects, compared with the three other combinations (Hamby, 1977); the former may simply be the most socially desirable of all. Bell Adjustment Inventory scores showed no relationship to age at first date or first romantic experience or to the number of such experiences, though those students who reported either difficulty in attraction to the opposite sex or a very high number of romantic experiences scored slightly lower in adjustment (Kephart, 1970). Women who had been infatuated or in love with younger men also scored less adjusted and had lower college grades (Kephart, 1967).

Types of love have been assessed by several authors. For instance, a factor analysis of 383 items dealing with behaviour and feelings towards a loved one yielded such behavioural factors as statements of affection, self-disclosure of personal information, and physical affection (Swensen, 1972). On the resulting scale of feelings and behaviour of love (Swensen and Gilner, 1973) spouses seeking marital counselling reported receiving less love from each other than happy couples and less than they expected (Fiore and Swensen, 1977). Alternatively, the recognition that people love in different ways while continuing to label it love inspired Lee (1974, 1977) to devise a scale to distinguish among six styles of love: *Agape* and *eros* are styles we are already familiar with; *ludus* turns love into a playful game, a series of obstacles and riddles to be mastered; *mania* is a clinging kind of obsessive love; *pragma* is sensible love, the search for an appropriate partner in a balanced relationship; *storge* is companionate love, a friendly bond of affection which seems akin to liking. High self-esteem is characteristic of ludic or playful lovers, while mania is found more often in people with low self-esteem. The distinction between romanticism and love experience is reinforced by Lee's (1977) discovery of a contradiction between subjects' opinions about true love (based on a modified version of the Gross scale) and their actual behaviour in love relationships.

Another attempt to assess the components of love as independent constructs was made by Pam, Plutchik, and Conte (1973). They found that of their five subscales, attachment best distinguished love relationships from dating or friendships, though respect, altruism, and physical attraction also were higher in love.

The Rubin Love Scale

The most widely used love scale to date, developed by Zick Rubin initially for his Ph.D. dissertation, is based on a definition of love quite similar to that of Pam *et al*. The components attachment, caring, and intimacy, taken together yield a love score based at first on 13 items (Rubin, 1970) but subsequently were reduced to nine items. Rubin also constructed a parallel liking scale, measuring respect, admiration, and perceived similarity to self. Though love scores correlated with liking (0.56 for men's responses, 0. 36 for women's), mean love scores were much higher for one's dating partner than for same-sex friends, but mean liking scores were closer, supporting discriminant validity (Rubin, 1970, 1973). Women gave higher summed love-and-liking ratings to partners and friends than men did (Black and Angelis, 1974). This is primarily because women liked their partners more than they were liked in return (Rubin, 1970) and loved their friends more than men did (Black and Angelis, 1975).

Further evidence of discriminant validity comes from a study in which men who read an erotic article reported being more in love and gave elevated love scores to their romantic partner than before the reading, but liking scores were no higher (Dermer and Pyszczynski, 1978). Face validity was indicated when women were more likely to endorse love than liking items as statements that they "most appreciated hearing from people who came to love" them, and men reported saying more love than liking items when sexually aroused by their current partner.

Love for the partner correlated higher with reports that the couples were in love and with the probability of marriage than liking for the partner (Rubin, 1973). In a follow-up study of the same couples six months later, love and, to a lesser degree, liking scores correlated with indications that the relationship had become more intense over that period, but only for those who scored above average on Rubin's romanticism scale. These correlations were even higher when both partners adhered to the romantic ideal. This is the only published attempt to relate romanticism as an ideology to love for one's partner in a relationship. A "known-groups" form of validation showed that casual-dating partners had lower love scores than exclusive-dating, engaged, or married couples but comparable liking and trust scores (Dion and Dion, 1976a).

Love scores also relate to sexual intimacy in dating relationships (Peplau *et al.*, 1977). Of the 82% of couples who had had sex with their current partners, those who had postponed sex until beyond the first month of dating had higher love scores, reported greater closeness to the partner, and were more likely to say they were in love than those who had had sex sooner. Love scores correlated moderately with ratings of sexual satisfaction in both sexes. If the woman had lost her virginity with her present partner, both had higher love scores and indicated a higher probability of marriage than if she had been sexually experienced. No such relationship was found for men's loss of virginity. The authors argue that the "later-sex" couples, more traditional in their attitudes and behaviour, may feel that only love justifies sex and that when it occurs, sexual experience may enhance love feelings through self-attribution. That is, in such couples recognition of love may lead to sex, and sexual behaviour may be rationalized on the grounds that they are in love.

In terms of the survival of relationships over one- or two-year periods, those couples who had broken up had had lower love scores and ratings of being in love at the start and, understandably, much lower scores at the end than those who were still together (Hill *et al.*, 1976; Rubin *et al.*, 1980). But these trends were more accentuated for women's scores than men's, suggesting that women's feelings are better predictors of the fate of a relationship than men's are. This again suggests the greater sensitivity of women than men to their progress as a couple.

Despite indications of equal and high overall self-disclosure on 17 items covering a broad spectrum, total disclosure to the partner correlated strongly with love scores but more weakly with liking (Rubin, Hill, Peplau and Dunkel-Schetter, in press). In love, then, partners feel freer to reveal their inner thoughts and secrets, confirming Rubin's inclusion of intimacy as one of the three elements in love. In each case, though, lower correlations were obtained in a study which employed a different set of items, 32 in all (Critelli and Dupre, 1978); love still correlated significantly with overall disclosure.

Though Rubin (1970) defined romantic love as love between unmarried opposite-sex peers, it has become clear that his love scale applies equally to homosexual couples. In carefully matched samples gay men and women rated their romantic partners on the love and liking scales very similarly to heterosexual men and women (Peplau, 1979); romanticism scores, feelings of closeness, satisfaction, and commitment, and frequency of seeing the partner were also similar. A factor analysis of 20 statements relevant to a romantic/ sexual relationship, rated for importance, yielded two strong factors — dyadic attachment and personal autonomy — separately for gay women, gay men, and heterosexuals. Thus, despite differing sexual preferences, partners were all faced with basic questions of intimacy and independence. Dyadic attachment was positively associated with romanticism, love, liking, and closeness scores in both gay women (Peplau *et al.*, 1978) and gay men (Peplau and Cochran, in press); personal autonomy was negatively related to romanticism in both sexes.

Behavioural correlates of love

Thus far in our review studies have looked only at questionnaire responses. Is there evidence for love beyond paper and pencil? In the lab Rubin (1970) surreptitiously observed the amount of eye contact in his dating couples. Those couples in which both partners scored above the median on the love scale spent more time gazing at one another simultaneously ("mutual focus") than couples below the love median. This was not the case when strangers who were strongly in love with others were brought together. Though lovers conversed with each other nearly twice as long as strangers, explaining part of this mutual focus, they gazed at each other nearly eight times as long as strangers when silent (Goldstein *et al.*, 1976). Thus, in love there is a mutuality and exclusivity of interest in the partner which is absent from weaker relationships.

This loving focus on the partner is also found in heightened recall for words read aloud by both the partner and oneself, above recall for words announced by strangers, in groups of 12 couples (Brenner, 1971). In couples who had dated longer than seven months, memory correlated somewhat with Rubin love scores but not in more recent couples. A study by Dion and Pratt (reported in Dion and Dion, 1979) found a positive association between liking scores and recall, but only in women.

Selective perceptual distortion in the Ames room (the "Honi phenomenon") was also found only in women who scored high on an index of positive cathexis toward the partner — trust together with Rubin love and liking scores (Dion and Dion, 1976b). That is, the spouse, fiance, or dating partner was seen as less distorted in size than a stranger, when made to look disproportionately small or large in either corner of the Ames room, and thus was seen as normal in size after moving a shorter distance from the corner. Yet another female-only effect occurred in the positive relationship between romantic love and the partner's perceived physical attractiveness (Price *et al.*, 1974).

Causal models of love

The most sophisticated approach to identifying the antecedents and consequents of love has employed path analysis as a form of causal modelling. Tesser and Paulhus (1976) concluded that, measured two weeks apart in the same student sample, thoughts about the partner and Rubin love scores had positive effects on each other. Dating had a positive effect on reality constraints (new information refuting old expectations), which itself had a negative effect on love. Bentler and Huba (1979) rejected the Tesser–Paulhus model statistically and presented evidence that love, thought, reality constraints, and dating may all be manifestations of a latent unidimensional variable of general attraction. In this model and a modified Tesser–Paulhus model, initial belief that information about the partner confirmed the lover's expectations predicted greater love later, and more initial thought about the partner led to greater perceptions of disconfirmation of the lover's expectations. Findings on thoughts about the partner, dating frequency, and disconfirmation of expectations suggest that daydreaming about the loved one may lead to idealization, which may be swept away after further contact and hence greater familiarity with the partner.

An Empirical Study of the Development of Love

As we have seen, the empirical literature on love and romanticism is plagued by a profusion of *ad hoc* scales and a fixation on convenient samples, namely, university students. Most reports based on such scales confess dubious levels of reliability and validity, if these are reported at all. Distinctions between romanticism and love are rarely made, and many scales of romanticism have been dubbed "love scales". One measure lumps together items relevant to personal experiences (using "I" as the sentence subject) with others tapping romantic ideology, possibly eliciting a spurious consistency between the two (Lasswell and Lasswell, 1976).

Furthermore, the development of love in romantic relationships has scarcely been touched. When it has, most investigators have used a cross-sectional approach, comparing different sorts of couples measured at one time, instead of the more demanding longitudinal design, in which the same couples are contacted again after a period of time has elapsed. The dangers of inferring developmental trends from cross-sectional data are numerous (see Schaie, 1965, for general background).

As an early look at the development of love and progress toward commitment in couples, and to transcend some past methodological confusions, we designed the study reported here. We began by choosing Rubin's Love Scale which, besides having generated the most research, has proved to have satisfactory levels of reliability and validity. It is, however, subject to acquiescence bias, i.e. agreement with all items yields a high love score. To avoid sampling only students, we moved beyond the campus into the wider community and collected extensive questionnaire data from couples in dating (70 couples), cohabiting (96, including many previously married), and married (117) relationships — an advance on past studies which have questioned only one member of each couple. Our samples consist exclusively of volunteers — a situation dictated by the length of the questionnaire, its personal nature and the comparative rarity of cohabitation in the general population. While this method of obtaining our samples restricts us in the sorts of general statements we can make, e.g. about all cohabitors, we can validly compare our samples without a volunteer effect alone accounting for any differences we might find. A longitudinal perspective is provided by our follow-up questionnaires, sent a year and a half after the initial return; these data will be reported on at a later time. The findings we present here are only a preliminary descriptive set.

There has been considerable media interest in our study, and hence we have been able to request volunteers in three Australian national magazines, three newspapers with state-wide circulation and two from local districts, and five Sydney-area radio stations. On request, questionnaires were mailed to each member of a couple to complete independently. The six sections of the 16-page questionnaire covered the following areas:

A. Individual background: age, education, employment, income, religion, etc.
B. Family background: parents' marriage, relations with parents, childhood, siblings.
C. Opposite-sex relationships: sex, cohabitation, and marriage to persons other than the present partner.
D. History of the present relationship.
E. The relationship now: division of labour, leisure, happiness, problems, sexual activities within and outside the relationship, contact with and attitude of parents, children. This section included Rubin's (1973) nine-item love and liking scales.
F. Attitudes and self-description: attitudes to marriage, cohabitation, feminism, political affiliation, and the Bem (1974) Sex-Role Inventory. Included here was Rubin's (1973) six-item romanticism scale, adapted from earlier scales by Gross (1944) and Hobart (1958).

Our respondents included some residents of each of the six Australian states and both territories. The socioeconomic status of the local sample as indicated by suburb of residence was somewhat above the general Sydney-area distribution. In terms of education, 41% had completed at least some secondary school, a further 39% had done at least some tertiary study and the remaining 20% had post-secondary technical or professional training. Overall, the distribution of religious preference was 54% agnostic/atheist, 26% Protestant, 15% Catholic, and 5% nominating other religions. However, the cohabitors included far more atheists and agnostics (70%) than either the marrieds (51%) or the daters (37%). Thus, the religious still appear to regard cohabitation as "living in sin". See Table 1 for mean ages and other descriptive statistics.

Romanticism

While romanticism tends to wane over time, especially as one becomes more experienced with relationships, the closeness or depth of a relationship can maintain the flame of romantic idealism. Thus, younger people in our sample tended to be more romantic, while those who had had a greater number of significant relationships or who were more sexually experienced exhibited less romanticism. At the same time, progress toward exclusivity in a current relationship, as indicated by engagement or probability of marriage, was associated with an affinity for the romantic ideal, as previously found for males (Hobart, 1958).

In comparing our different relationship groups, we found that for both males and females, daters were more romantic than married people, with cohabitors the least romantic (Table I). When the cohabitors were divided into those who had been married before and those who had not, the former

TABLE I   Descriptive statistics on the sample

	Daters	Cohabitors	Marrieds
Number of couples	70	96	117
Male's age	23.8	29.4	32.3
Female's age	22.6	25.6	29.5
Male's romanticism	19.5^a	18.0^b	18.7^{ab}
Female's romanticism	19.6^a	17.1^b	18.2^c
Male's love	56.7^{ab}	55.7^a	58.9^b
Female's love	58.8^{ab}	55.9^a	59.3^b
Male's liking	52.7^{ab}	51.0^a	54.1^b
Female's liking	55.3^a	51.7^b	54.2^{ab}

Note. Different superscripts (a, b) indicate a significant difference within the row ($p < 0.02$).

group was found to be less romantic than the latter (significant for males). Similarly, marrieds who had lived together prior to marriage (62 couples) were less romantic than those who had not (nonsignificant for either sex). As age tends to be negatively correlated with romanticism (Table II), this could explain some of the group differences. However, inclusion of age as a covariate left all significant group differences intact.

Evidence that romanticism is negatively related to the number of significant relationships and the amount of sexual experience an individual has had is quite strong. The more people with whom a person has had sexual intercourse, the lower the romanticism score is in all six (sex × relationship) groups. Also for all groups, there was a significant negative correlation between romanticism and the view that, given the opportunity, the person would readily have intercourse with someone other than his/her partner. Married people who had lived with someone other than their spouse prior to marriage were significantly less romantic than those who had not. Similarly, males in all relationships were significantly less romantic if they had previously been married.

Generally, the length of the present relationship is unrelated to romanticism. In terms of depth or strength of the relationship, the findings are far more clearcut. Cohabiting and dating females who are engaged are significantly more romantic than those who are not, while for daters and cohabitors of both sexes, there is a positive relationship between romanticism and the probability of marriage. Yet further evidence is available suggesting that the strength of the present relationship is associated with higher levels of romanticism. In all groups, the happiness of the relationship is positively related to romanticism; a similar result is present for sexual satisfaction. Both results support the findings of the survey of *Psychology Today* readers (Athanasiou *et al.*, 1970). Regardless of type of relationship or sex, individuals who have thought of ending their relationship — either considered it or seriously discussed it — tend to have less romantic views.

Consistent with the report by romantics that they are less sexually experienced than non-romantics are their negative views regarding sex before marriage (cf. Reiss, 1964), living together, and other permissive issues, such as legalizing prostitution and relaxing censorship regulations. Finally, the Bem Sex-Role Inventory masculinity and femininity scales were correlated with romanticism. While masculinity showed no relationship, femininity (seeing oneself as considerate, sensitive, understanding, etc.) was positively associated with romanticism for both married and dating males and females. If masculinity and femininity were regarded as broadly analogous to the independent dimensions personal autonomy and dyadic attachment, respectively, then our findings for femininity replicate those for dyadic attachment obtained by Peplau (1979).

TABLE II Correlates of romanticism

	Daters male	Daters female	Cohabitors male	Cohabitors female	Marrieds male	Marrieds female
Age	−0.19	−0.08	−0.28[b]	−0.36[a]	−0.12	0.07
Education	0.03	−0.11	−0.01	−0.23[c]	−0.06	−0.04
Occupational status	−0.05	−0.30[d]	−0.27[c]	−0.26[d]	−0.19[d]	−0.09
Suburb status	−0.25[d]	0.15	−0.08	0.10	−0.35[a]	−0.03
No. of sexual partners	−0.18	−0.26[d]	−0.22[d]	−0.05	−0.22[c]	−0.13
Age at first intercourse	0.05	0.02	−0.10	−0.20[d]	0.02	−0.08
Willingness to have sex with others (1 = no, 2 = yes)	−0.31[b]	−0.26[d]	−0.24[c]	−0.31[a]	−0.19[d]	−0.17[d]
Previous cohabitation (1 = no, 2 = yes)	−0.09	−0.10	−0.06	0.03	−0.19[d]	−0.29[a]
Previous marriage (1 = no, 2 = yes)	−0.20[d]	0.05	−0.21[d]	−0.10	−0.16[d]	−0.04
Length of relationship	0.05	0.03	−0.11	−0.15	−0.11	0.03
Currently engaged (1 = no, 2 = yes)	0.07	0.21[d]	0.11	0.21[d]	—	—
Probability of marriage	0.42[a]	0.33[a]	0.13	0.15	—	—
Happiness of relationship	0.25[d]	0.21[d]	0.14	0.12	0.27[b]	0.19[d]
Sexual satisfaction	0.28[c]	0.16	0.03	0.20[d]	0.15[d]	0.21[d]
Considered ending relationship	−0.21[d]	−0.07	−0.20[d]	−0.18[d]	−0.19[d]	−0.19[d]
Discussed ending relationship	−0.23[d]	−0.02	−0.16	−0.02	−0.16	−0.01
Sex before marriage (6 = positive)	0.00	−0.13	−0.16	−0.22[d]	−0.30[a]	−0.34[a]
Positive view of cohabitation	−0.11	−0.23[d]	−0.12	−0.18[d]	−0.28[a]	−0.20[c]
Permissiveness	−0.04	−0.07	−0.08	−0.13	−0.20[d]	−0.24[b]
Positive view of marriage	0.31[b]	0.38[a]	0.13	0.13	0.26[b]	0.07
Feminism	0.09	0.05	0.00	−0.25[a]	0.01	−0.16[d]
Religiosity	0.00	−0.01	0.07	0.16	0.27[b]	0.23[c]
Masculinity	0.14	0.16	−0.07	0.01	−0.09	−0.08
Femininity	0.33[b]	0.20[d]	0.02	0.00	0.39[a]	0.15[d]
Love	0.42[a]	0.18	0.13	0.32[a]	0.40[a]	0.15
Liking	0.35[b]	0.14	0.25[c]	0.12	0.26[b]	0.04

Because of the varying number of observations on which each correlation is based, correlations within each column may have different degrees of freedom.

[a] $p = 0.001$ [c] $p = 0.01$
[b] $p = 0.005$ [d] $p = 0.05$

Love

Conceptually separate from romanticism are Rubin's love and liking scales, which concern an individual's feelings toward a particular person rather than dealing with his/her view of love more generally. For men, however, there is a tendency to see both of Rubin's concepts as moderately similar to romanticism (average $r = 0.30$), while for women the association is lower (average $r = 0.16$). Although love and liking are proposed as representing different aspects of one's feelings toward another, the correlation between the two ranges from 0.49 to 0.64 in the six samples of the present study, as in previous research. It is not surprising, then, that love and liking have similar relationships with other variables.

In both men and women, love scores are highest for married people, followed by daters and then cohabitors (Table I; cf. Dion and Dion, 1976a). When the married sample is divided into those who lived together prior to marrying and those who did not, the latter group show the highest scores, with these significantly higher than cohabitors, particularly those who had previously been married. While women tend to have higher love and liking scores than men, the reverse is true for romanticism. Unlike past studies, however, neither of these differences is significant here. In contrast to romanticism, love scores show no discernible trends with age (Table III).

An interesting difference between men and women emerges when one looks at the degree of closeness which an individual claims between him/herself and parents during childhood and adolescence. Closeness to father is significantly correlated with love scores for all three groups of men but shows no such trend for women. Closeness to mother, however, tends to correlate with love scores for both men and women. Love for a romantic partner, then, may be fostered by an earlier love for one's parents as a youngster.

As with romanticism, there is evidence that love for one's current partner is negatively related to promiscuity, i.e. the number of sexual partners one has had. In addition, marrieds and daters who have lived with someone other than their current partner have lower love scores than those who haven't. Lower love scores are associated with having had sexual intercourse with a person other than one's partner since the start of the present relationship. The notion that they would, given the opportunity, have sex with another person under almost any conditions is significantly associated with lower love scores in all groups.

We have seen that love scores do not vary with age; neither do they vary with the length of a relationship, be it dating, cohabiting, or a marriage. However, as with romanticism, the depth of a relationship is important. Engaged men, both dating and cohabiting, have significantly higher love scores than their non-engaged counterparts. A similar but non-significant

TABLE III   Correlates of love

	Daters		Cohabitors		Marrieds	
	male	female	male	female	male	female
Liking	0.59^a	0.52^a	0.63^a	0.49^a	0.56^a	0.64^a
Age	−0.08	0.00	−0.15	−0.08	−0.04	0.07
Education	−0.02	−0.18	$−0.17^d$	−0.04	0.11	−0.02
Suburb status	$−0.28^d$	−0.10	0.18	0.14	−0.14	0.02
Occupational status	−0.14	−0.03	0.14	0.07	$−0.16^d$	0.04
Closeness to father	0.31^b	0.06	0.16^d	−0.04	0.17^d	0.10
Closeness to mother	−0.03	0.20^d	0.18^d	0.18^d	0.18^d	0.13
No. of sexual partners	$−0.32^b$	$−0.22^d$	−0.10	0.13	$−0.21^c$	−0.14
Previous cohabitation	$−0.27^c$	−0.13	0.08	0.21^d	−0.13	$−0.22^c$
Sexual partners since relation- ship began	$−0.48^a$	$−0.24^d$	$−0.21^d$	0.06	−0.11	$−0.19^d$
Willingness: sex with others	$−0.66^a$	$−0.44^a$	$−0.21^d$	$−0.23^c$	$−0.33^a$	$−0.15^d$
Length of relationship	0.07	−0.06	0.06	−0.13	−0.02	−0.04
Currently engaged	0.23^d	0.16	0.24^c	0.12	—	—
How long relation- ship will continue	0.35^b	0.35^b	0.24^c	0.41^a	0.18^d	0.27^b
Probability of marriage	0.68^a	0.62^a	0.31^a	0.24^c	—	—
Happiness of relationship	0.59^a	0.57^a	0.34^a	0.38^a	0.60^a	0.54^a
Considered end- ing relationship	$−0.27^c$	$−0.38^a$	$−0.31^a$	$−0.25^c$	$−0.41^a$	$−0.46^a$
Positive view of marriage	0.62^a	0.35^a	0.18^d	0.19^d	0.39^a	0.31^a
Femininity	0.31^b	0.30^b	0.32^a	0.40^a	0.22^c	0.32^a
Feminism	−0.07	−0.13	0.05	$−0.21^d$	−0.03	$−0.25^b$
Positive view of sex before marriage	$−0.36^a$	$−0.20^d$	$−0.16^d$	−0.14	$−0.33^a$	$−0.26^b$
Positive view of cohabitation	$−0.41^a$	$−0.29^c$	−0.10	−0.03	$−0.30^a$	$−0.19^d$
Permissiveness	$−0.28^c$	−0.12	0.07	0.05	$−0.29^a$	$−0.18^b$

$^a p < 0.001$ $^c p < 0.01$
$^b p < 0.005$ $^d p < 0.05$

trend is present for their partners. The length of time the relationship is likely to continue is significantly related to love scores for all groups, as is the likelihood of getting married for all dating and cohabiting groups, corroborating Rubin (1973).

Understandably, the perceived happiness of the relationship is highly correlated with love scores (average $r = 0.58$ for dating and married people), but this is less true of cohabitors. Similarly, thoughts of ending the relationship are significantly and negatively related to love in all groups.

Positive views about the institution of marriage are significantly related to love of partner in all samples, and as with romanticism, so too is femininity. The expression of feminist views is negatively related to the expression of love in all female samples.

Another result which parallels that of romanticism concerns the conservative position taken on issues such as sex before marriage, cohabitation, and sexual issues more generally. For both married and dating men and women, there is a highly consistent and significant trend for the expression of love to be associated with conservative attitudes on these issues. This does not apply to cohabitors, for whom there may be far less variability of viewpoint.

Discussion

In sum, those who are romantic tend also to be in love, and both express more conservative opinions and have had less experience in opposite-sex relationships (whether sex, marriage, or cohabitation) than the tough-minded remainder. These results generally corroborate earlier studies. The particular contribution of the present study is to look at cohabiting couples, who, it turns out, by no means fall halfway between daters and marrieds in their views. As an unconventional relationship, cohabitation attracts those who seem to reject the conventional wisdom of the romantic ideal. On the other hand, to posit that cohabitation makes partners less romantic than they were before requires the discovery of a reason why — something beyond our present knowledge. Similarly, divorce had a "deromanticizing" effect on those of our respondents who had experienced it, not so surprising as the findings on cohabitors. But despite their increasing incidence both divorce and cohabitation continue to be frowned upon by many members of society. Those who would risk the occasional or frequent opprobrium that such statuses elicit may also stand outside mainstream opinion on the importance of love and romance in relationships.

Among the daters and marrieds, dedication to love and romance appears to keep the partners together and away from the temptations of alternative partners. Though this inwardness may seem a fool's paradise to the advocates of open marriage (O'Neill and O'Neill, 1972), we have indications that far from a threat to marriage as an institution, romantic love strengthens the bonds between partners and gives them a reason for maintaining their commitment. Feminists have argued that love is impossible between unequals (Firestone, 1970), which modern men and women are taken to be. If their love is an illusion, then it is an illusion which gratifies them and gives purpose to their relationship.

Conclusion

Our study provides a perspective on certain points discussed earlier. First, though they can be distinguished theoretically, love and romanticism do tend to go together in practice. Both are characteristic of people with fewer past or present lovers, regardless of age now. For these individuals, there is "one and only" whom they feel they have found. Love and romanticism do not follow a simple increasing trend over time; rather, commitment to the partner in engagement or marriage enhances feelings of love, as Braiker and Kelley (1979) found. Referring to our conception of the development of love, movement towards permanence in the relationship means movement towards an identity of interests and equality of outcomes. Such progress is associated with stronger love for the partner, in the sense of Rubin's elements of intimacy, caring, and attachment.

Secondly, after previous experience in cohabitation or marriage, people are more likely to temper their love and enthusiasm for their new partner, perhaps cognizant of possible obstacles in the road ahead. Their starry-eyed romanticism may earlier have come to grief, or their past life convinced them that no one partner is indispensable. There is no evidence here for lesser love in couples together or married for longer periods of time (*contra* Cimbalo *et al.*, 1976). This may reflect an increasing willingness to divorce rather than acquiesce to a loveless marriage out of duty or security.

Thirdly, in a broader frame of reference, love and romanticism were found to be related to conservative attitudes on permissive issues, religion, and feminism. It is paradoxical that romance, so castigated by early sociologists of marriage for threatening family and societal stability, is now the firm bedrock of the *status quo*. In the aftermath of the "sexual revolution" long-term commitment to only one partner may often be regarded as quaint. But rather than fostering love or appreciation for one's spouse or long-term partner — a well-worn rationalization — liaisons outside the primary relationship seem to dilute that love. Thus, there is some evidence that the more that love is shared with a variety of partners, the less love is available for each of them. In love, then, the breadth advocated by ideologies of personal liberation seems to occur at the expense of depth.

Finally, and most importantly, we remain desperately short of longitudinal studies of loving relationships. With the rapidity of change in the divorce rate, sex roles, child-bearing patterns, and cohabitation, cross-sectional comparisons can be grossly misleading. We hope that our panel data will be of some use in this regard. But investigations must follow couples across time to determine who lives happily ever after.

Acknowledgements

We are grateful to L. Anne Peplau and Zick Rubin for their helpful comments on an earlier draft. Thanks are also due our research assistants, Sandra Cotton and Beverley Tulloch, for their able contributions to the research reported here, which was supported by Grant A77/15244 from the Australian Research Grants Committee and by a Macquarie University Research Grant.

CHAPTER 3

From Courtship to Marriage: Mate Selection as an Interpersonal Process

Ted. L. Huston, Catherine A. Surra,
Nancy M. Fitzgerald and Rodney M. Cate

Surprisingly little is known about why people marry particular partners or how couples' relationships change as they progress through courtship and into marriage. Information about the development of relationships is important for several reasons, not the least of which is that they serve as the point around which many people focus their lives. Klinger (1977) found that people identify social relationships more than anything else as making their existence meaningful. The significance of the marriage relationship, in particular, is implied by data indicating that people who report they are satisfied with their marriage tend to feel satisfied with their lives as a whole (Campbell *et al.*, 1976).

Gathering detailed information about courtship can help us to understand why people choose to marry particular partners. Mate selection as a topic of social scientific inquiry has a long history, but this work has not produced a coherent body of knowledge, as we shall show in the following sections. Part of the reason is that investigators have developed their theoretical analyses of mate selection without access to systematic information concerning what actually happens during courtship. Moreover, the experience of courtship may differ for men and women, although this issue has not been adequately taken into account in research. An appreciation of differences between males and females is the proper basis for creation of more sophisticated and empirically supportable theories of mate selection and might provide insights into the premarital origins of sex differences in marriage (Bernard, 1972). More generally, features of premarital relationships may predict patterns of marital interaction and satisfaction (Burgess and Cottrell, 1939; Burgess *et al.*, 1963). Burgess and his colleagues found that length of engagement, the closeness of the relationship during engagement ("engagement success"), and the length of acquaintance prior to marriage were important predictors of the subsequent happiness and stability of the marital relationship. Other researchers have studied whether the occurrences of certain events, such as premarital pregnancy (Christensen and Meissner, 1953; Christensen and Rubinstein, 1956; Lowrie, 1965) or cohabitation (Bentler and Newcomb, 1978; Newcomb, 1981), affect the subsequent quality of marriage. However, noone has yet pursued the idea proposed by Burgess and his co-workers that general qualities of the courtship bear a relationship to marital outcomes.

This situation is the result, at least in part, of the lack of descriptive data concerning the ways in which courtships differ from one another. In this chapter we will summarize two studies, both of which describe the processes through which partners select each other as a mate, the data about the courtship being provided independently by husbands and wives who had been recently married. The fact that we had information from both partners afforded us the opportunity to cross-check our factual data and to examine courtship in terms of both men and women. The data, taken as a whole, are rich, internally consistent, and yield a number of important insights concerning how relationships change as couples move through their courtship and into marriage.

An Overview of Research on Courtship

Compatibility models

The dominant focus of theory and research on courtship has been on testing compatibility models of mate selection. Compatibility models began to take root when studies conducted by sociologists in the 1940s and early 1950s revealed that persons similar to each other on a variety of personal and social characteristics, such as age, social class, religion, and attitudes and values, are likely to choose one another as mates (see Burchinal, 1964; Kerckhoff, 1974; and Udry, 1974, for reviews of this literature). Winch (1958) argued that homogamy in mate selection occurs because people have more opportunity to interact with others who are similar to themselves in social attributes and because people are socialized to prefer socially similar others. Winch suggested that within a "field of eligibles" partners are chosen on the basis of complementary personality needs (Winch, 1955; Winch *et al.*, 1954).

The view of courtship as compatibility testing was elaborated by Kerckhoff and Davis (1962), who found that value consensus and need complementarity were tied in different ways to "courtship progress" (i.e. movement toward marriage over about a six-month period), depending on how long the couples had been involved with one another when the study began. For short-term couples (together less than 18 months), value consensus was associated with progress toward permanence. For long-term couples, however, courtship progress was related to complementarity of needs. These data, when considered in conjunction with the high degree to which the partners were similar in social attributes, led Kerckhoff and Davis (1962) to propose what is now known as their "filter theory" of mate selection.[1] According to this filter theory of courtship selection, persons compare themselves first in terms of social characteristics; later, filtering proceeds with regard to similarity in values; and finally, for those couples still together, continued progress towards marriage depends on the complementarity of needs.

Murstein (1970, 1976, 1977) has reinterpreted Kerckhoff and Davis's (1962) sequential filter theory of courtship in terms of social exchange concepts. He suggested that partners first select one another on the basis of stimulus characteristics; that is, attributes that are observable (such as physical qualities or demeanour). Once potential mates have begun to interact, they begin to assess how similar they are on matters such as political views, religion, sex, and attitudes towards life. In the final stage, the degree of "role fit" in the realms of personal adequacy, spousal role expectations, and sexual compatibility is tested. Murstein (1970, 1976, 1977) presents data which he interprets as support for the theory that partners make a series of decisions about whether to continue the relationship, based on their compatibility on stimulus, value, and role characteristics.

More recently, Lewis (1972, 1973) has posited a developmental stage model of premarital relationships which emphasizes the partners' growing abilities to perceive and identify with each other. In contrast to the models proposed by Kerckhoff and Davis (1962) and Murstein (1970, 1976, 1977), Lewis's (1972, 1973) model focuses on six sequential interpersonal processes: (1) perceiving similarities; (2) achieving pair rapport; (3) inducing mutual self-disclosure; (4) achieving role-taking accuracy; (5) achieving role fit; and (6) achieving dyadic crystallization. The model, like other developmental task formulations, assumes that each process gives rise to the next and that movement to a higher process depends in part upon the successful achievement of the antecedent process. Lewis (1973) reports that 19 out of 24 developmental hypothesis were confirmed by data gathered on two occasions, separated by a span of two years, from 91 dating pairs.

The compatibility view of mate selection and these sequential filter theories share some important assumptions. First, relationship escalation and continuation are seen as a function of the extent to which partners match up on a variety of individual characteristics that they bring to the relationship at its inception. Mate selection, then, is conceptualized as a series of decisions about the degree of fit between the partners' individual attributes. The bases of the decisions about the viability of the relationship are thought to change as increasingly personal information about the partner becomes available. Secondly, these models assume that compatibility of individual attributes influences the selection of a mate for everyone, and the models overlook the fact that other forces, such as the nature of interaction between partners or social network influences, can affect the mate selection process for some persons. Thirdly, implicit in the above, is the assumption that premarital relationships are quite intimate, with the partners revealing to one another (sometimes indirectly) very personal, and hence ordinarily hidden features of their personality and private facts about their lives prior to committing themselves to marriage. Finally, the decision to marry is seen as continuously open to modification as new information is gathered and assessments of different types of compatibility are made.

Recent research is beginning to unsettle this tidy picture of mate selection. In an attempt to replicate the study which prompted Kerckhoff and Davis (1962) to postulate their sequential filter model, Levinger *et al.* (1970) found no evidence that the value similarity or need complementarity indicated in the Kerckhoff–Davis model predicted couples' courtship progress, regardless of whether couples had been together for a long (18 months or more) or a short period of time. Data from a recent study by Hill, Rubin, and Peplau (1976) also indicate the present inadequacy of such sequential filter models of mate selection. Hill and his colleagues used a sample of couples already "going together" and found evidence of filtering regarding social characteristics. Among these established pairs, matching on age, physical attractiveness, educational plans, and intelligence distinguished couples who stayed together from those who broke up. Similarity in attitudes, however, did not predict which couples remained together over the two-year period. Hill *et al.*'s (1976) data suggest that "filtering" on the basis of social background and physical characteristics continues to occur after partners have become involved with one another.

Murstein's (1970, 1976) and Lewis's (1973) formulations of premarital relationship processes have been criticized because the supporting data are methodologically weak (Rubin and Levinger, 1974; Kerckhoff, 1977). The samples used to test both theories appear poorly suited for studying the early stages of premarital involvement or for establishing the posited sequences. Murstein's (1970, 1976) couples were either going together or engaged and 84% of Lewis's (1973) were either considering marriage or engaged at the first time of measurement. Although both investigators postulated that causal processes operate in a particular sequence, neither supplied evidence demonstrating the sequential ordering of the causal processes (Rubin and Levinger, 1974). The investigators, for instance, did not break down their data by the partners' level of involvement in order to examine whether different predictors are important at various stages of involvement. Lewis (1975) and Murstein (1974b, 1976) now concede that their data do not provide evidence for the operation of a fixed sequence of filters or processes. What remains open, however, is whether sequential filter frameworks, if put to a careful test, would be able to account for the progression of premarital romantic relationships, as other more sophisticated models may do for other types of relationship (Duck and Craig, 1978).

Other attempts to examine courtship progress in terms of compatibility of attitudes, values, and personality have not, on the whole, been successful. With regard to attitudes and values, studies by Byrne et al. (1970) and Coombs (1966) have shown that similarity is related to the attraction partners feel towards one another after their first date. Attempts to connect attitude similarity to courtship progress or courtship stability, however, have generally failed (Hill et al., 1976; Levinger et al., 1970; Levinger, 1972), except for the study by Kerckhoff and Davis (1962). Centers (1975) compared five groups of partners ranging in involvement from "most preferred date" to married and found no difference in their degree of attitude similarity. Murstein (1976) found, in two of his three samples, that couples who seriously contemplated marriage were somewhat more similar than random pairs; his data, however, are cross-sectional and do not allow determination of whether attitude similarity, independent of its correlation with social background, contributes to the escalation of involvement.

With regard to compatibility models of courtship stressing personality fit, the data are equally weak. Winch's (1958) theory of complementary needs and the data which he gathered in support of it have been criticized on conceptual and methodological grounds. Seyfried (1977), among others, points out that Winch's theory fails to specify which needs complement one another and that the theory does not consider cases in which highly similar needs (e.g. when both partners are high in need for affiliation) might be complementary. Tharp (1963) has observed that the three data sets used to support Winch's theory are interdependent. Two of the supporting sets were drawn from one source (a needs interview) and the third set correlated highly with the other two ($r = 0.60$ and 0.80). Tharp (1963) further questioned Winch's (1958) results on statistical grounds, pointing out that the 388 correlations used to test the complementary needs hypothesis were not independent, which inflates the risk of a Type I error. After reviewing other research, Tharp (1963) concluded that "the complementary need hypothesis as now stated is not tenable" (p. 107). Even though Winch (1974) reformulated his position by incorporating role concepts, the theory has no more support today than it did when Tharp (1963) made his pronouncement.

After reviewing the literature on compatibility testing and courtship, Huston and Levinger (1978) indicated two major reasons why attempts to predict the evolution of premarital relationships on the basis of the degree of compatibility between the partners' personal attributes have failed. First, they note that little is known about the ways in which combinations of attributes affect the behaviour of premarital partners towards one another. Recent attempts to reconceptualize personality (e.g. Bem and Allen, 1974; Carson, 1979; Mischel, 1973) have stressed the mediating effects of situational and interpersonal contexts on the expression of individuality. This literature suggests only a weak correlation between traits and needs, as traditionally measured, and particular forms of social behaviour exhibited within a specific relationship. Secondly, Huston and Levinger (1978) suggest that social psychologists studying premarital relationships may have overestimated the degree to which such relationships are intimate, and hence the degree to which partners' psychological attributes come into play.

Another criticism of research on interpersonal attraction and premarital relationships has been that data have been gathered primarily from samples of college students (Huston, 1974; Huston and Levinger, 1978). Both Lewis's (1973) and Murstein's (1976) models of mate selection, for example, were supported by data drawn from couples who were students. Consequently, what we know about mate selection is limited to conclusions based on samples comprised of young, largely white, middle-class adults, most of whom have never been previously married.

Mate selection as an interpersonal process

Waller (1938), using what are now known as exchange and symbolic interactional concepts, was the first to describe mate selection as an interpersonal process. According to Waller (1938, pp. 271-272):

> Once a courtship passes its earlier stages, an interaction of idealization takes place which carries the couple farther from contact with reality. . . . As the love relationship develops, A idealizes B, replacing the actual B to a considerable extent with a creature of his own imagination. Because of this idealization of B, he displays to her only a limited segment of himself; he puts his best foot foremost . . . he tries to be in

her presence the sort of person who would be a fit companion for the sort of person he thinks she is; all of this facilitates the idealization of A by B, and B in turn governs her behavior in such a way as to give A a false impression.

Waller (1938), in addition to suggesting that relationships are propelled forward by idealization, stressed that relationships are also moved toward marriage by interpersonal events and episodes, many of which appear likely to be more influenced by the partners' immediate needs and desires than by global values and generalized traits. Bolton (1961) has amplified Waller's (1938) perspective by identifying additional commitment mechanisms and suggesting that the mix of factors influencing commitment varies considerably from one couple to another. Commitment for some couples may emerge from deeply personal interaction extended over a long period of time; for others, it may result from a series of misunderstandings. The following account, provided by a participant in L.R. Rubin's (1976) interview study of working-class couples, illustrates how a relationship might move to marriage in a seemingly more casual manner, at least from the male partner's perspective, than the compatibility design posits:

> We met at this place and I kind of liked her. She was cool and kind of fun to be with. Before I knew it, we were going steady. I had this class ring from high school and she kept wanting me to give it to her. So finally one night I took it off and did. And the next thing I knew, she took it down and had it made smaller. She made a big thing out of it, and so did her family. Don't get me wrong; I liked her good enough. But I just didn't think about getting married — not then anyhow. But then, after we were going together for almost a year, it just seemed like the thing to do. So we did (p. 164).

Social exchange theorists (e.g. Altman and Taylor, 1973; Huesmann and Levinger, 1976; Huston and Burgess, 1979; Kelley, 1979; Scanzoni, 1979) and social scientists working within a symbolic interactional framework (e.g. McCall and Simmons, 1977) have offered interpretations bearing on how the interdependence between premarital partners evolves through time. Studies of the interpersonal processes and experiences that bear upon the decision to marry are rare, however, and investigations of developmental change are even more rare. An excellent study by Braiker and Kelley (1979) is illustrative of the promise of such research.

Braiker and Kelley (1979) utilized a thematic analysis of unstructured, retrospective interviews of newly-wed couples to identify the content dimensions used to describe stages of courtship. Then a structured questionnaire, based upon these content dimensions, was administered to 22 young married couples, who completed the questionnaire four times, once for each of these stages: casual dating, serious dating, engagement, and marriage (first six months). A principal components analysis resulted in the identification of four dimensions of relationship development: (1) *love*, which relates to the extent of belongingness or attachment; (2) *conflict*, the degree of negative affect and overt argument; (3) *maintenance*, the degree of self-disclosure between partners about their relationship; and (4) *ambivalence*, the extent of confusion or hesitancy about continuing the relationship.

Among the most interesting parts of Braiker and Kelley's (1979) work is their finding that scores on each of these dimensions changed significantly over the four stages of involvement. Scores on the love and maintenance dimensions increased over all four stages, although increases on the maintenance dimension were more gradual than on love. In contrast, ambivalence tended to decrease over the four stages while reported conflict increased from the period of casual to serious dating but levelled off in the later stages. Changes in the factor loadings suggest that the meaning of ambivalence and maintenance was different, depending on the partners' level of involvement. Ambivalence and conflict went together early in relationships; later on, ambivalence was tied to the amount of love; when the partners were seriously involved, however, maintenance behaviours co-varied with level of reported conflict.

Apart from the Bolton (1961) and Braiker and Kelley (1979) studies, which were based on data gathered from married couples, research efforts have not been mounted to describe either the interpersonal processes through which partners select mates or the changes in features of relationships which accompany the movement to marriage. No study has examined the beginnings of premarital relationships which eventuate in marriage, or attempted to follow relationships from their early stages of involvement into marriage. Longitudinal studies of premarital relationships have been limited to examinations of the determinants of "courtship progress" — measured in terms of perceived changes in the likelihood of marriage over a restricted period of time (generally 6–8 months). Problems of subject attrition, coupled with the wide variation in the length of premarital relationships, make the conduct of extended longitudinal research extremely difficult.

Cross-sectional comparisons of couples varying in commitment are apt to provide a misleading picture of how relationships change as partners move through the premarital phase of their relationship up to and into marriage. The most notable complication is that the proportion of couples who eventually marry in each cross-sectional grouping varies from a small proportion (in the low commitment categories) to a large majority (in the "engaged" category, for instance). Cross-sectional data can provide information about the characteristics of relationships at various stages of involvement, but the different mortality rates of relationships for the cross-sectional groupings make the leap from cross-sectional data to longitudinal inference particularly problematic.

Investigating Courtship Development

Developing a descriptive procedure

The purpose of the investigations described below was to gather basic information about the evolution of premarital relationships from their early stages into marriage. A basic task was to develop an efficient procedure for gathering reliable and valid information concerning the events and processes associated with courtship.

Ideally, we would have liked to be able to study the interpersonal events and larger circumstances that affect partners' commitment to one another as relationships evolve and to contrast relationships that result in marriage with those that do not, but from a practical standpoint this was not feasible. We focused instead upon devising a procedure which would help newly-wed husbands and wives reconstruct in a time-ordered fashion, those events and circumstances that led up to their marriage. These data were then used to develop a portrait of how courtships, in general, move to marriage, and also allowed us to examine differences among couples in their courtship, as well as how courtships are experienced differently by men and women. The procedure was articulated through a series of pilot interviews, and then used with encouraging results in a study by Cate and Huston (Study 1 below) involving 50 husband–wife pairs. On the basis of the Cate and Huston investigation, the procedures were further refined by Surra (Study 2).

Retrospective techniques such as those used in the present investigations are commonly used with intellectual profit in the social sciences. Studies of individual development and research on sexual behaviour, for example, often require respondents to recall information about their life histories or significant life events (cf. Baltes and Goulet, 1971; Spanier, 1976). Problems with retrospective techniques include threats to validity and reliability of data due to faulty recall or falsified accounts (Sudman and Bradburn, 1974; Spanier, 1976). According to Spanier (1976), faulty recall results when respondents unintentionally distort the past because they either forget events or alter their perceptions of their history. Falsified accounts, on the other hand, are deliberate misrepresentations of the past, which often result from respondents' attempts to provide socially desirable information (Spanier, 1976).

It is important to recognize that the degree of accuracy in recalling the past is probably related to the salience of what respondents are asked to remember (Spanier, 1976). The events of the courtship period are undoubtedly among the most important a person ever experiences and they are apt to be particularly salient to newly-weds. It was not uncommon in our studies, for example, for husbands and wives to relate in considerable detail the events of particularly important days in their courtship, the timing of sexual experiences (such as the first kiss or first sexual intercourse), and occurrences shared with family or friends.

Nonetheless, we took several steps commonly recommended (Spanier, 1976; Sudman and Bradburn, 1974) to minimize faulty recall and to increase the likelihood of obtaining honest accounts. In order to enhance the participants' ability to remember events, they were asked to provide an open-ended description of their courtship early in the interview. Data on the events of the courtship and features of the relationship were gathered in chronological order, with the respondents using a timeline to order the significant events. Finally, we gave the participants several opportunities to check on the accuracy of their recollections, to add new material, and to make changes in their report.

The shortcomings associated with falsified accounts are probably less hazardous in our studies than some others for at least two reasons. First, the nature of a socially desirable response may be less clear than in studies of other phenomena. It is likely that conceptions of a socially appropriate courtship are not as well defined as, for example, perceptions of appropriate ways of initiating a relationship or acceptable sexual behaviours. However, our respondents were aware of the fact that their spouses were reporting on the same events and experiences and knew we had a way of checking on the information they provided. Thus, one way for our respondents to present themselves in a favourable light was to be as accurate as possible in the data they provided. Nevertheless, we took precautions to minimize the problem of respondents' giving false information. First, in order to eliminate collusion between spouses, we made sure that the exact purpose and nature of the investigation were unknown to participants before the interview. Secondly, we started each interview with the following statements:

> We realize that there is *great* variability in how relationships develop over time and that there is no *typical* relationship. Each relationship is also unique in the experiences that characterize it over time. We are *not* interested primarily in how your relationship is similar to others, but in the ways in which it might be different and unique.

This caveat was intended to communicate to respondents that we had no preconceived notions about what we expected to hear from them, thereby reducing the tendency to give false accounts.

Although we took steps to enable respondents to relive the actual experience of their courtship throughout the interview, there is still the possibility that respondents unintentionally reported to us an inaccurate reconstruction of the past. A common criticism of retrospective data is the accounts of the past are altered to be congruent with the present state of affairs. Our data on the extent of agreement between the reports of husbands and wives, however, suggest that if our respondents modified the past, they created a shared fiction. One part of our procedure, for example, required that husbands and wives represent their courtship history on a graph, as a series of changes in the probability of marriage to their partner from the time they met until their wedding day. The correlations of estimates provided independently by husbands and wives of the probability of marriage for each month of the courtship averaged 0.79 for the first study and 0.80 for the second study. Data on husband–wife agreement are surprisingly strong across all levels of courtship and marriage, indicating either that couples created a common reconstruction or that they were fairly accurate in their reports. It is notable that partners' reports on the characteristics of their marriage (which are concurrent) are as similar as their reports concerning the premarital stages of their relationship.

Study I: tracing the development of premarital relationships into marriage

The initial study to be reviewed (Cate and Huston, in prep.) was designed to establish how relationships changed from the time partners met until they eventually married. One hundred newly-weds (i.e. 50 couples) were asked to reconstruct, from first meeting to marriage, alterations in the probability that they would marry their partners. They divided their relationship into four periods — akin to casual dating, serious dating, commitment, and marriage — and then with reference to each period filled out questionnaires designed to assess love, ambivalence, conflict, and self-disclosure and problem-solving activities (labelled "maintenance").

The specific goals of the investigation were: (a) to obtain a typology of courtships, based upon how the participants perceived the evolution of their commitment from first meeting to marriage; (b) to examine, in general, how relationships are perceived to change from the early stages of involvement into marriage; and (c) to determine if and, if so, how courtship and marriage are perceived and experienced differently by men and women.

Method

Couples, who were married for the first time and for less than one year, were recruited for participation in Study I (Cate and Huston, in prep.). The average age of the participating husbands was 23.9 years; the wives averaged 21.8 years in age.

Husbands and wives are interviewed by separate interviewers during the same period of time, out of earshot of one another. The interviewer began by saying that there are many ways people arrive at the decision to marry and that we were interested in getting a picture of this variety. After ascertaining the date of the beginning of the relationship and the wedding date and marking them on the horizontal axis of a blank graph, the interviewer asked the respondent to provide a brief rendition of the courtship. Next, other important events that occurred during the courtship were marked on the baseline of the graph, as shown in Fig. 1.

To get a more detailed description of the premarital relationship, the interviewees were asked to construct a graph of it, showing how the probability of marriage changed from the time the relationship with their spouse started until the wedding day. The interviewer indicated that each division along the bottom of the graph represented one month of courtship, and the chance of marrying the partner was indicated along the side of the graph. Participants were told that with this graph they would show the changes that occurred over time in the probability that they and their partner would marry one another. In estimating the "chance of marriage" the participants were asked to consider both their own feelings about marrying their partner and how they thought their partner felt about marrying them.

The interviewer and the respondent then proceeded to draw the trajectory according to these instructions:

> Remember, we are interested in *your* perception of changes in the chance of you and (name) becoming married. Of course, the day of your wedding you were 100% sure you would marry (at this point, the interviewer marked 100% with a dot on the

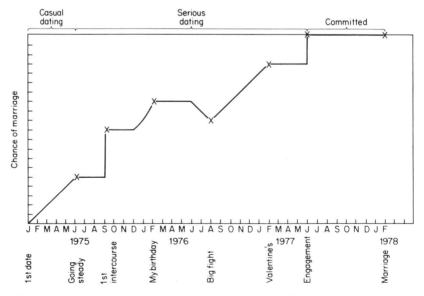

FIG. 1   An example of a graph of changes in the probability of marriage.

graph above the month of the wedding). On your first meeting or date the chance of your becoming married may have been zero or it may have been something above zero. It is very important to keep in mind that changes in the chance of marriage are based on changes in both your feelings about marriage and (name's) feelings. So this is *not* an indicator of how much you wanted to marry or how much you were in love. It is an indicator of the chance that you and (name) would get married. Now what do you think was the chance of marrying (name) at this time when you say your relationship began?

The interviewer then pointed to the first month of the graph and marked the respondent's answer. The graphing procedure continued with:

> We realize that once people meet, the relationship can go up, go down or stay at the same level. At what month were you first aware that the chance of marrying was different from this point? (Interviewer pointed to the chance of marriage for the first month in the relationship.) What was the chance of marriage at that time? (Interviewer marked the chance of marriage.) Now we must connect these two points with the proper line. Was this a gradual change or were there things that caused it to change suddenly? (Interviewer probed until appropriate extension of the line could be drawn.)

Next, the interviewer asked about why the chance of marriage changed during the period indicated, and probed for details until a complete description was obtained. The above sequence of questions was repeated with appropriate changes in wording until the trajectory was graphed to the wedding day. Upon completion of the graph, the respondent was again given the opportunity to make necessary changes. (Figure 1 illustrates the raw data obtained from the graphing procedure for one male respondent.)

The next task was to have the participants indicate on the graph the period or periods when they and their partner were (a) dating, but not identified as a couple (casually dating); (b) dating, and identified as a couple (seriously dating); and (c) certain of marriage (committed). Figure 1 shows how one person marked his graph to indicate these levels of involvement. It is important to note that not all respondents experienced all three levels and that the three levels were usually, but not always, sequential.

Participants were next asked to fill out a 25-item questionnaire that sought to measure features of relationships for each of the three premarital periods as well as for the time since marriage. The questionnaire was developed by Braiker and Kelley (1979) for use with a similar sample of newly-weds and required participants to rate on a nine-point scale the degree to which each statement represented their experiences in the relationship during the particular time of interest. On the basis of their data, Braiker and Kelley (1979) derived four dimensions: (a) *love* (feelings of belongingness, attachment); (b) *ambivalence* (confusion or anxiety about the relationship); (c) *conflict* (disagreement, negativity); and (d) *maintenance behaviour* (characterized primarily in terms of the respondent's inclination to disclose feelings about the relationship to the partner, efforts to solve problems, and willingness to change behaviour to please the partner).

To control for order effects, the sequence of questionnaire administration was counterbalanced. Half the couples filled out the instrument from the first involvement level to the present, while the other half completed the instrument in reverse order. Those persons who reported experiencing a particular level of involvement more than once filled out the questionnaire for the most recent period, and respondents who reported skipping an involvement level did not complete the instrument for that stage. Before the respondent completed the questionnaire for each period, the interviewer set the stage by pointing to the appropriate time span on the graph and by reviewing events and experiences which the respondent had used earlier to depict that period.

Results

The first step in the analysis was to group individual trajectories to marriage into meaningful courtship styles. A set of procedures developed by Tucker (1966), aimed at reducing a sample of graphed data to a small number of representative curves, was applied to the monthly estimates of changes in the probability of marriage. Tucker (1966) originally proposed his techniques as an alternative to the traditional approach for the analysis of learning curves, where an average curve is generated to represent a sample of learning curves. He pointed out that the average curve provides a misleading representation when the learning process differs considerably from one person to another. Tucker's (1966) analysis, which is conceptually similar to a principal components analysis, generates a parsimonious number of derived curves that underlie individual graphs. The Tucker (1966) procedures were ideally suited to our purposes because they allowed us to convert the graphed data into a manageable form and still retain the important variations in the sample of graphs.

The analysis yielded three components that accounted for 97% of the total sum of squares for the data plotted on the 100 graphs. The three components retained were selected on the basis of the mean square ratios for each component and the percent of the total sum of squares accounted for by each component. The mean square ratios for the three derived components were considerably larger than those remaining.[2]

The Tucker (1966) analysis also provides a component score for every person on each derived curve. In a general way, the magnitude of the component score indicates the degree to which a derived curve underlies an individual's curve.[3] To group the original graphs according to their similarity, the component scores for each person on the three derived curves were used.

Individuals scoring most highly on the same component were grouped into relationship types. Seventy percent of the individuals (35 couples) fell into the same type as their partner by means of this method. Curves representing an average trajectory for each type were drawn using the raw data, as shown in Fig. 2. Based on the differences in the trajectories visually evident in the graphs, three types of courtships were identified as follows:

Type I: *Accelerated Courtship*, a type which began at about 13% chance of marriage, on the average, and climbed rapidly to a high probability.

Type II: *Intermediate Courtship*, a form which fell between Types I and III in the rate they proceeded to high levels of commitment and, on the average, moved toward marriage in a smoother fashion than the others.

Type III: *Prolonged Courtship*, a type characterized by a slow, rocky ascent to marital commitment.

In order to get a more refined picture of how the types differed in terms of properties of the graphs, a series of Sex × Relationship Type analyses of variance were conducted. Men and women, in general, graphed their relationships and demarcated their levels of involvement within them in a similar fashion. There were two exceptions to this generalization, and these will be noted in the context of our discussion of sex differences below. No significant Sex × Relationship Type interactions were found.

The differences among the types are summarized in Tables I and II. Persons in prolonged relationships spent significantly more time, both in absolute and proportionate terms, in the "dating" and "a couple" stages; they also took longer to move from low (25%) to high (75%) probability of marriage, and they experienced more downturns in their relationships. As

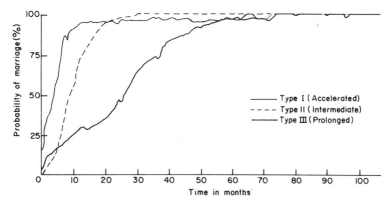

FIG. 2 Average trajectories to marriage for relationship types for Study 1.

TABLE I Comparison of courtship types on length of relationship and involvement level variables for Study I

Variable	Accelerated	Relationship type Intermediate	Prolonged	Significance level
A. Length of relationship (months)	17.9	23.0	50.5[a]	$p < 0.05$
B. Length of involvement levels (months)				
1. Dating	3.3	2.6	6.4[a]	$p < 0.05$
2. A couple	6.9	6.4	24.9[a]	$p < 0.05$
3. Certain of marriage	7.5	10.4	15.5	n.s.
C. Ratio of time in level to total length of relationship				
1. Dating	0.11	0.17	0.13	n.s.
2. A couple	0.31	0.27	0.50[a]	$p < 0.05$
3. Certain of marriage	0.42	0.40	0.27[a]	$p < 0.05$
D. Probability of marriage by level of involvement				
1. Dating	0.24[b]	0.99	0.13	$p < 0.05$
2. A couple	0.50	0.48	0.39	n.s.
3. Certain of marriage	0.89	0.89	0.89	n.s.
E. Time in months to move from low probability (25%) to high probability (75%) of marriage	2.6	5.5	17.2[a]	$p < 0.05$

[a] Significantly different from "accelerated" and "intermediate" relationships.
[b] Significantly different from "intermediate" relationships.

TABLE II Summary of findings for turning point variables

Variable	Accelerated	Relationship type Intermediate	Prolonged	Significance level
A. Number of turning points	5.4	5.3	$\underline{11.4^a}$	$p < 0.05$
B. Number of downturns	1.1	0.8	$\underline{3.2}$	$p < 0.05$
C. Index of turbulence (ratio of downturns to total length of relationship)	0.08	$\underline{0.03}$	0.06	$p < 0.05$

[a] Underlined figures are significantly different from non-underlined figures.

one might expect from looking at Fig. 2, persons in accelerated relationships reported a significantly greater chance of marriage at the earliest stage of premarital involvement than those in either intermediate or prolonged relationships. The intermediate relationships were distinguishable from the other two types primarily in that they were significantly less turbulent. Thus, the analyses of the specific properties of the graphs verify and elaborate what we can see in Fig. 2.

The next step in the analysis considered whether the types could be further differentiated in terms of participants' reports of the evolution of love, conflict, ambivalence, and maintenance activities. These analyses were conducted using the data from the 35 couples where both partners fell into the same relationship type. Four $2 \times 4 \times 3$ (Sex $\times$ Involvement level $\times$ Relationship type) analyses of variance were performed, one for each of the four relationship dimensions. Involvement Level and Sex were treated as repeated measures factors.

Significant Involvement Level differences were found for all four relationship dimensions. Love and maintenance activities both increased through the four levels of involvement. Conflict and negativity increased as the couple moved from dating to identifying as a couple, but levelled off at the last two levels. Ambivalence was high during the precommitment phases, but was perceived to decrease when the couple became committed and married. These results are almost identical to those reported by Braiker and Kelley (1979).

A significant Sex $\times$ Involvement Level interaction was found for love. Men reportedly experienced more love for their partners than women during the first stage of involvement: "dating, but not a couple". They also reported that they moved from the dating stage to the couple stage significantly earlier (2.6 months to 5.5 months, respectively) and that they spent proportionately less time in the dating stage (10–19%, respectively). There were no sex differences in love at the last three involvement levels. The findings that men fall in love faster and report their relationships escalating to deeper involvement levels sooner is consistent with the results of several previous investigations (Burgess and Wallin, 1953; Kanin *et al.*, 1970; Rubin *et al.*, 1980). Rubin *et al.* (1980) have suggested that this sex difference in love early in relationships is due, in part, to the greater economic stake women traditionally have had in selecting a mate. They postulate that women must be more practical than men since the success of their husbands often determines their social status and financial well-being.

"Maintenance" behaviours pertain to such things as self-disclosure about the relationship, telling the partner about wants and needs, and changing behaviour to alleviate problems. A significant Sex $\times$ Involvement Level interaction was found for maintenance behaviours, with men reporting significantly more such activity early in the relationship (when they were dating, but not a couple), and with the reverse pattern obtaining for the period of time since the couple was married. The finding that men reported more maintenance behaviours than women early in the relationship might be partially explained by the findings having to do with sex differences on love. Several researchers report a significant relationship between liking and self-disclosure (see Huston and Levinger, 1978, for a review) and Rubin (1970) has shown that liking and loving are highly correlated in dating couples. Consequently, since the men in this study reported more love early in their relationship, then it seems appropriate that they would also report more maintenance behaviours, given that maintenance behaviours include self-disclosure activities. On the other hand, women reported engaging in more maintenance behaviours than men at marriage, but did not report significantly higher levels of love at this level. These findings suggest that maintenance oriented self-disclosure and related activities may be anchored in love only during the early stages of involvement. Indeed, Braiker and Kelley (1979) found that early in the premarital relationship love was associated with maintenance activities, while later, amounts of love had little connection with such activities. Thus, it could be that as couples move to marriage, maintenance activities not only increase, but also get increasingly tied in with sex roles which specify that women take over the day-to-day maintenance of the relationship (Parsons and Bales, 1955).

Do the relationship types differ with regard to their reports of love, ambivalence, conflict, and maintenance behaviours? The answer, in general, is in the affirmative. For love, a significant interaction between Relationship Type and Involvement Level emerged. A *post hoc* analysis of the means showed that participants in prolonged and intermediate relationships reported that they felt more love for their partner at each of the first two levels of involvement than those in accelerated relationships. The three relationship types did not differ in the reported amount of love at either of the two committed levels of involvement. With regard to ambivalence, there was no significant main effect for Relationship Type, nor did Relationship Type and Involvement Level interact significantly.

The relationships differed in the degree to which the participants reportedly experienced conflict, as was indicated by a significant main effect for Relationship Type with regard to conflict. *Post hoc* comparisons of the means revealed that participants in prolonged relationships reported more conflict than those in either accelerated or intermediate relationships.

A main effect for Relationship Type and an interaction effect between Relationship Type and Involvement Level were found for the maintenance behaviour dimension. The main effect for Relationship Type showed that participants in accelerated relationships reported significantly lower levels of maintenance activity than those in both the prolonged and intermediate types. Analysis of the interaction, however, revealed that the differences between the accelerated relationship and the other two types held for all three premarital phases, but not for the marital phase.

Conclusions from Study I

The results of the various analyses, when viewed together, provide a clear picture of the three courtship types identified in this study. Prolonged relationships, as the name suggests, moved towards marriage in a gradual and uncertain fashion. Relative to the other two types, participants in prolonged relationships reported the highest level of conflict. This finding is consistent with that showing that prolonged relationships are marked by more downturns, showed a longer time spent in the precommitment levels of involvement, and took longer to move from low to high levels of probability of marriage. The high level of conflict in these relationships, however, was not associated with lower levels of love. In fact, people involved in prolonged relationships reported high levels of love early in the relationship relative to those in accelerated relationships, and their reported levels of love increased with each stage of involvement. Maintenance activity was also reported to increase as the relationship evolved and was particularly high throughout the premarital relationship for couples in prolonged and intermediate relationships, as compared to that reported by those in accelerated relationships.

Intermediate courtships differed from the prolonged relationships in that the trajectories of these relationships moved to certainty at a faster rate. Relative to prolonged courtships, this more rapid movement was reflected in short courtships, rapid movement from uncommitted to committed levels of involvement and a fast progression from a low to high probability of marriage. As might be expected, these couples indicated less conflict than those in prolonged relationships, and reported fewer downturns in the probability of marriage. Participants in these courtships, as in the prolonged ones, reported high levels of love for their partners early in the relationship, with their amount of love escalating with their level of involvement.

Accelerated relationships, in comparison to the other two types, were short, with the partners' wedding day on the average less than 18 months after their first meeting. Commitment to marriage came rapidly in these relationships, and the partners spent relatively little time in the initial stage of involvement. Again, as with intermediate relationships, the rapid movement to marriage was characterized by low levels of conflict. Participants in this type of relationship reported the lowest amount of love early in the relationship, as well as the lowest amount of activity aimed at maintaining or enhancing the intensity of the relationship throughout the courtship. Participants in accelerated relationships "fell quickly" for one another. In contrast to the love-struck image sometimes portrayed by the mass media, however, they reported they were neither notably in love nor particularly involved in the relationship.

Study II: Courtship patterns and changes in other interactions

The second study, conducted by Surra (in preparation), was designed to examine how different styles of courtship might be linked to patterns of dyadic interaction. We were curious about whether the particular path a couple took to marriage, conceived in terms of the kind of typology generated in Study I, might be reflected in the way that the partners structure their relationship with each other as well as with other people. To determine this, we needed an instrument that would allow us to gather data on the extent and nature of independent and joint activities.

Developing a measure of premarital and marital interaction

The first step in the development of the Premarital and Marital Activities Checklist was to discover what dimensions of interaction typically have been used to classify premarital and marital relationships. Although social scientists have not done much methodological and substantive work in this area with regard to the premarital relationship, students of the marital relationship have been intensively interested in identifying the ways in which spouses interact. A review of the literature on styles of marital interaction (Bernard, 1964; Bott, 1971; Burgess and Locke, 1945; Burgess and Wallin, 1953; Cuber and Harroff, 1965; Farber, 1962; Goodrich et al., 1968; Ryder, 1970a, 1970b) turned up six dimensions commonly used to differentiate marriages: (a) the frequency and character of interaction with kin; (b) the extent to which activities performed take place in the home or in the community; (c) the extent to which leisure activities are done alone, with the partner, and with others; (d) the degree of affect present in the relationship; (e) the amount of positive as compared to negative affect; and (f) the extent to which instrumental role performance is sex-typed. It is interesting to note that the features of interaction mentioned by observers of marriage capture not only the way in which the spouses relate to one another, but also the manner in which they organize their social world in terms of their relationship.

The dimensions of interaction derived from the literature on marriage seem to be equally relevant to premarital relationships. We began to develop an Activities Checklist with a roster of activities identified by Weiss and his colleagues (see Weiss and Margolin, 1977) as representing those typically performed by married persons. To generate activities for premarital couples, we asked 50 people involved in varying degrees (i.e. casually dating, seriously dating, etc.) to keep a complete diary of their activities over a two-day period. A representative list of activities relevant to both unmarried and married couples was then developed with the goal of covering three basic domains: (a) affectional activities, (b) leisure activities, and (c) instrumental activities. The instrumental activities were subclassified in terms of whether they were typically done by men, typically done by women, or non-sex-typed. The activities were put into a questionnaire which was administered to the participants in our second study, who provided information on how often and with whom activities were performed for different periods of their premarital relationship and for marriage.

Procedure

The Activities Checklist was used in conjunction with the graphing procedure to gather data for Study II. A sample of 50 couples, married for the first time and for 10 months or less, was secured using the same techniques as were used in the first study.

The procedures used to construct the graphs of changes in the chance of marriage were generally the same as in Study I. After drawing the graph and separating it into levels of involvement, the respondent was asked to complete the Activities Checklist once for each of the premarital levels and once for marriage. For each activity, the respondent indicated how many days the activity was performed at least once in a typical month of each period of the relationship. Respondents were asked to fill out the questionnaire items regarding affectional activities in reference only to their partner. For leisure activities, they were asked to indicate the frequency with which the activity was done: (a) alone, (b) with their partner, (c) with their partner and others together, and (d) with others only. Participants were asked to indicate for each instrumental activity how often they engaged in the activity alone and how frequently they did the activity with their partner. To ascertain the extent to which the relationship was central to our participants' lives, we also asked them to indicate the proportion of time spent alone, with their partner, with their partner and others, and with others only, when all of the time available to them was considered.

Prior to completing the checklist for each of the premarital involvement levels, the interviewer pointed to the appropriate period on the graph, briefly reviewed with the respondent what had happened during that period and asked the respondent to try to remember the kinds of activities that were performed and with whom these activities were done. Respondents who said they did not experience a particular involvement level were asked to skip the checklist for that level; those who experienced the same level more than once filled it out for the most recent period. As in Study I, the order of questionnaire administration was counterbalanced across couples.

The Activities Checklist yielded information on several facets of premarital and marital interaction, including the degree to which the total life space of the individual was organized around the partner, the extent to which instrumental activities were done according to traditional roles, and the way in which leisure activity was allocated in terms of the partner and others.

Results

The data analytic procedures used to identify courtship types in this study paralleled those applied in the first study. The analysis was conducted to derive a small number of component curves which captured individual variation in the sample of 100 graphs.

The monthly changes in probability of marriage had to be analysed twice in this study by means of the Tucker (1966) procedures. The first time the analysis was performed, two components (accounting for 98% of the total sum of squares of the graphed data) were derived. Subsequent analyses demonstrated, however, that individuals' scores on the two components were almost perfectly negatively correlated ($r = -0.985$). Essentially, this result meant that the information contained in one component score was reflected almost entirely in the second score. In short, one component curve could adequately represent the 100 graphs in this data set. This conclusion seemed inconsistent with the diversity apparent in individual trajectories to marriage and with the results of the Cate and Huston (in press) study. The most obvious explanation for this discrepancy stems from differences in the pool of graphs in each study in combination with the specifications required to perform the analysis. Tucker's (1966) analysis requires that all graphs in the sample cover the same number of months (or trials). For this reason, all graphs were assigned a score of 100% probability of marriage for each month beyond the wedding day, until each graph was as long as the longest courtship in the pool. Although this method of extending the graphs was used in both studies, a larger proportion of courtships reached asymptote fairly rapidly in Study II as compared to Study I, which made it more difficult to detect differences in the shapes of individual curves in the second study.

To generate curves that would reflect the variation in individual trajectories and still reduce the sample of graphs to a workable form, a decision was made to drop couples with relationships longer than 41 months (seven couples in all) and then to reanalyse the remaining data. This time, three components were derived, and these accounted for nearly 99% of the total sum of squares of the raw data. Correlational analyses revealed that individuals' component scores obtained from this analysis were only moderately correlated (*r* for Components I and II = − 0.49; *r* for Components I and III = − 0.29; *r* for Components II and III = − 0.68).

As in the first study, couples were grouped into courtship types according to the similarity of their scores on the three derived curves. In this study, however, we made use of more of the information contained in the component scores by clustering persons according to whether they were "high" or "low" on each component, rather than according to their highest component score. A natural split in the distribution of component scores (the largest gap in the entire range of scores) was determined for each component. Seven categories of persons emerged when individuals were grouped on the basis of whether they were above or below this split for the three components.[4] Because these seven categories captured very refined differences in the graphs and we wished to form a smaller, more workable number of clusters, we had to collapse persons in some of the categories to form relationship types. When it was necessary to combine categories, they were collapsed over Components II and III, since these components were the most highly correlated and, therefore, contained the most similar information about individual graphs.

Three relationship types resulted from these procedures, and a fourth type was formed by grouping those seven couples with longer courtships who had been dropped from the first Tucker (1966) analysis. Seventy-six percent of the individuals fell into the same relationship type as their partner. An average trajectory to marriage was drawn for each relationship type (see Fig. 3) and the types were named:

Type I: *Accelerated–Arrested Courtship*, a type which began, on the average and relative to other relationship types, at the highest initial probability of marriage moved rapidly to higher probabilities of marriage, but slowed down in its final progression to marital commitment.

Type II: *Accelerated Courtship*, a category of relationships which escalated more slowly than Type I at first, but then proceeded directly and smoothly to asymptote.

Type III: *Intermediate Courtship*, a type that evolved to marriage at a pace that was slower than the first two types, but more rapid than the fourth; turbulence is most evident, on the average, in the final shift from 80% to 100% probability of marriage.

Type IV: *Prolonged Courtship*, a group consisting of relationships that took a relatively retarded and rocky path to marriage.

To examine whether observed differences in average trajectories to marriage were statistically reliable, the relationship types were compared with regard to features taken from the graphs, as we had done in Study I.

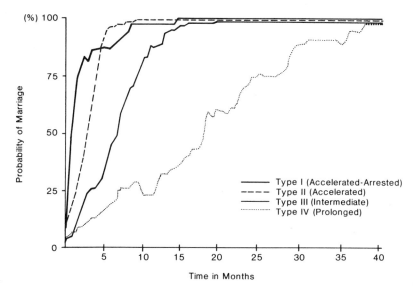

FIG. 3   Average trajectories to marriage for relationship types for Study II.

Data from the first involvement level, "dating, but not a couple", were dropped from these and subsequent analyses because sixteen respondents reported they had by-passed this stage during their courtships. Only the 38 couples where the partners fell into the same type were included in this and the remaining analyses.

The analyses of variance on graphic properties revealed that types in this study were particularly distinct from one another on variables having to do with the length of the relationship and its various stages, as well as the rate at which the relationship reportedly moved to marriage (see Table III). Accelerated and accelerated-arrested relationships were characterized, of course, by shorter courtships and shorter amounts of time in the "couple" involvement level, as compared to intermediate and prolonged relationships. The visual impression of accelerated-arrested courtships depicted in Fig. 3, where the trajectory first escalates rapidly and then loses momentum, was substantiated by the results on several variables. Couples in accelerated-arrested relationships reported the highest mean probability of marriage at the "couple" stage of all the types, and spent significantly less time in this level, relative to the total length of relationship, than did couples in intermediate and prolonged relationships. Once "certainty of marriage" was reached, couples in accelerated-arrested relationships spent a significantly greater proportion of time at that level than the remaining types. This finding helps to explain the somewhat extended "tail" evident in the average trajectory

TABLE III Comparison of courtship types on length of relationship and involvement level variables for Study II

Variable	Relationship types			
	Accelerated-arrested	Accelerated	Intermediate	Prolonged
A. Length of relationship (months)	14.3^a	10.9^a	27.6^b	59.4
B. Length of involvement levels (months)				
1. A couple	2.6^a	3.2^b	11.5^b	37.1
2. Certain of marriage	9.6	3.1	7.7	11.6
C. Ratio of time in level to total length of relationship				
1. A couple	0.25^b	0.40	0.45	0.57
2. Certain of marriage	0.60^c	0.31	0.30	0.21
D. Probability of marriage by level of involvement				
1. A couple	0.67^c	0.47	0.43	0.44
2. Certain of marriage	0.86	0.93	0.91	0.86
E. Time in months to move from low probability (25%) to high probability (75%) of marriage	2.46	3.31	9.35	28.15^c

Note— All differences are significant at 0.05 level or less.
^{a} Significantly different from intermediate and prolonged.
^{b} Significantly different from prolonged.
^{c} Significantly different from all other types.

for these courtships. Prolonged courtships, as the name implies, were significantly different from the others with regard to the overall length of courtship, the amount of time spent in the "couple" stage, and the slow progression from low (25%) to high (75%) probability of marriage. Intermediate relationships were most distinct from prolonged; these partners had shorter courtships and spent less time in the "couple" involvement level than prolonged. In contrast to the results of the first study, no significant differences were found among the types on any of the variables reflecting the degree of turbulence in the relationship (number of turning points, number of downturns, or the index of turbulence).

These findings point to some of the similarities and differences between the types in the two studies. Prolonged relationships in both studies were comparable in terms of the long, delayed path to marital commitment. The average trajectories to marriage for accelerated and for intermediate relationships were similar in the two studies, although these two types were more distinct from the prolonged type on length-related variables in the second study than in the first. In addition, intermediate courtships were less turbulent than the other types in Study I while no such differences were found in Study II. The accelerated-arrested type bears little resemblance to the types in Study I, except in its rapid movement to "certainty of marriage" and its higher probability of marriage at the "couple" stage. In these respects, it is most like the accelerated type in Study I. Accelerated-arrested relationships differed from all of the types identified previously, however, in the relatively high proportion of time spent in the "certain of marriage" involvement level.

The next set of analyses was conducted to describe level of involvement, sex, and relationship type differences in the performance of affectional, instrumental, and leisure activities. A series of Sex(2) × Involvement Level(3) × Relationship Type(4) analyses of variance were performed for this purpose. Because a number of the couples skipped the "dating, but not a couple" level, only data on the remaining two premarital periods and marriage were included in these analyses. The frequencies of instrumental activities performed alone and with the partner and the frequencies of leisure activities performed alone, with the partner, with the partner and others, and with others only were converted to proportional variables, and customary arc sine transformations were applied. As in Study I, Sex and Involvement Level were treated as repeated measures factors.

The level of involvement findings indicated that courtship and early marriage for these couples were characterized by an expansion of companionate activities in several domains. The frequency of *affectional* activities performed with the partner increased significantly through both premarital involvement levels and into marriage. This finding corresponds to the increase in love across involvement levels reported in Study I, but it is not possible from our data to ascertain whether the increase in affectional activities in Study II is tied directly to enhanced feelings of love for the partner.

The overall pattern of findings for *instrumental* activities suggests that partners share practical tasks more and more as they approach and move into marriage. In general, instrumental female and instrumental male activities were reportedly done increasingly with the partner as the relationship moved through courtship and into marriage. This increased sharing was accompanied by a decrease in the proportions of instrumental male and non-sex-typed activities performed by either partner alone as couples moved from premarriage to marriage. No such effect for female activities done alone was discovered, however. Taken together, the results suggest that mutual participation in the practical side of life is an important feature of partners' interaction during courtship and early marriage that has been ignored by most researchers.

The distribution of *leisure* activities over involvement levels showed a pattern of increased sharing of recreation with the partner, but a general withdrawal from others (see Fig. 4). The proportion of leisure activities performed with the partner grew significantly over all three stages while the proportion of these activities performed with the partner and others declined significantly for the "couple" and "marriage" involvement levels. Similarly, the proportion of leisure activities done only with others decreased over all premarital stages and marriage. The results on percentages of time spent with the partner and other persons were like those for leisure, and suggested a pulling away from others and a drawing towards the partner as couples moved into early marriage. Partners focused on one another and neglected others, at least in the area of leisure activities, as they courted and married.

Only one sex difference emerged on variables derived from the graphs: men reported a significantly higher mean probability of marriage throughout their courtship than women. This suggests that men have greater confidence than women that the relationship will end in marriage and may partially reflect the traditional tendency for males to be in control of the decision to marry. When the findings on sex differences on interaction variables are considered, an interesting picture of male–female differentiation emerges. When the overall distribution of domestic tasks between the sexes is considered, women did proportionately more of these tasks alone than with their partners, regardless of the sex-specific nature of the activity. Secondly, with regard to sex differences in the use of time, women, as compared to men, reported significantly more time spent with the partner, less time spent alone, and more time spent with the partner and others. Thirdly, a significant Sex by Involvement Level interaction indicated that the withdrawal from leisure activities with the partner and others which accompanied the movement to

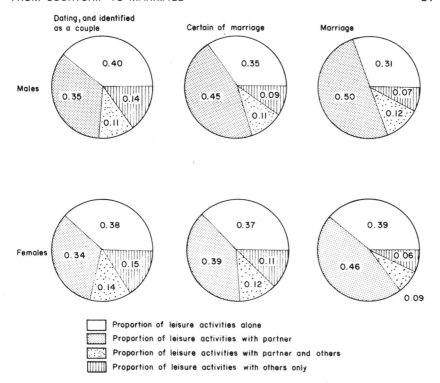

FIG. 4   The proportion of leisure activities in the two sexes at different levels of involvement.

marriage was primarily due to the increasing withdrawal of women, but not men. As shown in Fig. 4, for women the distribution of leisure activities shifted so that the proportion of these activities shared with the partner and the network was reduced, while for men there was little change in this domain.

The data summarized above are consistent with traditional views of heterosexual relationships, where men are thought to be more independent and women are believed to focus on the home and their partners. In general, relationship- and home-centred activities are more central to the total life-space of women than men. Moreover, changes in activities with the network that accompany the transition to marriage are more severe for women than men. It appears that women may not integrate relationships with family and friends with their marital partnerships to the extent that men do.

Further analyses of variance also showed how relationship types differed in structuring of interaction between the partners, on the one hand, and between the partners and others, on the other hand. For example, a significant main effect for Relationship Type was found to suggest that partners in the two accelerated types reported a higher frequency of affectional activities than did couples in prolonged and intermediate courtships, but *post-hoc* tests revealed that these differences were not statistically significant. The relationship types also differed in the extent to which household tasks were segregated along traditional lines, with women in accelerated–arrested, intermediate, and prolonged courtships reporting that they perform more female tasks alone. Similar findings for the relationship types were obtained when other indicators of the amount of sex-typing in domestic tasks were examined. A significant main effect for Relationship Type was found for the proportion of leisure activities performed with the partner, with this proportion being significantly greater for couples in accelerated–arrested relationships than for couples in prolonged courtships. These two types were also found to differ in a similar way on the proportion of leisure activities performed with the partner and others. A significant Relationship Type × Involvement Level interaction revealed that the proportion of leisure activities done with the partner and others reported by couples in accelerated–arrested relationships was significantly less than that reported by partners in prolonged relationships for both the ''certain of marriage'' and ''marriage'' involvement levels.

Summary and conclusions

The concepts of internàl versus external relatedness are useful for summarizing differences among the types on interaction variables, since the types differed from one another in both internal and external relatedness. Leisure activities and use of time variables can be viewed as measures of the extent to which partners associated with persons external to the dyad. Affectional and instrumental variables, on the other hand, can be construed as indicators of the extent of bondedness between partners on two internal domains of relationships.

Partners in intermediate courtships were the most disaffiliated, especially in the affectional and instrumental domains. In addition, these couples were characterized as spending greater amounts of time alone than couples in the other types, although this difference was not statistically significant in *post-hoc* test. Intermediate relationships, then, can be characterized as noncohesive in both internal and external relatedness. Partners performed fewer affectional activities, showed up as having segregated roles on instrumental variables, and tended to spend more time alone rather than with the partner and with others, as compared to the other types.

Prolonged relationships are similar to intermediate in some respects. Partners in prolonged relationships performed proportionately more instrumental male activities alone than couples in either of the accelerated types, and were characterized by segregated roles in the realm of typically female instrumental activities. With regard to affectional activities, partners in prolonged courtships tended to report lower frequencies than either of the accelerated types, and were more similar to intermediate relationships. The separateness apparent in these internal dimensions of relatedness carried over into interaction with others for couples in prolonged relationships. These partners reported lower proportions of leisure activities with the partner and withdrew less from leisure activities with the partner and others as they progressed to marriage, compared to partners in accelerated–arrested relationships.

In contrast to prolonged and intermediate relationships, partners in accelerated–arrested courtships were closely affiliated on most internal and external indicators of relatedness. On the indicators of instrumental male activities performed alone, instrumental female activities performed with the partner, instrumental non-sex-typed activities done alone, and affectional activities, these partners were highly affiliated. Yet these couples maintained segregated task performance with regard to typically female activities. In terms of associations with others, the accelerated–arrested type was characterized by extensive leisure with the partner and a greater withdrawal from leisure with the partner and others, especially when contrasted with the prolonged type. Thus, accelerated–arrested relationships were distinguished by cohesiveness with regard to associations with other persons and by a mix of bondedness and separateness on internal relationship domains.

Couples in accelerated relationships were the most highly affiliated on internal domains of the relationship. These partners reported sharing the performance of female instrumental activities, performing fewer instrumental male activities alone, and tended towards higher levels of affectional activities. Accelerated couples did not show up as more cohesive in terms of activities and time shared with others.

Conclusions

The data gathering procedures used in the two studies were designed to provide a descriptive portrait of how relationships change from their inception to marriage. The graphing procedure yielded a representation of the premarital relationship as a series of changes in the perceived likelihood of marriage, and was an efficient means of gathering information on several characteristics of the courtship, including, for example, the length of the relationship, the occurrence and perceived length of different involvement levels, and the degree of stability of the likelihood of marriage. The graphed data were then analysed in a way that would allow us to extract relationship types, based on the degree of similarity in the paths taken to marriage. Other data collection procedures provided material on dimensions of relationships (love, conflict, ambivalence, and maintenance) and on the activity patterns of partners for various stages of involvement. We used this information to characterize the movement to marriage for relationships in general and to describe how the progression to marriage varied for different types of relationships. The ways in which men and women differed in the experience of courtship and marriage were also delineated.

The data on sex differences during courtship and marriage suggest that the development of romantic relationships is not the same for both sexes. Men seem more attuned than women to the escalation of the relationship to marriage, as indicated by data showing that men, as compared to women, reported more love and maintenance activities at early involvement levels, reportedly moved from the "dating" to the "couple" stage sooner, spent proportionately less time in the "dating" stage, and perceived greater likelihood of marriage throughout the courtship. Men seem to have greater certainty that the relationship is a viable one, while women appear to be more cautious with regard to falling in love and making judgements about the marriageability of their relationships. These observations reflect traditional roles of men and women in heterosexual relationships, where men are seen to be in control of the decision to marry and women to follow their partner's leads. Some of the hesitancy on the part of women may also be due to the fact that often they are choosing an economic and social status as well as a spouse when they decide to marry (Rubin *et al.*, 1980). The decision to marry may require greater forethought for women than for men.

Other findings from the two studies also fit conventional views of men and women in relationships. Once couples were wed, women gave greater attention to the sustenance of the relationship; they reported more involvement in activities aimed at maintaining the relationship than men. In addition, as women moved closer to and into marriage, they reduced the extent to which they included others in their leisure activities with the partner, but men did not. Women also reported that their time was more partner-centred and that they spent less time alone than men throughout their relationships. With regard to instrumental activities, women reportedly did proportionately fewer domestic tasks with their partners than did men. These data imply that women expend greater energy than men in sustaining the expressive qualities of the relationship at marriage and in attending to instrumental tasks throughout the history of their relationships. Moreover, women may adjust associations with the network to a greater extent than men in order to accommodate their increasing involvement with their partners. Such an interpretation is consistent with Bernard's (1972) argument that marriage is a more demanding lifestyle for women than men, and, therefore, takes a greater toll on the well-being of women. Our data suggest, however, that women's adaptations to their relationships may begin before they marry.

As one might expect, the findings on changes in relationships for different involvement levels characterize the movement to marriage as a process whereby partners become increasingly close and, at the same time, resolve doubts and conflicts about their partnership. On indicators of love and maintenance activities and on measures of shared activities in different interaction domains, partners showed up as increasingly involved as the relationship advanced towards and into marriage. Concomitant with these changes was a reduction in ambivalence about becoming involved and a decrease in the amount of conflict and negative feelings toward the partner.

The evidence on relationship types suggests, however, that the processes which accompany the development of relationships to marriage are not the same for all couples. Those courtships that were shorter and moved rapidly to marital commitment (i.e. the accelerated relationships) were characterized by low levels of love and maintenance at early involvement levels in Study I. Relationships falling into the two accelerated types in Study II, however, were the most closely affiliated on indicators of the degree to which various kinds of activities were shared between partners. Couples who had a long, rocky, delayed path to marriage — the prolonged courtships in Study I — reported high levels of love and maintenance activities early in their relationships, and high levels of conflict throughout their courtship and marriage. In the second study, partners in the prolonged type were disaffiliated on most internal and external interaction domains. Finally, the intermediate type in Study I, which included courtships that escalated to marriage more rapidly than prolonged courtships, was high on love and maintenance activities, especially during early involvement levels, but low on conflict. Relationships in the intermediate type in Study II, in contrast, were the most disassociated on the extent to which partners performed affectional and instrumental activities together.

Although our data are descriptive, they do suggest that the relationship types differ in the forces that prompt them to marry. Partners in prolonged and intermediate relationships reported considerable amounts of love for their partners before certainty of marriage was reached, even though these partners did not perform activities together as extensively as did partners in accelerated types of relationships. It may be that intermediate and prolonged kinds of relationships move to marriage on the basis of subjective feelings of closeness and attachment to the partner rather than because of the intertwining of their day-to-day lives. A corollary to this explanation, as our data suggest, is that such relationships require extensive maintenance to sustain feelings of love. Since partners are not sharing activities to any large extent, they may find it necessary to concentrate on the emotional aspects of the relationship by resolving problems and self-disclosing about their feelings. This explanation fits data gathered by from Braiker and Kelley (1979), who found that love was tied to maintenance activities early in premarital relationships.

Couples in accelerated kinds of relationships, on the other hand, were highly bonded in their daily activities throughout their courtship and marriage. Strong beliefs that the relationship would end in marriage preceded the development of love and attention to the maintenance of the relationship for these couples. Perhaps these men and women were inclined to marry even before they met their prospective partners. Diverse life situations (for example, transitions in work, school, or even other relationships) may prompt individuals to align themselves closely in a short period of time. For these individuals, love may have grown out of their intense companionship by the time they reached certainty of marriage, or these couples may have labelled their feelings to be consistent with the romantic view that if they are committed to marriage, they must be in love. Involvement in the maintenance of their relationship also came later for these couples, once they were wed.

The data on relationship types further indicate that the salience and role of conflict in relationships may be associated with the amount of interaction and the nature of the commitment to marry between partners. Furthermore, the mechanisms which underlie this association seem to vary, depending on the relationship type. Braiker and Kelley (1979) have noted that different styles of courtship have different sources of conflict. They propose that the degree and type of conflict varies with the difficulty partners encounter in making transitions to deeper involvement levels and with the amount of interdependence between partners. Thus, for prolonged kinds of relationships, high levels of conflict may be connected to the apparently disassociated nature of these relationships, especially if partners are working to maintain feelings of closeness, or to the difficult transition to marital commitment that is characteristic of these couples. The low levels of conflict in accelerated relationships, in contrast, may result from the partner's agreement on their degree of commitment to marriage and on their extent of bondedness. The very lack of interaction between partners in intermediate relationships may preclude opportunities for conflict in these partnerships.

We can only speculate about the subsequent marital cohesion and stability of the different relationship types. The work of Cuber and Harroff (1965) is especially relevant here because these authors have evidence that the kinds of adjustments that partners make in marriage vary with the type of relationship. Partners who had prolonged and intermediate courtships may need to concentrate their efforts on sustaining their intense emotional involvement in relationships seemingly based on disaffiliated interaction. These partnerships may be especially susceptible to the devitalization processes described by Cuber and Harroff (1965), in which some relationships lose the intense emotional quality they once had. Marital stability in these marriages seems especially dependent on the partners' acceptance of reduced emotional involvement and their satisfaction with other aspects of their lives, such as their work, children, and friendships. Partners in accelerated courtships probably will be faced with maintaining the high levels of affiliation that characterized their courtships. During courtship and early marriage, at least, partnerships seem to resemble the "vital" and "total" marriages described by Cuber and Harroff (1965), where partners are highly interdependent in their interaction. These authors have noted that marital instability for such couples may be linked to one or both partners' withdrawing from the other, thereby disrupting the total quality of the relationship that the partners had known in the past.

The studies reviewed here add depth to our descriptive knowledge about the development of relationships to marriage. The findings emphasize the need for researchers to allow for differences in the mechanisms that lead couples to marriage and in the meaning of courtship and marriage for men and women. The information provided here may serve as an impetus for future investigations directed at explaining the mate selection process and at predicting marital outcomes.

Acknowledgement

Work on this chapter was supported by a grant from the National Institute of Mental Health (No. 1 R01 MH33938-01), Ted L. Huston, Principal Investigator.

Notes

[1] Although the Kerckhoff–Davis Filter Theory of Mate Selection is the first and most important such theory, other independent filter theories have been proposed to describe other forms of relationship growth, and criticisms made here of the Kerckhoff–Davis model do not *necessarily* apply to those other theories which are founded on an entirely different data base. For discussion of these other models, readers should consult Morton and Douglas (p. 3 this Volume), Duck (1977a), Duck and Craig (1978), and McCarthy (1981) — (*Editors*).

[2] Each component curve generated by the Tucker (1966) analysis is defined by a set of monthly component loadings. These loadings can be plotted to obtain a visual representation of the derived curves, which can be compared for differences in overall

shape. It is inappropriate, however, to make month-by-month comparisons of the loadings.

[3] Individual trajectories to marriage can be reproduced, within the limits of error, by multiplying the monthly loadings for each derived curve by the appropriate component score and then summing the products (for a detailed explanation of the analysis, see Tucker, 1966).

[4] One category, for example, consisted of twelve persons who were grouped together because they each scored "high" on Component I, "low" on Component II, and "high" on Component III. Another category, with 20 persons, was formed by grouping those who were "low," "high," and "high" on Components I, II, and III, respectively.

Section II

Relationships Across the Lifespan

CHAPTER 4

Friendship over the Life-cycle

Wenda J. Dickens and Daniel Perlman

"It may be true of friendship as it is of jazz. If you need a definition for it, you'll never understand it." (Donelson and Gullahorn, 1977, p. 156). The word has many interpretations as is evident from the numerous psychological, sociological or philosophical definitions dating back at least as far as Aristotle. Friendship can imply casual acquaintances, persons with whom one shares social or occupational activities, or a more intimate relationship with reciprocal feelings of tenderness, caring, and sincerity. For the purposes of this chapter, we wish to distinguish between interpersonal attraction and personal relationships: *interpersonal attraction* refers to the positive attitude of liking another person; by *personal relationships*, we mean people's ongoing friendships and kin relations. Admittedly, this distinction is a matter of nuance rather than radical difference but, in essence, whilst we usually like our friends, friendships involve more than attraction *per se*.

The bulk of the existing social-psychological literature in this general area has focused on interpersonal attraction. Much of the relevant research has been experimental in nature and involved college students as subjects and, based on the findings from this work, social psychologists have formulated a number of principles and theories. The implicit assumption in formulating such principles is that they operate across the life cycle and, in going through the attraction literature, one can undoubtedly find evidence consistent with this assumption. Consider, for instance, the following propositions, each of which has been tested with various age groups ranging from children to senior citizens:

(a) We like those who like us (Hartup *et al.*, 1967; Backman and Secord, 1959).

(b) We like those whose attitudes are similar to our own (Byrne and Griffitt, 1966; Byrne and Nelson, 1965).

(c) We like individuals whose personalities are similar to our own (Duck *et al.*, 1980; Duck, 1975).

(d) We like physically attractive people (Dion and Berscheid, 1974; Stroebe *et al.*, 1971).

(e) We like people who live near us (Festinger *et al.*, 1950; Furfey, 1929; Nahemow and Lawton, 1975).

(f) We like people of approximately our own age (Verbrugge, 1977).

(g) We are friends with people of the same sex (Hartup, 1970; Booth and Hess, 1974).

The results, then, generally show that these principles function across the life-cycle but, even though such principles can be demonstrated with people of different ages, we are reluctant to accept the traditional study of interpersonal attraction as a complete view of personal relationships *in vivo*. As Huston (1974) has noted, over 80% of the attraction research has involved strangers as subjects and the collection of data at only one point in time, which is usually after only a brief period of getting acquainted. Although the laboratory research is carefully controlled, the results lack generalizability to everyday relationships.

For describing people's personal relationships, several limits of the traditional laboratory approach can be noted. First, our most significant friends are people we know for extended periods of time: certainly duration adds a complexity to our relationships that is not captured in the typical laboratory experiment. Secondly, the laboratory approach focuses attention on who we like rather than on the amount of contact we have with friends, the affective fluctuations in relationships over time, and the like. Thirdly, the heavy reliance on statistical analyses in hypothetico-deductive research obscures the fact that many of the statistically significant influences on friendship formation are so small in size as to be of little practical importance. Fourthly, social–psychological research typically uses "college sophomores": thus, some findings from the interpersonal attraction literature may hold only for better educated, more affluent individuals of a certain age group. Finally, traditional social–psychological research does little to examine how factors associated with friendship formation are distributed among people: for instance, it may be that some groups in society have more reinforcers at their disposal to use in forming friendships than others.

In the present chapter, we will examine friendship patterns from a life cycle perspective and such criticisms of the traditional laboratory approach get further compounded when one takes such a perspective. Life cycle fluctuations in friendship may depend less on liking alone than on those exterior features of the life stages which limit or enhance opportunities for social contacts. Such age-related factors as cognitive development, employment status, marital status, and health all intuitively seem important to us, but such factors are usually held constant or ignored in laboratory studies. Thus, we feel that attention to a wider network of variables, as well as the use of other research methodologies (especially longitudinal and cross-sectional surveys) can help to round out our understanding of people's social relationships. As we shall demonstrate, people's friendships are clearly influenced by their stage in life: friendship expectations change, network sizes change, and the functions of friendship change. The importance of various antecedents (i.e. propinquity) of friendship as well as the specific operation of fundamental influences on friendship formation may change. For instance, in Duck's (1975) research, personality similarity promoted friendship throughout adolescence but the relative importance of various dimensions of similarity (e.g. physical, psychological, role) showed developmental changes.

The primary purpose of this chapter is, therefore, to integrate information on friendship across the life-cycle from diverse sources. In 1972, Beth Hess (p. 360) wrote "Little is known about the age patterns of friendship, either at a given time or over the life course." More is known now, of course, but the state of our knowledge has not changed dramatically and the volume of relevant work is still surprisingly small. Thus, the present review can be considered fairly comprehensive rather than highly selective.

Naturally, some selection of material did occur. We have paid more attention to recent, empirically based work, and have tried to cite other review articles. We have also paid more attention to studies of friendship involving several age groups and analyses of the unique properties of friendships at a given stage in life. The large body of research on interpersonal attraction *per se*, undertaken without reference to life-cycle considerations, could be organized by age of the subjects to develop a catalogue of findings at each stage in life. This approach was rejected as an unfeasible task for a single chapter (but see Section Two of this Volume).

The present chapter also attempts to blend evidence together with theory. Greater weight is given, however, to descriptive evidence since very few theories have been articulated to explain friendship across the life cycle. Of the theories that have been advanced, most either focus on only one stage in life (e.g. Bigelow, 1977) or have yet to serve as the basis for programmatic research (Kimmel, 1979). The development of a comprehensive theory is beyond either the scope or the intent of the present chapter.

One might assume that changing friendship patterns are caused by developmental changes *per se*. We have not made this assumption: instead, we consider it a question to be answered. It is equally plausible that changing friendship patterns are caused by some third set of factors that are linked to chronological development. We should also note that the relationship of development to friendship is not a one-way stream: an individual's friendships undoubtedly influence his or her development.

This chapter is divided into four major sections: childhood, adolescence, adulthood, and old age. In the first two sections of the chapter, attention will be focused on the importance of cognitive and social development. In examining friendship in adulthood and old-age, attention will shift to socio-economic status and such age-linked life events as marriage, parenthood, and becoming widowed. Throughout the chapter, attention will be focused on gender. We believe such demographic and age-related factors as these play an important role in the patterning of personal relationships across the life-cycle. Finally, since the life-cycle fluctuations in friendships may differ from the life-cycle fluctuations in kin contact, both will be examined, but more consideration will, nonetheless, be devoted to friendships.

Childhood

In childhood, friendships play a role in the individual's socialization (Donelson and Gullahorn, 1977; Gamer *et al.*, 1975; Newman and Newman, 1975) and, indeed, Brenton (1975) calls friendship a necessity for children, vital for their assimilation into society.

The current literature on children's friendships can be divided into two broad categories.[1] First, psychologists have examined friendships at various stages in childhood and we will deal with this literature later, dividing childhood into four segments: infancy, preschool, the early elementary years, and preadolescence. Based on this body of research, but organized into a separate section, we will also examine gender differences in friendships during childhood. Secondly, there is a body of work in the Piaget–Kohlberg cognitive development tradition. In this area, Selman and his associates (Selman and Jaquette, 1977; Selman and Selman, 1979) have offered an analysis of children's understanding of their relationships, whilst Bigelow (1977; Bigelow and La Gaipa, 1975) has done work on what children expect (or want) in a friend. Both Selman and Bigelow see children's friendships as passing through an invariant sequence of stages related to the individual's cognitive development. We shall now examine this approach in more depth.

The cognitive development tradition

Selman has identified five separate stages in children's views of friendship which evolve so that they form an increasingly comprehensive set of insights. As a child moves from one stage to another, s/he builds upon the understanding gained from the earlier levels of development, and advances in awareness about friendship are related to advances in the child's perspective-taking ability. Table I outlines the stages in Selman's model.

In the first stage of development (ages 3 to 7), Momentary Playmate, friends are defined by their proximity; also the child has difficulty differentiating other children's viewpoint from his/her own and friends are valued for their possessions and physical attributes. The second level of development (ages 4 to 9) is called One-Way Assistance: children are able to distinguish another's viewpoint from their own, but they have not recognized the necessity of give-and-take in a relationship and friends are valued for what they will do for the individual. Stage three (ages 6 to 12) is called Fairweather Cooperation: children at this stage realize that reciprocal cooperation is important for interpersonal relationships, but they see the basic purpose of the friendship as serving self-interests rather than mutual interests. At the fourth level (ages 9 to 15), Intimate–Mutual Sharing, the child has advanced to the point that s/he can take an objective, third-person perspective of the friendship: friendship is seen as a collaboration with others for mutual and common interests, but it is also seen as an exclusive and possessive relationship. The final level of development (age 12 +), Autonomous Interdependence, is characterized by complex relationships: the adolescent or adult realizes that in his/her friendships with other individuals, one person cannot fulfill all emotional and psychological needs. Therefore, friends are allowed to develop independent relationships and there is respect for both dependence and autonomy in friendships.

Selman and Jaquette (1977) tested their model by presenting hypothetical dilemmas to a cross-sectional sample of people ranging in age from 4½ to 32 years old. Each story of interpersonal conflict was the basis for an interview on close friendships. An additional sample of 48 males (6–12 years old) was interviewed and then re-interviewed two year later. Data from both the cross-sectional and longitudinal samples supported Selman's hierarchical levels of friendship development. There was evidence of increasing friendship awareness in children between 6 and 15 years of age in that, in this age range, the average increase was approximately two stages, from Stage 1 to Stage 3. As is evident from Table I, there was large variability in ages at each level of awareness: however, the longitudinal data showed that there was advancement across stages rather than random fluctuations (Hartup, 1978).

Bigelow's (1977) work, on the other hand, was based on content analysis

TABLE I Two major theories of children's friendships

	Selman and Jaquette[a]		Bigelow and LaGaipa[b]		
Stage	Friendship awareness	Perspective-taking	Stage	Dimension	Grade at onset
0 (3-7)[c]	Momentary physical playmate	Undifferentiated; egocentric	I.	Situational 1. Common activities 2. Evaluation 3. Propinquity	2 3 3
1 (4-9)	One-way assistance	Subjective; differentiated	II.	Contractual 4. Admiration	4
2 (6-12)	Fairweather cooperation	Reciprocal; self-reflective	III.	Internal-Psychological 5. Acceptance 6. Loyalty and commitment	4 4
3 (9-15)	Intimate-Mutual understanding	Mutual; third person		7. Genuineness 8. Common interests 9. Intimacy potential	5 6 7
4 (12+)	Autonomous Interpendence	In depth; societal			7

[a] Adapted from Selman and Jaquette (1977) and Selman and Selman (1979).
[b] Adapted from Bigelow and LaGaipa (1975) and Bigelow (1977).
[c] The numbers in parentheses are rough guidelines of the age range in each stage.

of children's essays on what they expected in a best friend. He identified at least nine key dimensions of children's friendship expectations which form a three-stage hierarchy (see Table I for a listing). The first stage, Situational, is characterized by dimensions such as common activities and propinquity. At this level, the child evaluates his/her friends in concrete, superficial terms such as how close the friend lives and if the friend shares certain activities with the child. In the second stage, Contractual, dimensions of friendship expectation are normative. At this stage, children expect friends to have an admirable character and to abide by certain rules and norms, with violations of friendship expectations resulting in disapproval and negative sanctions. In the final stage, Internal–Psychological, dispositional personality factors such an intimacy potential, commitment, genuineness, loyalty, are relevant to friendship expectations.

Bigelow's (1977) research was done with children aged 6 years to 14 years from two different cultures, Anglo-Canadian and Scottish. Across both samples, 11 out of 21 friendship expectations showed a significant increase in importance with age but one (play) decreased in importance. Many of the more cognitive dimensions, e.g. understanding, mentioned by the older children were not evident in the expectations of the younger children. Interestingly, though, there appears to be a cumulative effect in friendship expectation development since the older children also mention dimensions from developmentally lower positions. Basic friendship expectations such as reciprocity and ego reinforcement were evident across all ages and affective dimensions, e.g. ego reinforcement, develop early in friendship expectations of children, whereas the cognitive elements of friendship more closely follow general intellectual development (Hartup, 1978).

The results of two other cross-sectional studies provide further evidence on children's descriptions of their friendships. In both these studies, children of various ages were asked to describe liked and disliked peers (Peevers and Secord, 1973; Scarlett et al., 1971). Peevers and Secord (1973) examined written descriptions of friends by kindergarten children, third graders, seventh graders, high-school students and university students. There were four dimensions of the descriptions that changed with age. First, older participants gave more description ("she's talkative") providing information about their friends as unique invididuals whereas younger participants gave more descriptions of their friends in global terms ("he's nice") as well as more descriptions in which the friends were undifferentiated from the environment ("Chris lives in a big house"). Secondly, over a third of the descriptions given by kindergarten children were egocentric in nature ("Leslie gave me a cookie"): that is, the younger children described friends in self-orientated terms — a tendency that declined with age. Thirdly, evaluative consistency (i.e. the tendency to mention only positive qualities of friends and only negative qualities of disliked persons) was high in third and seventh graders. Fourthly, the descriptions of friends provided by older participants manifest more "depth": that is, older children were more likely to offer explanations of their friends' attributes and to recognize contradictory or changing aspects of their friends' behaviour.

In a related study, Scarlett *et al.* (1971) found that preschool children's concept of friendship was based on the simple and/or observable dimensions they used to differentiate others ("she's nice", "he has blond hair"), results which are also consistent with the findings of Bigelow and La Gaipa (1975). The friendship choices of young children were related to the situational factors of the interaction and tended to fluctuate with the child's subjective feelings, whilst the onset of dimensions of friendship expectation such as admiration or loyalty did not occur until around age eight or nine.

Overall, from the cognitive perspective, it appears that children's views of their friends are initially simple, egocentric, and based on physical or external factors. As they get older, children's views of their friends become more complex, less egocentric and based more on the person's internal dispositions or character. Let us now turn from children's views of their friendships, to studies of friendships at specific stages in childhood. In doing so, we might expect to find some general correspondence between children's views of friendships and the friendship bonds they actually form.

Studies of childhood friendships

Infancy studies

Some authors stress the importance of the social attachment between the young infant and mother on the development of later interpersonal relationships (cf. Chapter 5, this Volume). In the early establishment of a primary bond with the mother, the infant experiences trust and closeness, and learns of his capacity to love and be loved. On the basis of these experiences, the child is later able to form friendships (Newman and Newman, 1975).

As infants develop they become more aware of their environment and the people surrounding them, and with this growing awareness, infants begin to realize that there are other individuals separate and independent from themselves. Infants less than a year old are capable of social interaction, although these interactions often resemble contacts made with play materials (i.e. manipulation, exploratory looking, etc.; Maudry and Nekula, 1939). Also in infancy, repeated exposure to another same-age child may be crucial in getting babies to manifest peer-orientated behaviour (Becker, 1977).

Around the age of two, children begin to engage in parallel play: that is, they do not interact with the other child in their play, but play unto themselves alongside the other child. Peer interactions that do occur are mainly object-orientated (e.g. Eckerman *et al.*, 1975).

Studies of preschool children

In the preschool years children's friendship patterns are very unstable, changing with age. Generally from the age of two to three, the number of a child's playmates increases whereas from the age of three to five there is an increase in the degree of closeness of a few friends rather than in the total number of friends (Green, 1933). This change is considered to be a consequence of the child learning about new interpersonal relationships since in initial experiences with others, the child learns that certain relationships are more gratifying than others and the child forms closer attachments to these children (Mussen *et al.*, 1969).

The nature of children's friendships also change between three and six years of age. The older a child becomes, the less likely s/he is to engage in negative social interactions such as crying, sucking, or submissive behaviour (Smith and Connolly, 1972) and also positive behaviour such as talking, laughing, playing with other children, or smiling, increase with age. Parten (1932) found that children participate more in cooperative and associative play with increasing age. Piaget and other cognitive developmental psychologists believe that cooperative and associative play reflect a higher level of cognitive development than does parallel play or on-looker behaviour.

Rubin and Maioni (1975) found that measures of preschool children's cognitive development were negatively correlated with functional or parallel play, but were positively correlated with measures of associative play. They also found that the incidence of parallel and constructive play was greater than the incidence of the more mature forms of play (associative play or game with rules). Although the children did not often display the more mature forms of play, when it did occur, it was positively related to higher cognitive measures.

In preschool children, the normal predeterminations of friendship appear to be gender, age and play skills: Challman (1932) found that friends were usually the same age and gender, and similar in level of activity and, furthermore, children who engaged in cooperative activities tended to form more friendships.

Middle childhood — early elementary years

Around the time that children enter school, their social perceptions and awareness start becoming less self-centered and they are more responsive to others. Personal characteristics appear to play some part in friendship formation at this age: for instance, Furfey (1929) found that friendships pairs of nine-year-old boys were most similar on a measure of social maturity and somewhat alike in intelligence and physical characteristics (age, height, weight). Furfey concluded that it was similarities in the non-intellectual traits that were more important in friendship formation than resemblance in intelligence.

Another finding from Furfey's (1929) study was that propinquity was an important determinant of friendship choice since most of the friendship pairs were from the same classroom (89%) or lived in the same neighbourhood (45%). Other researchers have found similar results for different ages of grade school children (e.g. Gallagher, 1958; Seagoe, 1933). The fact that propinquity has such an influence on friendship ties for children ages six to nine is not surprising, for, when children are this age, they have little opportunity to meet or interact with others except for children from their neighbourhood or classroom at school. If they do meet other boys or girls who do not live close by or are from their school, the children are dependent on parents or older siblings to bring them together, and therefore any mutual contact is difficult. Children still do have friends outside their neighbourhood and schoolroom, so there are other factors which motivate the children to form and maintain their more remote friends.

Thus personal characteristics of the other child start to influence friendship choice for the child aged five to nine. However, the characteristics that children attribute to their friends are at a simple, concrete level — appearance, proximity, possessions. Dymond et al. (1952) provide some empirical evidence for this conclusion: second graders chose five phrases from a list of 25 which best described the children they liked the most, and the most popular responses were: "is good looking", "has nice home", and "has lots of spending money" — concrete characteristics.

Later childhood — preadolescence

Three major changes in the friendship patterns of children begin to emerge around the age of nine. Consistent with the cognitive development models of Bigelow and Selman, children start to make attributions about the behaviour of their friends to internal traits (Gamer et al., 1975). The children realize that others have internal thoughts and feelings and this knowledge begins to influence the selection and keeping of friends.

The second change in children's patterns of friendship is related to their social development. Childhood friendships begin the transition from family commitment to commitment to the larger social community (Brenton, 1975; Fine, 1980; Newman and Newman, 1975) and through peer interaction, children learn to deal with others in order to maintain their friendships. The need for peer friendships provides children with an increasingly complex social network and they learn the necessity of conforming to norms for approval, and learn that friendships provide close emotional experiences which are different from those at home (Newman and Newman, 1975).

Thirdly, around the age of eight to twelve, close dyadic friendships between children of the same gender begin to have greater intensity and importance. Researchers have noted not only the importance of friends to the preadolescent (e.g. Sullivan, 1953) but also that chum relationships play an important role in the preadolescent's development of social interactional skills (Fine, 1981; Hartup, 1978).

Fine (1981) believes that preadolescent friendships involve three components which are directly related to the child's socialization into adulthood. First, friendships are a staging area for behaviour which would otherwise be improper: for example, children can explore aggressive and sexual feelings with their friends which they would not discuss with their parents. The second component is friendship as a training area to learn culturally appropriate methods of dealing with the new problems of growing up: the preadolescent learns how to handle and react in new situations. Thirdly, friendships contribute to the development of the child's self-image.

Sullivan (1953) believes that preadolescents develop a need for personal intimacy. At this stage children have the capacity for forming same-sex friendships, or chumships, that are dramatically different from their earlier relationships as the "child begins to develop a real sensitivity to what matters to another person" (Sullivan, 1953, p. 245). Through closeness with a chum, the child is able to validate his/her own self-worth since chums take on each other's successes, and derive satisfaction, prestige and status from their friends' accomplishments. According to Sullivan, it is only with the advent of such relationships that the preadolescent can experience the extremes of relationships (i.e. loneliness, intimacy).

Finally, Sullivan noted that interlocking networks of chums provide the basis for the formation of cliques and gangs. We will examine this type of friendship further in our discussion on adolescence; first, however, we wish to discuss gender differences in children's friendships, and certain age-related aspects of adolescent friendships.

Gender differences

There is a large literature on gender differences in children. Several stereotypes regarding differences between boys and girls exist in the folklore, some of the more common of which pertain to social interaction, and are relevant to children's friendships. Girls are supposed to be more socially orientated than boys; to be more motivated to receive social rewards; and to have a greater need for affiliation (Eder and Hallinan, 1978). Reviewing the literature, Maccoby and Jacklin (1974) found little empirical support for these stereotypes. However, one consistent finding from studies of play in children has been that girls tend to interact in twos and threes while boys will interact in larger groups or gangs (e.g. Laosa and Brophy, 1972; Waldrop and Halverson, 1975).

Waldrop and Halverson (1975) conducted a longitudinal study of children's friendships in which, for children aged 7–8, they collected 12 measures of the child's relationships with their peers and factor analysed the data separately by sex. A main factor was extracted for each gender. Some variables loading on the main factor were common for both sexes (i.e. social ease, importance of peers, and total hours with peers) but some variables loading on the main factor were gender specific. The variables that loaded only on the main factor for boys were "extensiveness" (i.e. participation in group activities), hours spent with more than one peer, and number of peers seen; whilst the variables that loaded only on the main factor for girls were hours spent with one peer and intensity (importance of a best friend). Based on this analysis, Waldrop and Halverson (1975, p. 19) conclude:

> The highly social boys, when with peers, tended to have *extensive* peer relations; that is, they usually played with a group of boys. The highly social girls, when with peers, tended to have *intensive* peer relations; that is, they usually played with only one other girl.

Waldrop and Halverson also reported longitudinal effects. The children who had been peer orientated at 2½ years (friendly, involved with peers and assertive) tended to become children who were socially at ease and who spent a great time with peers at 7½ years. Interestingly, the female peer-orientated 2½-year-olds were likely to be highly intensive 7½-year-olds, while the male peer-orientated 2½-year-old tended to become highly extensive 7½-year-old boys.

Based on these results, Eder and Hallinan (1978) hypothesized that girls' dyadic friendships would be more exclusive than dyadic friendships of boys. They tested this proposition by looking for sex differences in patterns of sociometric choice of fifth and sixth graders throughout the school year. To analyse the exclusiveness of the friendship dyads, the authors examined the dyads in relation to a third person. As predicted, there was a tendency for girls to have more exclusive friendship dyads than boys, and boys participated more in non-exclusive friendship triads than girls. Looking at changes in the triads over the school year, results showed that boys' dyadic friendships expanded to include others, but girls generally continued to associate in pairs. The results of these studies imply that there is a relationship between friendship and sex-role socialization: via socialization, boys' relations become more extensive and girls' become more intensive.

Comment

In summing up this stage, we see that as children mature, the qualities that they value in a friend also change and so do the nature of peer interactions. Toddlers relate to their friends or playmates on a superficial, self-centred level but around the time children enter school, personal characteristics of the other child begin to influence friendship choice. The personal characteristics are still at a simple level, though; for example, appearance or possessions of the other child are important. As they grow older, the children become less self-centred and start to attribute their friends' behaviour to internal traits.

Discussed in terms of the cognitive developmental theories (i.e. Bigelow and La Gaipa, 1975; Selman and Jacquette, 1977), the literature suggests that by pre-adolescence, children's friendships have advanced through the earlier stages — One-way Assistance, Fairweather Cooperation (Selman and Jacquette, 1977) or Situational, Contractual relations (Bigelow and La Gaipa, 1975). There may be some recognition of the needs of the other individual, but the basic purpose of the friendship is to serve self rather than mutual interests. As the child approaches adolescence, the need for a close friend and mutual intimacy develops.

Finally, from a life-cycle approach it is evident that something more than attraction is associated with children's friendships. There is an obvious parallel between children's cognitive development and changes in the nature of children's friendships. In his discussion of the cognitive nature of social development, Youniss (1978) has described cognition as

> ". . . an *enabling* device which mediates social development. As capacities, skills, and processing develop, children become able to know more and different things about other persons. With each step toward maturity, children are more able to free themselves from private interpretations and come closer to understanding social reality as other persons understand it" (pp. 206-207).

Thus, both theory and evidence lead to the conclusion that cognitive and social development are related. But, we are reluctant to specify whether, as Youniss implies, cognitions influence children's friendships or vice versa, because research on this issue has so far been merely correlational in nature.

Adolescence

During adolescence, friendships play an increasingly important role in socialization. This period is characterized by change — both physiological and psychological, and these changes are reflected both in the nature and the structure of friendship relationships. Moreover, the adolescent's social network changes as s/he gradually disengages from their his/her family of orientation and prepares for future roles.

The literature suggests that the importance of the relationship between cognitive development and friendship declines during adolescence (Bigelow and La Gaipa, 1980; La Gaipa, 1979). For instance, La Gaipa (1979) extended the study of friendship expectations to adolescents. Granted there were some changes — some expectations declined and others become more important (evaluative/global and moral/character qualities declined, and intimacy, authenticity and loyalty increased in importance) — but three expectations (similarity, helping and common activities) remained the same. Overall, as La Gaipa (1979, pp. 204, 212) states "few differences were found between 13 years and 16 years of age . . . The meaning of friendship appears to become stabilized in early adolescence and shows little change afterwards". What emerges to replace cognitive development in importance is the peer group.

The support and security of the peer group provide adolescents with the opportunity to work through the new aggressive and erotic feelings often associated with physiological changes through puberty (Douvan and Adelson, 1966; Fine, 1981). Moreover, the adolescent turns to the peer group to learn the acceptable norms for behaviour in the changing adolescent subculture (e.g. manner of dress, ways of speaking and acting within the peer group; Donelson and Gullahorn, 1977).

Adolescents choose friends whom they can trust and depend on, but also, they wish to be associated with popular individuals (Hurlock, 1973). The number of friends is one measure of popularity, but in later adolescence it becomes more important who the friends are (Hurlock, 1973). Increased self-awareness and self-criticism are associated with the psychological changes, and the potential for personal growth through friendship may be greatest during adolescence (Donelson and Gullahorn, 1977). Younger children take themselves and others for granted, adults are more rigid in their social roles, but adolescents have increased self-criticism, self-awareness, and flexibility.

Those findings parallel the three components of friendship that Fine (1981) describes in preadolescent friendships. For adolescents, a fourth component may be added to the relationship between socialization and adolescent friendships. As the child increasingly disengages from the family s/he needs the intimacy that friendships provide to compensate for the loss of intimacy in the family relationship. When asked to rate the understanding of friends, teachers, and parents, Soviet adolescents from age 14 to 20 all consistently rated their friend as the most understanding. Furthermore, the adolescents felt more comfortable with and were more apt to confide in a friend than parents or other adults (Kon and Losenkov, 1978). In all measures of psychological closeness and at every age level, the best friend was given the highest rating. The mother was rated second highest, then the father or favourite teacher depending on the gender of the child: boys usually rated father higher, but girls were more apt to give a favourite teacher higher ratings than father (Kon and Losenkov, 1978).

Age-related aspects of friendship

We turn now to examine age-related aspects of adolescent friendships. One classic study was done by Douvan and Adelson (1966) and was based on two large national surveys of adolescent boys (age 14-16 years) and adolescent girls (age 11-18 years) from a variety of types of schools, social backgrounds and communities. The age-related differences will be discussed in terms of three aspects of friendship relations: (a) the qualities of friends which are important; (b) the emotional commitment of the relationship; and (c) heterosexual relationships.

Preadolescent girls (11-13)

The qualities of a friend which are important to girls at this age are more basic in terms of cognitive development. Qualities which facilitate cooperation and shared activities are important. Friendships are not yet the primary focus of emotional commitment; the preadolescent girl's emotional commitment is still centred on the family. The girls who were interviewed felt closer to their family than friends and most of their leisure time was spent with the family. Boys and dating are not important yet.

Middle adolescent girls (14-16)

At this age, friendships are more than sharing activities, they now centre on the personality of the other girl and her response to the self (Douvan and Adelson, 1966). During the interviews, girls aged 14-16 stressed the importance of security in friendships and they wanted friends to be loyal, trustworthy and a source of emotional support. Intense emotional commitments develop in friendships since a close intimate same-sex friendship is needed to help the girls deal with the doubts, confusions, and anxieties associated with puberty but because of the emotional involvement of the relationships, friendships are more unstable and prone to disruption due to jealousy. Girls have started dating but sexual feelings are discussed and explored within same-sex friendships.

Middle adolescent boys (14–16)

The characteristics of friendships of teenage boys of 14–16 years were more similar to the friendships of the preadolescent girls. The boys named concrete and impersonal qualities as criteria for choosing a friend. They felt a friend should be aimiable and cooperative and able to control aggressive impulses; a friend should be a companion you share activities with. The two main obligations that a friend had in the relationship were to provide support in trouble and do favours for the other person. Compared to girls of the same age, boys in early adolescence are less concerned with intimacy, emotional support, or security. They have no great interest in dating, yet. Consistent with the lack of desire for intimate friends, the teenage boy's friends centre around a gang that is the basis of support against authority. The major difference in the friendships of teenage boys and girls is in the type of support they provide: for the boys the emphasis is on group support in confronting authority, whereas the girls stress emotional support in personal crises.

Late adolescent girls (17–18)

The qualities important in friendships have become more subtle and abstract. They focus on the individual talents of the friend and what the friend can contribute to the relationship. The older girls have developed a self-awareness and begun to establish a personal identity. They have developed a complex understanding of friendship. Girls in this age group had more to say about the important qualities of friendship than girls in the younger age groups. The intensity of the emotional commitment in same-sex friendship has now subsided, and girls aged 17–18 apply important qualities of same-sex friendship to heterosexual friendships and relationships. As the characteristics of like-sex friendships are generalized to heterosexual relationships, friendships take on a more disinterested, playful and diversified quality.

So we see from preadolescence through to late adolescence, the development of important qualities in friendships and the emotional commitment of the relationships correspond to the cognitive developmental models of Bigelow and Selman. The progression is from dealing with friends on a concrete level to a recognition and acceptance of the other's internal, psychological characteristics. In line with Douvan and Adelson's results, Duck (1975) found that early adolescents chose their friends on the basis of similarities of objective fact constructs, but that middle and late adolescents used more psychological constructs than did the early adolescents. Now we turn to a discussion of the structure of adolescent peer groups.

Cliques and crowds

The literature suggests that play groups and peer groups assist pre-adults in gradually disenganging from their family of orientation and preparing for future roles in their own family of procreation (Dunphy, 1963; Hess, 1972; Smith, 1962). Sullivan (1953) has also noted that the interlocking networks of chums provide the basis for the formation of cliques or gangs. In this section we shall discuss a major field study by Dunphy on the changing structure of adolescent peer groups and we shall show the development of the peer group from a one-sex crowd to cliques of cross-sex pairs.

Dunphy collected his data over a two and a half to three year period in Sydney, Australia, through interviews and observations of 303 adolescents between the ages of 13 and 21 years. The findings can be summarized into two main categories: (a) group demographics; and (b) developmental changes.

Group demographics

Dunphy found basically two types of groups — the clique and the crowd. The clique was a smaller, more intimate group usually composed of three to nine members. The membership was more exclusive and there was usually an established social hierarchy within the clique, the members of which all lived within close proximity. The crowd was essentially an association of cliques. The size of the crowd ranged from 15 to 30 people and was usually composed of three cliques. The cliques associated in a crowd were usually from adjacent residential areas and the members were about the same age and at the same level of social development. All the crowds that Dunphy observed were heterosexual and he found a consistent age difference between boys and girls within a crowd: the boys were older than the girls with whom they associated. In the heterosexual cliques of the older adolescents, the same difference in ages was present.

The two types of groups perform different functions. The function of the clique centres around talking and the dissemination of information about crowd activities whilst the function of the crowd focuses on the organized social activities. The crowd provides a pool of acceptable people to socialize with and the opportunity for heterosexual interaction. Crowd interactions occurred mostly on weekends while the majority of interactions in the clique setting occurred during the week.

Developmental changes

Dunphy observed certain general trends in the developmental changes of peer group structure across the adolescent period. Certain group structures consistently appeared before others. Figure 1 presents an outline of the changes.

The first stage of group development in adolescence is the pre-crowd stage where associations are isolated same-sex cliques and there is no interaction with cross-sex cliques. At the next stage, the crowd starts to develop with interaction between cross-sex cliques at the group level and any interaction on an individual basis is rare and seen as very daring. The crowd begins structural transitions at stage 3. Upper-status members of same-sex cliques initiate heterosexual interaction which leads to the formation of cross-sex cliques. The adolescents who have begun to date and belong to the cross-sex cliques, also maintain membership in their same-sex cliques, so that they belong to

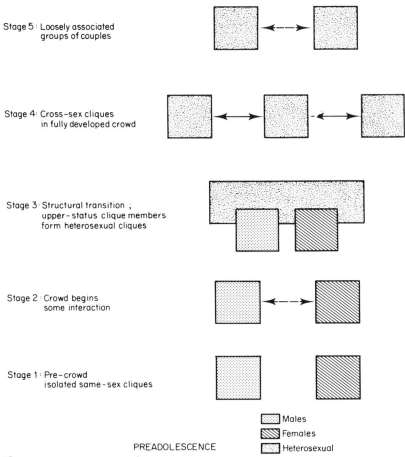

LATE ADOLESCENCE

Stage 5 : Loosely associated groups of couples

Stage 4: Cross-sex cliques in fully developed crowd

Stage 3: Structural transition ; upper-status clique members form heterosexual cliques

Stage 2 : Crowd begins some interaction

Stage 1 : Pre-crowd isolated same-sex cliques

Males
Females
Heterosexual

PREADOLESCENCE

FIG. 1　Natural history of adolescent groups (adapted from Dunphy, 1963).

two intersecting cliques. During the next stage, the intersecting same-sex and cross-sex cliques re-form to comprise separate cross-sex cliques which associate in a crowd. At the final stage, the crowd begins to disintegrate into loosely associated groups of couples.

Thus there is a "natural history" of the peer group structure from predominately same-sex to cross-sex groups. The crowd plays an integral role in the developmental schema since membership in the crowd provides adolescents the chance to establish a heterosexual role and because of the social hierarchies within the cliques which comprise the crowds, an individual's social development is influenced by his/her position within the hierarchy (Dunphy, 1963).

Comment

From the research of Douvan and Adelson (1966) it is evident that adolescents' friendship expectations are similar to children's friendship expectations but at a more advanced level. The peer group and its structure emerge with increasing importance in relation to adolescent friendships replacing cognitive development which was important during childhood. The friendships of adolescents become more intimate and cross-sex relationships develop (Dunphy, 1963). The group structure of peer relationships changes so that the end of adolescence the group is a loose association of couples, preparing the adolescent for the roles of adulthood.

Adulthood

In doing research on adults, two major approaches have been used for dividing the life-cycle: the first has simply been to divide people according to age; the second has been to divide them by stages in the family life-cycle. We shall examine adult friendship patterns using both approaches.

We should forewarn readers that in adulthood, social contacts are subtle: the determinants of friendship ties are not necessarily the determinants of kin ties; the determinants of frequency of contact are not necessarily the same as the determinants of closeness. Furthermore, as adult friendship patterns are appreciably influenced by social class and by gender, these factors must also be considered.

Four major studies

Four cross-sectional studies of adult friendships are especially important.

The first, analysed by Stueve and Gerson (1977) was the 1965–66 Detroit Area Study which consisted of a large (n = 985) representative sample of white males, aged 21–64, living in the Detroit metropolitan area. Friendships were assessed by asking respondents to name "the three men who are your closest friends and whom you see most often".

The second study was conducted in Toronto, Canada by Norman Shulman (1975) and the sample included 347 respondents (146 males, 201 females), aged 18–65. Respondents were asked to name their closest relationships outside their own household to a maximum of six persons.

The third study was conducted in 1977 by Claude Fischer in Northern California. Fischer's team interviewed 1050 randomly selected adults from 50 different urban census tracts and small towns. No upper limit was imposed on the age of the respondents, resulting in interviews with 128 people 65 and older. Fischer used a series of ten questions to determine each respondent's social network. Illustrative (paraphrased) questions were: Who would take care of your home if you went out of town? With whom do you talk about decisions at work? With whom do you engage in social activities? and, From whom would you borrow money?

The fourth study, consisting of 216 men and women from the San Francisco area, was done by Lowenthal and her associates (Lowenthal *et al.*, 1975). Lowenthal had four groups: she began her sampling by identifying high-school seniors who were the youngest children in their families; parents of these students, who were in the "launching" stage of family life, were the second group; the third and fourth groups were newly-weds and people about to retire. All the groups were from the same neigbourhoods and the mean ages of the three adult groups were as follows: newly-weds, 24; parents, 50; and pre-retirement seniors, 60. Friendship data were collected as part of a series of intensive interviews with each respondent.

The rise and fall of friendship

In Fischer's study, respondents named an average of 18.5 members in their social networks. Fischer (Fischer and Phillips, in press) has reported his data in terms of the question: Who is alone? He divided people's networks into kin and non-kin and found that, with reference to non-kin relations, the proportion of social isolates (especially among men) increased steadily with age.

In Lowenthal's study, the average number of friends mentioned was 5.7 with high-school students reporting the fewest friends (n = 4.8), newly-weds the most friends (7.6). Number of friends dropped for parents of teenagers (n = 4.7), but increased modestly in pre-retirement (n = 6.0).

Frequency of contact with friends declines as people get older — a consistent finding across studies. For instance, in the Detroit Area Study, 73% of young singles' friends were seen at least weekly whereas the corresponding figure for people in the post-parental stage of the family life cycle dropped to 39%.

The intimacy of relationships was investigated only in the Detroit study. Intimacy with friends did not vary by stage in the family life cycle but did decline slightly with age. Fischer (Fischer and Phillips, in press) similarly found that as people, especially men, got older, they lacked confidants.

Thus, despite some nuances, friendships seem to decline over the life-cycle. This picture is further reinforced when one examines the influence of two major life events, marriage and parenthood, both of which generally constrain friendships. For instance, in Shulman's study, single individuals were most apt to report a high frequency of social contacts, childless married respondents were intermediate, and parents were least likely to report a high frequency. Fischer and Phillips reported similar results.

Several plausible reasons can be offered for life-cycle changes in friendships. For instance, in early adulthood, people may have the time and resources to engage in frequent interaction with friends and this tendency may be further promoted by the high social comparison needs of young adults. With marriage, people may satisfy many social needs via their conjugal relationship, rather than via friendship contacts whilst the arrival of children may add new responsibilities and restrict people's free time.

As people age, they appear content with their old friends and seem to lack initiative in forming new relationships. In line with this interpretation our key studies (Stueve and Gerson, 1977; Shulman, 1975; and Lowenthal et al., 1975) consistently show that older people have known their friends longer and, further, friends who were known longer are seen less often (see Jackson et al., 1977). Obviously, one could argue that this correlation is an artefact of the age of people with long-standing friendships. However, we would entertain the possibility that the long duration of close friendships lowers contact with those friends and contributes to the general decline of contact in the aging adult.

Friendships of longer duration tend to be more intimate (Jackson et al., 1977) and the tendency of older adults to have a high proportion of long-term relationships should thus serve as a buffer against the decline of intimacy. In the light of this, it is not surprising that frequency of contact declines more dramatically than the degree of intimacy in friendships.

Sources and characteristics of friendships across adulthood

Besides mapping the rise and fall of friendships, studies of friendships over the life-cycle have demonstrated a number of additional points. Findings on four topics are noteworthy: namely, the context of friendship formation, the places where friends meet, the density (interconnectedness) among one's friends, and the age similarity between individuals and their friends.

In analysing the contexts of friendship formation over the family life-cycle, childhood friends were the most important type of friends for young, single men in the Detroit survey (Stueve and Gerson, 1977) but in the later stages of the family life-cycle, the importance of childhood friends declined. Work and one's neighbourhood became the major contexts in which friendships flourish. Having children played an important role in linking neighbours; when grown children left home, the percentage of friends in the neighbourhood dropped. In the launching and post-parental stages in the life-cycle, it became more difficult to classify the context of men's friendships. Presumably, as men age they retain friendships based on past, no longer current connections.

The context of interpersonal relations influences the reported intimacy and frequency of contact. Detroiters reported high intimacy and moderately frequent contact with childhood friends but they felt their relations with co-workers and neighbours were generally less intimate, and, finally, they got together with neighbourhood friends the most often and co-workers least often. Naturally, these changes in the contexts of relationships may contribute to life-cycle changes in the relationships themselves.

At all stages in the family life-cycle, Detroit men were apt to get together with friends in someone's home. This tendency was most pronounced for young husbands without children and for young fathers.

Density refers to the degree to which one's friends know each other. Shulman found density was highest in the 31–44-year-old age group and among married respondents with children but in the Detroit study, the relationship between density and age was non-significant (see Laumann, 1973, pp. 121–122).

People generally have friends of roughly their own age. Fluctuations in this tendency over the life-cycle have been examined in three separate samples (see Lowenthal et al., 1975; Stueve and Gerson, 1977; and Verbrugge, 1977). Despite minor inconsistencies across studies, one finding stands out: people under 25 are more apt to have similar-age friends than people over 25. For instance, for Detroit men in their early twenties, 68% of friendships involved people of the same age (± two years). Not surprisingly, in discordant relationships, young men had friends who were older than themselves and old men had friends who were younger.

Kin

Kin constitute an important component of people's social networks. For instance, when Shulman asked respondents about their closest relationships,

41% of those people named were kin and a slight majority (51%) of relationships ranked first in closeness were kin.

Kin contact varies over the life cycle. Table II shows data from Shulman's study indicating two points: close kin relations are more common for married adults than for the never married and such relationships are more common in older adults, aged 45–65. Fischer and Phillips' (in press) data on isolation from kin demonstrate roughly equivalent patterns for people aged 22–64, although for their women the affect of age on isolation from kin held for only one of two dependent measures.

TABLE II   Kin in social networks by age and life-cycle stage (adapted from Shulman, 1975)

Life-cycle stage	Percentage reporting one + kin	Percentage reporting over 50% kin
Age		
18–30	60	32
31–44	66	29
45–65	77	36
Marital life-cycle		
Single	41	16
Married, Childless	70	42
Married, Children	83	32
Other	81	51

One should note that life-cycle factors generally have reverse effects on kin and non-kin relations. As an overall generalization, contact with friends declines during the adult stage of the life-cycle while contact with kin increases.

This raises the question: when are network sizes the largest? Table III presents Fischer's (1979) data on this issue and indicates what may best be described as a curvilinear association, especially for men. Overall network size is smaller for single young adults without children but the networks of seniors (65 years old +) are quite small compared to all other groups.

A few speculations on why kinship contact fluctuates over the life-cycle are in order. In late adolescence and young adulthood, people may be trying to establish their autonomy and independence; so they are more involved with peers who have similar interests and life-styles than with kin. At this point in life, older relatives (especially parents) may not be very important to respondents, even though these same relationships may be reported as

TABLE III   Total network sizes across the marital life-cycle (adapted from Fischer, 1979)

Stage	Men	Women
Young adults ≤ 35		
Single	19.8	18.1
Married, Childless	22.4	21.4
Married, Children	22.4	19.3
Mid-life adults, 36-64		
Married, Childless	18.4	20.4
Married, Children	19.4	19.8
Senior, 65 +	13.3	15.5

important by the older adults. Marriage and children make family life salient since the cultural norms surrounding these events undoubtedly promote extended family relations. With the arrival of children and again with old age, we have additional needs that we turn to kin for help in satisfying.

Socioeconomic status

Throughout adulthood, people tend to form friendships with other individuals of their own socioeconomic status. However, social networks are class linked. Existing research (e.g. Adams, 1970; Hendrix, 1979) generally suggests that kin are a more important component in the networks of working-class individuals than in the networks of middle-class respondents. Consistent with this generalization, Fischer and Phillips (in press) found that people with graduate training were considerably more apt to be isolated from kin than were people without a high-school diploma. (Fischer and Phillips excluded kin living more than an hour's drive from the respondent in analysing their data. If long-distance relations with kin are more important in the lives of better-educated individuals than in the lives of less-educated individuals, then these data may systematically underestimate the importance of kin to well-educated groups.) Fischer and Phillips also found that isolation from friends (non-kin) declined steadily with increased education.

One reason for class differences in social networks may be the manner in which friendships develop and what social activities people believe to be relevant to the friendship. From a small, intensive survey conducted in a suburban village, Allan (1977) reported that the friendships of working-class people tended to be situation specific and confined to a particular setting. For example, if the working-class respondent met someone on the job, the friendship was confined to the work setting and they would not entertain a co-worker at home: working-class people tended to entertain only relatives at home. In contrast, friendships of middle-class respondents from one situation (work) would develop to include other activities and settings. Middle-class friendships emphasized the individuals within the relationship, but friendships of working-class individuals were bound to the setting in which they developed (Allan, 1977).

Gender

The evidence on who has more friends, adult men or adult women, is mixed. Lowenthal and her associates (1975) found that women consistently reported a greater number of friends but Booth (1972) found the opposite. Men in the latter study had more friends than women, although this difference approached statistical significance ($p < 10$) only among white-collar workers, and among blue-collar workers it was non-significant.

In Fischer's study, men and women had equivalent network sizes but the overall means mask differences that occurred at specific points in the life-cycle. As shown previously in Table III, young married men had larger networks than young married women, but among older adults the reverse was true; older women had larger networks than older men. At the early stage of the life cycle, Fischer explained the sex difference in terms of work and family responsibilities since men are more apt to be in the labour force, and the gender difference in network sizes largely reflected men's tendency to have a larger number of co-workers in their networks. Parenthood may restrict the networks of women more than of men. The sex differences of seniors will be considered later in the section of this chapter on the elderly.

Turning to the qualitative aspects of friendship, clearer gender differences emerge. For instance, Booth (1972) concluded that women have "affectively richer" relationships since women were more apt to confide in their friends and to do things with them on the spur of the moment. In a similar vein, in a study of college students, Caldwell and Peplau (in press) found that women place greater emphasis on emotional sharing and talking in their relationships whilst men emphasized shared activities. Thus, it appears that adult women are generally more orientated towards emotional intimacy in friendships than are adult men.

Lewis (1978) argues that cultural norms in North America prohibit men from developing intimate friendships. Traditional male roles, such as the pressure to compete, homophobia (fear of homosexuality), or aversion to vulnerability and openness, produce barriers to emotional intimacy in men; and also discourage adequate male role models of healthy emotional behaviour.

Same- and cross-sex friendships

Friendships tend to be homogeneous with regard to gender: that is, the friends of men tend to be men and the friends of women tend to be women. However, Lowenthal and her associates found that as people got older, their opposite-sex friendships declined. Over 60% of high-school students and newly-weds had at least one opposite-sex person among their three best friends but this dropped to 30% for parents of high-school seniors and 18% for people about to retire.

Booth and Hess (1974) explored the determinants of cross-sex friendships in a sample of respondents, 45 and older. They especially focused attention on the cross-sex friendships of women where both work status and marriage were found to play important roles. Employed women, whether married or not, had more cross-sex friendships than non-working women. Being in the labour force, presumably, gives women an opportunity to develop relationships with men; not surprisingly women reported first meeting many of their cross-sex friends at work. Membership of professional and trade associations, which probably consist mainly of men, was also positively correlated to the number of cross-sex friends among women. Men's cross-sex friendships were virtually unaffected by work status. Thus, the opportunities to develop cross-sex friendships at work are apparently more salient and important for women than for men. In part, of course, this may be a statistical artefact. If men are more numerous in the work force, then each cross-sex relationship would increase the mean number of cross-sex relationships for women more than for men.

Comparing employed single women with unemployed married women, the employed singles reported a slightly higher number of cross-sex friends, but, holding employment status constant, married women were more likely to report more male friends than were non-married women. There are two probable reasons for the effects of marital status. First, friends of their husbands provide married women with a large pool of potential male friends. Prior research has shown that in middle-class couples, the men are more likely to initiate and maintain mutual friendships (Babchuk, 1965; Babchuk and Bates, 1963). Booth and Hess found that women who reported they shared mutual friends with their husbands were four times as likely to have cross-sex affiliations as women who did not share friends with their spouses. Secondly, because many married women meet their male friends through their husbands, the relationship was considered to be appropriate by both husband and wife.

Not all cross-sex relations are the same. Although married persons had a larger number of cross-sex friends, they had less frequent interactions with opposite-sex friends than did unmarried persons. The degree of intimacy, as measured by confiding behaviour, of the cross-sex friendships was also lower for married people. Further, married people interacted less with their cross-sex friends than with same-sex friends. Thus, marriage places certain normative constraints on the amount of time spent with people of the opposite sex and the degree of intimacy of the relationship.

Comment

In reflecting on studies of adult friendship, perhaps the most notable feature is the extent to which demographic or sociological type variables have been investigated and the results of these studies show that gender, marital status, social class and the like all influence our personal relationships. Perhaps because they are more stable in adulthood, cognitive factors have largely been overlooked at this stage. However, differences between the patterning of friendships and the patterning of kin relations are clearly evident in adulthood. Collectively, the research done with adults testifies to the importance of external forces such as one's social position in shaping such relationships.

The Elderly

The onset of retirement provides people with more free time and many senior citizens maintain friendship bonds well into later life, but popular writers frequently associate being old with being alone — a view that many gerontologists share. As one noted contributor to this area of study wrote:

> The aged live in a contracting social world in which participation declines, notably sharply after age seventy-five. . . . (The aged) apparently lose friends, and their informal associations with them diminish (Rosow, 1970, p. 59).

Studies analysing quantitative differences in the friendship patterns of mid-life and older adults are surprisingly difficult to find. In an earlier review, Riley and Foner (1968, pp. 562-563) concluded that friendship participation generally declines with age, but, unfortunately, earlier studies used inferior research designs. For instance, instead of getting longitudinal or cross-sectional data, early investigators simply asked elderly respondents whether they felt their social contacts were increasing or decreasing.

Probably the best available evidence is Fischer's northern California survey which was discussed at length earlier. Fischer's data show a clear decline with age in both people's overall social networks and in their friendships. Given our life-cycle perspective, we believe older adults find themselves less able to maintain social contacts, in part because of incidental life changes that occur during this period. For instance, senior citizens are apt to have increased difficulty with transport and they are more apt to have physical disabilities. Such factors as these undoubtedly curtail their personal relationships (see Riley and Foner, 1968, p. 565).

Gender differences

The second point demonstrated by Fischer's data is a gender difference in senior citizens' social networks: old women reported larger networks than old men. However, this conclusion is of limited generality. In Philblad and Adams' (1972) sample of people over 65, men reported more friends than did women (see also Booth, 1972). In terms of frequency of contact with friends, the results of several studies are mixed: one found males higher (Powers and Bultena, 1976), two found females higher (Rosow, 1967, p. 86; Philblad and Adams, 1972) and a fourth found no significant sex difference (Petrowsky, 1976). One seemingly consistent finding is that older women are more apt to have confidants (or intimate friends) than are comparably aged men (Lowenthal and Haven, 1968; Powers and Bultena, 1976).

One possibility in resolving these studies is that men have less stringent criteria of what constitutes a friend. Depending on how the questions are asked, men may score higher on number of friends, as in Philblad and Adam's study. This larger circle of relationships adds to their total amount of friendship interaction. Women, having more stringent criteria of what constitutes a friend, may list fewer names but interact more frequently with each person.

Another aspect of sex differences in social contact at this stage in life is the impact of retirement. If work is the source of many friendships, then retirement should cause a decline in these contacts — a decline that should be especially noticeable among males, since males have traditionally been more likely than females to be in the labour force. This logic is consistent with Fischer's data as well as other results reported by Blau (1961). Among older males, Blau found that friendship participation was higher among working respondents than among retired respondents but among females, no effect of employment was detected.

Marital status

The bulk of the evidence (see Booth, 1972; Philblad and Adams, 1972; Riley and Foner, 1968, p. 570) suggests that married individuals score higher than widowed seniors on quantitative friendship measures. Furthermore, the available evidence (Booth, 1972; Philblad and Adams, 1972) suggests that widowhood is detrimental to the friendship patterns of men more than of women. Exceptions to these two generalizations do, however, exist (e.g. Powers and Bultena, 1976; Petrowsky, 1976).

Reporting on data gathered from 968 people 60 years and older, Blau (1961) hypothesized that widowhood had an adverse influence on friendships only when the status change placed the person in a deviant position in relation to his/her age, sex, and class peers. For example, the data showed that loss of spouse had an adverse effect on the friendships of both men and women in their sixties, but the effect was greater for men than women. In the sample there was a much smaller proportion of widowers than widows under 70 years of age, so that the widowers were in a more deviant position than were the women who had lost a spouse. In the older age groups the majority of the men and women had lost a spouse so that being married would have a negative effect on an individual's social participation. Married people in their seventies reported fewer friends than those who had lost a spouse. Being in a deviant position relative to a person's age and sex peers differentiates his/her interest and experiences and "reduces the mutual bonds that serve as the basis for the formation and persistence of friendships" (Blau, 1961, p. 432).

Socioeconomic status and age homophily

In many ways, the patterns of friendship in the elderly are similar to patterns observed for mid-life adults. For instance, with few exceptions (Powers and Bultena, 1976), the existing evidence indicates that friendship contacts are more frequent among seniors of high socioeconomic status (see Riley and Foner, 1968, p. 563; Booth, 1972; Lowenthal and Haven, 1968). Furthermore, older people from the working class are still more dependent on their neighbourhood as a source of friends than those in the middle class (Rosow, 1967).

Senior citizens, like other adults, demonstrate a tendency to form friendships with others of their own age group. In a West German data set, this form of homophily was greatest in young adults (under 25), declined in mid-adulthood, and increased modestly again for seniors over 70 (Verbrugge, 1977). Unlike other adults, seniors cannot form age-discrepant relationships with individuals older than themselves. This constraint as well as the life changes promoted by retirement may enhance the formation of same-age friendships.

Kin

The importance of friends versus kin to the elderly is controversial. On the

one hand, gerontologists have made pro-kin statements such as the
following:

> Whatever their disengagement or loss of contact with other groups, old people's
> relations with their children are maintained (Rosow, 1970, p. 61).

> Friends and neighbours play an important part in the lives of many older
> people. . . . They are, however, generally less important to older people than
> children and relatives (Riley and Foner, 1968, p. 561).

Relatives, especially adult children, provide older people with emotional
support, help and a buffer against institutionalization (see Wood and
Robertson, 1978, p. 367).

However, from a second perspective, it seems that relationships with kin
are not as important to the elderly as are associations with friends. Several
studies (Philblad and Adams, 1972; Arling, 1976; Wood and Robertson,
1978; Perlman et al., 1979) have examined the contribution of kin and friends
to life satisfaction and loneliness and these studies consistently show that
friendships contribute more to morale than do relations with kin.

Perhaps contact with family members persists, but the enjoyment gained
from such interaction lessens. Rosow (1967) has argued that frequent contact
between the elderly and their children may be ritualistic — based on obligation rather than on warmth or closeness. At the end of the life-cycle, contact
with children may be a consequence of poor health and other needs rather
than a causal variable.

Comment

In summing up research on old age, two points are salient. First, as in adulthood, demographic and sociological factors such as gender and marital
status continue to influence one's personal relationships. Secondly, as
suggested by popular stereotypes, old age appears to be a period of declining
social contacts due to such factors as retirement, poor health, and loss of
spouse or friends.

Conclusions

During childhood and adolescence, the nature of friendships changes as the
child matures. Infants can recognize one another; around the age of two,
children begin to engage in parallel play. In the early preschool years, peer
interactions tend to be negative but become more constructive as children
approach school age. Around the time children enter school, personal
characteristics of the other child begin to influence friendship choice. The

personal characteristics are still at a simple level, though; for example, appearance or possessions of the other child are important. As they grow older, children become less self-centred and start to identify internal attributes that promote friendships.

Around puberty, friendships become more intimate. The child begins to disengage from the family and turns to his/her network of friends for support. From chumships in puberty, cliques and crowds emerge. In late adolescence, heterosexual partnerships are important.

While there are inconsistencies in the available data, we believe friendships peak in late adolescence and early adulthood. At this stage in the life-cycle, people list a large number of friends (Reisman and Shorr, 1978), and the frequency of social interaction is high. Marriage and parenthood reduce social, but not necessarily kin, relationships. Nonetheless, as people get older, they maintain a feeling of intimacy with their friends. In old age, friendships decline, although they remain important in the morale of senior citizens.

Across the life-cycle, there are important gender differences in friendships. Men have more extensive, activity orientated relationships whilst women have more intensive relationships; they have more confidants in old age and the like. Across the life-cycle, same-sex friendships predominate.

Social relations are class linked: available data support the generalization that upper-class groups have more friendships and lower-class groups have more kin contact.

Throughout this chapter we have argued that personal relationships are not only influenced by whom we like but are also influenced by life-cycle factors. We believe the available evidence clearly supports our view. We have emphasized the importance of cognitive development in childhood, but demographic or sociological influences in adulthood and old age. These reflect the kind of variables that previous researchers have chosen to investigate, not a careful listing of factors essential to the development of a theory of friendship over the life-cycle. We feel further attention should be given to developing a life-cycle theory of personal relationships. Such a theory needs to specify: relevant variables, a model of how these influences operate, and how the traditional principles of interpersonal attraction are affected by life-cycle considerations. We believe the development of theory profits from reference to empirical evidence; thus, we are confident that this chapter can contribute to the theory-building task that lies ahead.

In doing this review, we have reached several conclusions about the state of the literature which, we feel, have implications for future studies of friendship over the life-cycle. In particular, we would like to note two observations. The first is the problem of measuring friendship. The simplest assumption would be that friendship is a unified concept which can be assessed via a single item or set of items. This assumption seems incorrect to us. In this review, we have seen several measures used: number of friends, number of confidants, social network size, frequency of contact, kin contact, intimacy, and the like. It seems most likely that each of these measures has its own unique pattern over the life-cycle and to expect studies using different measures to produce comparable results is, in our view, naive. Further investigations should undoubtedly attend more carefully to the measurement issue. We suspect that questions dealing with "number of friends" have different meanings for men and women.

There are at least two solutions to the measurement problem. First, investigators can use several different measures. Secondly, in posing questions to respondents, researchers can specify the meaning of friendship. This should reduce the tendency of different respondents defining friendships differently. We would also discourage investigators from relying heavily on a "number of friends" measure. The search for life-cycle fluctuations in number of friends has met with only modest success. We recommend that more effort be spent exploring how the qualitative nature and functions of friendship change over life.

A second problem with the existing work on friendship over the life-cycle is sample selection since very few studies involve large scale, representative samples. To reach conclusions about friendships in society, representative samples should be used. Furthermore, most studies focus only on one segment of the life-cycle and we know of only one investigation (Reisman and Shorr, 1978) spanning childhood to pre-retirement. (This study used quota sampling.) Certainly, more studies involving both mid-life adults and senior citizens could be conducted. While the inclusion of infants in research poses unique problems, greater effort should be expended to do studies spanning the years from late childhood to old age.

All in all, we feel the study of friendship in people's everyday lives is a fascinating but important pursuit which complements the laboratory study of interpersonal attraction. As social psychologists, we hope more of our colleagues will turn their attention in this direction whilst we also hope that, in their future work, social psychologists will join forces with developmental psychologists, survey researchers, and sociologists. It is only such a combined perspective that will fully illuminate the vicissitudes of friendship throughout life.

Note

[1] At the time this chapter was being prepared, work on children's friendships was in a flourishing period. At least three books were in preparation (Foot et al., 1980a; Asher and Gottman, 1981; Rubin, 1980). Unfortunately, none of these volumes was available to the present authors.

CHAPTER 5
Infant-Mother Relationships

Susan J. Pawlby

An infant's relationship with his mother is the first of many interpersonal relationships that he will form. As such it is of interest to researchers and clinicians from two standpoints. First, how does the infant form his first relationship with another human being? Secondly, does the way in which he forms this first relationship relate in any way to the infant's later development? Any attempt to answer either of these questions depends on adequate description of the relationship between a mother and her infant.

During the past decade there has been a growing awareness of the importance of a descriptive base for the study of human relationships. It is perhaps no coincidence that this realization has emerged amongst developmental psychologists at the same time as the interest of many ethologists, well rehearsed in the descriptive method, has been turning towards the study of human behaviour. Hinde (1976, 1979, 1981) cogently argues that "If we are to make progress in understanding relationships. . . we must start with a descriptive approach". The task of describing the human mother–infant relationship is not an easy one, not least because of its complexity. However, this has not deterred researchers and there now exists a comprehensive body of studies of mothers and infants aimed at describing the interactions which make up this relationship.

In this chapter I shall draw upon the descriptions found in both the normative and clinical literature in an attempt to answer my initial questions. In so doing, I shall use the terms "infant" to cover the first year of life, "neonate" to refer to approximately the first ten days after birth, and "child" to talk of the period from one to 16 years of age.

How Does an Infant Form a Relationship with his Mother?

It is now almost universally acknowledged among researchers at least, that the building up of the mother-infant relationship is a joint enterprise: the infant is no longer seen to be the passive recipient of all that his mother imposes upon him but he is actively involved in determining the course of their relationship. One reason for this change of view is that the human infant is much more competent than he was at first thought to be and right from birth he is well equipped to enter into a relationship with his mother. The most salient features of the infant's social behavioural repertoire are now well documented.

The biological equipment of the newborn infant

Visual contact is often considered to be one of the most important components of social behaviour in infants (Rheingold, 1961; Robson, 1967). An infant's visual motor system is fully operational at birth in that he can look at and see objects. To begin with, his focal range is limited to a distance of about 20-25 cms — the distance between the infant's face and his mother's when he is held in the normal feeding position. Thus the infant is biologically equipped with the ability to see his mother's face which provides him with the opportunity for face-to-face interaction. It is now well known that the infant is also highly selective in what he looks at (Fantz, 1961, 1966) and that it is the human face which best provides him with the qualities of a moving, self-deforming, three-dimensional "object" for which he shows preference (Schaffer, 1971; Newson and Newson, 1975).

The infant's auditory apparatus is similarly equipped with a preference for the human voice. Thus Hutt *et al.* (1968) write that:

> the structure of the human auditory apparatus at birth ensures both that there is a limit of basilar membrane excitation beyond which defensive reflexes are evoked and that the voice at normal intensities is non-aversive and prepotent. The survival value of this differential responsivity may lie in the part it plays in the development of the affectional bond between parent and child.

The newborn infant is also able to turn his head to the sound source (Bower, 1974), thus demonstrating auditory-visual coordination. Again, he is ready to engage in interaction with another human being.

Little attention has been paid to olfactory perception in the human neonate, but recently MacFarlane (1975), has shown that, by six days of age, infants are able to differentiate between their own mother and another mother on the basis of smell. Preference for his own mother's smell again illustrates how well the newborn is equipped to enter into a relationship with his mother.

A fourth feature of the newborn's highly developed repertoire of social behaviours is his ability to produce a wide range of facial expressions. The infant's first smile, sober expression, frown, grimace are thought to be produced spontaneously with no intention on the part of the infant to use them to communicate, but nonetheless they exist and are there to be exploited by anyone interacting with the baby. It is these same expressions which, when seen in the child or adult, have communicative significance.

Fifthly, the infant's ability to cry at birth and to emit more pleasurable vocalizations within the first few weeks of life (Papousek and Papousek, 1977) equips him with yet another set of behaviours which will play an important role in his interactions with his mother.

Although I have described each of the examples of the newborn's social behavioural repertoire individually, their adaptive value lies in the fact that they are combined and organized in such a way that right from birth the infant is able to enter into a dialogue with his mother. An essential characteristic of any smooth dialogue is that the two partners take turns but it is only recently that researchers have turned their attention to examining this ability in the very young (Kaye, 1977; Newson and Newson, 1975; Schaffer, 1974; Schaffer et al., 1977; Trevarthen et al., 1975; Trevarthen 1977). Microanalytic studies have shown that the infant's behaviour follows a cyclic and rhythmic pattern which gives the mother the opportunity of engaging in a turn-taking sequence with her infant in which each partner first acts and then attends to the activity of the other.

Recent research revealing the complexity of the infant's social behavioural repertoire at birth makes it increasingly difficult to avoid the conclusion that, in some sense, the infant is already biologically equipped for social intercourse. Nonetheless, however well prepared the infant may be, little purpose is served unless he has someone with whom to interact. In Western societies it is the mother who usually fulfils the role of principal caregiver and thus the person with whom the infant has most opportunity of interacting. How well equipped is the mother for social intercourse with her infant?

The mother's role in relationship formation

Newson (1979) suggests that a mother's social interaction with her infant is very little different from that between pairs of adult human beings in that when she interacts she credits her infant with possessing human qualities and treats him as a communicating individual.

However, the means by which the mother interacts are unique to the dialogue with her infant (Brazelton *et al.*, 1975; Stern, 1974, 1977; Papousek and Papousek, 1975). Observations have shown that the mother adapts and modifies her behaviour in response to the infant's display. Stern (1977) calls the mother's adaptation of her adult behaviour "infant-elicited social behaviour", and goes on to describe how the mother exaggerates her facial expressions and vocal behaviour in both time and space when interacting with her infant. He gives as an example the mock surprise expression in which, as the infant turns to look at his mother, she attempts to hold his attention by opening her eyes very wide, raising her eyebrows, tilting her head slightly upwards, and opening her mouth very wide, sometimes vocalizing. The expression is not only exaggerated in space but it will probably be built up very gradually as if being performed in slow motion, until it reaches its climax, then it will be held for a relatively long time.

Similar exaggerations are observed in the way a mother talks to her infant. Mothers almost always speak to their infants in a high-pitched voice (Klaus *et al.*, 1975). Stern (1977) also comments on changes in the intensity of sound which, he points out, span a range from "whispered sounds to exuberant exclamations". Mothers also vary the speed with which they talk to their infants, generally slowing down what they say and exaggerating certain words or phrases. Schaffer *et al.* (1977) and Davis (1978) have demonstrated how the mothers pause in anticipation of a response from the infant. The pauses themselves are longer than in adult-to-adult dialogues. Stern (1977) suggests that the mother remains silent for the normal adult pause length plus the duration of an imagined infant response plus a second normal adult pause length before she speaks again. An other example of exaggerated maternal behaviours are eye-to-eye contact which is both prolonged and often accompanied by vocalizations — features which are uncharacteristic of adult interaction. Face presentations such as those found in games of peek-a-boo are also exaggerated.

Another feature of the mother's behaviour to which attention has been drawn is the repetitiveness, not only of what she says (Snow, 1972) but also of what she does with her face, head and body (Stern *et al.*, 1977; Fogel, 1977; Papousek and Papousek, 1977). They each show how in interaction episodes between a mother and her infant, maternal repetition can sustain infant gaze, provide a basis for a "theme-and-variation format", and present information in small doses with high redundancy for the benefit of the infant's cognitive apparatus.

One further example of the way in which the mother adapts her behaviour to that of her infant is in imitation. I have shown elsewhere (Pawlby,

1977a, b) that the mother's imitation of her infant's own spontaneous acts is by no means an infrequent phenomenon.

The ubiquity of the exaggerated and repetitive nature of maternal social behaviour towards her infant suggests that it might be adaptive for the mother to organize her activity in this way. To evoke a response in her infant is one of the mother's main goals. Maternal repetition and exaggeration sustain the infant's gaze (Stern *et al.*, 1977), thus holding his attention and increasing the likelihood of a response and maintained interaction. They also provide the infant with a stable predictable pattern of interaction (Papousek and Papousek, 1977) which he will come to anticipate and from which he will derive much pleasure (Pawlby, 1977b). By engaging the infant in the same repetitive sequences, the mother also gives the infant the opportunity of learning that if he performs certain acts he can sustain the chain of reciprocal activity (Newson, 1977). Knowing the consequences of one's acts is fundamental to the development of the notion of intentionality.

It is not simply the means by which the mother interacts with her infant but also the way in which she organizes her behaviour which plays an important role in their dialogue. Particular attention has been paid to the way in which the mother synchronizes her activity with that of the infant (Newson, 1977). She selects acts which the infant performs spontaneously and responds to them as if the infant had deliberately initiated them for the purpose of social exchange. In doing this the mother appears to allow herself to be paced by the infant, filling in the pauses between his bursts of activity and anticipating their occurrence. To do this successfully she needs not only sensitivity but also an exquisite sense of timing. By careful placing of her responses the mother gives the infant the opportunity of finding out that his behaviour can be used as a means of interacting with another person. In this way he can learn that his behaviour is of interest to another, that it will be attended to and elicit responses and that it is worth his while to attend to these responses in turn. The infant thus begins to function in such a way that his own actions can be used purposively. His task in learning how to make sense to others is not so much learning new actions that he has never made before, as learning a social use for actions that he makes all the time (Shotter and Gregory, 1976).

The quality and nature of interactions

My own observations of the development of imitation in infants illustrates well the importance of the part played by the mother in building up interaction sequences. It is not only what she does which is important but the way in which she does it. I have suggested elsewhere that the infant's ability to imitate is rooted in the mother's initial readiness to imitate her infant's spontaneous acts (Pawlby, 1977a). In doing this the mother transforms what the infant performs spontaneously into something he can use in interaction with others. Thus, for example, when the infant repeats one particular action for a second or third time — in a kind of repetitive ritual — the mother may skilfully seize the opportunity to insert her own copy of that act between two of his repetitions and thus create a simulated form of an act of imitation on the infant's part. In this instance, the mother's imitation of her infant's acts seems to facilitate the development of intentional imitation by the infant because the mother's answering gesture provides the infant with an interest-holding event which is, in fact, temporally contingent upon his own performance of a similar event.

A mother, in her interaction with her infant, also becomes highly sensitive to those moments when her infant is about to produce some action or gesture which she has previously endowed with special social significance and reflected back to him. She thus knows how to anticipate actions which her infant is about to perform and produces them herself just before the infant does, thus creating yet another form of simulated imitation.

Observations of this kind provide evidence that the mother's timing and placing of her reproductions is a matter of crucial importance in understanding the development of a child's ability to imitate with intent later on.

Developing a relationship

It is obvious from the descriptions of the behavioural repertoire of the infant and mother that both partners are well equipped for engaging in interaction, thus providing them with the opportunity of establishing a relationship. Crucial to the study of the development of a relationship is the notion that it involves a series of interactions in time (Hinde, 1976, 1979, 1981; Hinde and Stevenson-Hinde, 1976). Each interaction within a relationship should not be viewed as an isolated event but as part of a chain, each link of which is based on a history of previous exchanges (Newson, 1977) and may also be influenced by the expectation of future ones (Hinde and Stevenson-Hinde, 1976). It, in turn, may affect the subsequent course of the relationship.

Infants are repeatedly and massively involved in sequences of interactions with their mothers (Newson, 1977). Such extended dialogues promote shared understandings as the infant begins to attach meaning to the discrete pieces of behaviour which make up the exchanges. As such understanding develops, it becomes progressively more dependent upon a specific history of exchanges which the participating individuals share as a function of joint remembering. Interaction episodes between a mother and her infant thus contain a cumulative element as communication competence grows. The corpus of shared understandings is progressively enlarged as a result of continual negotiations and renegotiations, and, in this sense, individuals who know one another well may share an idiosyncratic or restricted code the form of which, as Newson (1977) points out, is not necessarily available to the observer. Indeed, it may well be that at the preverbal level of communication, the mother herself will sometimes be the only person who can identify certain communicative gestures which her infant is currently making, because only she shares a history of common communication experience with that infant (Newson and Shotter, 1974). However, Newson suggests (Newson and Newson, 1975) that as human observers we are in a privileged position since we are able to look at the process by which the mother and infant build up their relationship from the point of view of a participant observer. It is possible for us to identify the significant events and chart the course of the development of shared under-standings by virtue of the fact that we ourselves are constantly engaged in interactions with other human beings.

I have tried in this chapter to illustrate how the content and the quality of both the infant's and the mother's behavioural repertoires are such that the two partners are well equipped to engage in interaction. By repeatedly involv-ing one another in interaction sequences certain acts begin to take on meaning in the experience of both infant and mother. This facilitates the development of shared understandings not only of events and happenings in the outside world but also of each other. Such knowledge is crucial to the formation and development of a relationship.

It has become comparatively easy for us as researchers to observe the con-tent and structure of individual interaction episodes between a mother and her infant, especially since the advent of the videorecorder which gives us the opportunity of analysing sequences in micro-detail. However, we are still faced with the difficulty of identifying the factors which make the interaction meaningful to the two partners involved. This is possible only if we approach the task from the point of view of a *participant* observer, and even then we cannot fully overcome the problem that the meaning of each interaction episode is to some extent dependent upon the history of exchanges that have preceded it. However, even though each sequence is in some sense unique, detailed observations across time have shown that each behaviour does not occur with equal probability and it is possible for us to identify the common and salient features. We thus have access, albeit restricted, to an under-standing of the dynamics of the interactions between a mother and her infant which may determine the course of their relationship.

As an example let me trace the development of one type of interaction sequence observed during the course of my study on imitation (Pawlby, 1977b). One of the limited number of spontaneous acts produced by the infant which the mother selected and marked out by responding imitatively was a cough. All infants cough in response to irritation in the throat. Observations have shown that it is highly likely that early on in the infant's first year, mothers will respond in some way to this act. It need not necessarily be an imitative response; it could be a verbal response. "Oh dear!" or "What a bad cough!". Whatever her response, the mother is highlighting the infant's act and encouraging him to attend to her. Repeated episodes of this nature mean that the infant becomes aware of the consequences of his action. He then becomes capable of performing an act *in order to* get a desired response. Thus I observed how the infant's cough (brought about in response to irritation in the throat) was transformed into an effortful gesture which, combined with other gestures such as eye contact and smiling, became a deliberate invitation to the mother to engage in interaction. What was an isolated event in the behavioural repertoire of one individual has become a meaningful gesture in the experience of two interacting partners although it may not necessarily be understood by an outsider. It is interaction episodes such as these upon which the developing relationship between mother and infant is founded.

Does the First Relationship have Consequences for Later Development?

It has been suggested by Hinde and Simpson (1975) that the usefulness of descriptive studies of the mother–infant relationship lies in the degree to which they enable us to predict future social behaviour. Few would deny that the nature of this early relationship in some way influences the course of the child's later development. But what evidence is there to support this view? I shall first look at those studies in which the developmental consequences of variations in the mother–infant relationship within the normal range have been assessed, and then turn my attention to those studies which have examined the effects of a disruption in the relationship between a mother and her infant.

Essential to the task of examining consequences is the need for longitudinal studies. In the field of mother–infant interaction long-term follow-ups are unfortunately rare, not least because the detailed studies which I have described in the first part of this chapter are relatively recent and we are, as yet, unable to assess the long-term consequences of their findings. However, I shall attempt to summarize those that do exist.

Effects of normal range variations in mother-infant relationships

In her studies of social development Ainsworth (1977) has tried to show how the nature of the interaction that an infant experiences with his mother is one of the most important influences on the kind of attachment relationship he eventually forms with her. She examined several aspects of mother–infant interaction in different situations — responsiveness to infant crying, early feeding interaction, contingent pacing and encouragement of interaction in face-to-face situations, and tender, careful handling while in close bodily contact — and found that the characteristic which related most strikingly to the eventual security of the infant–mother attachment relationship at the end of the first year was maternal sensitivity to infant signals in the earliest months of the first year. In her study of mothers and their infants between the ages of nine and 18 months, Clarke-Stewart (1973) also found that the child's optimal, secure attachment to the mother was significantly related to high maternal scores on dimensions of affection, stimulation and responsiveness. Findings such as these provide support for the view put forward by Schaffer and Emerson (1964) in which they suggest that it is the *quality* rather than the quantity of the interaction between a mother and her infant which is important in maintaining the attachment relationship.

A recent finding by Blurton Jones *et al.* (1979) again emphasises the importance of the contingent nature of the mother's response upon her infant's signals. They found that aggression at 21 months, defined as the number of times a child attacked or took objects from another child, was positively correlated with a slow maternal response to crying at 15 months.

There have been several studies which have looked at the consequences of differences in the early interactions between a mother and her infant and the child's later language and cognitive development. Blurton Jones *et al.* (in preparation) found that a child's performance on a language test at 21 months and at 27 months and on an I.Q. test at 39 months was positively correlated with measures of maternal responsiveness to her child's vocalizations at 15 months. On the other hand, Dunn (1977) found no relationship between her simple frequency measures of maternal responsiveness made during the first year and I.Q. at 4½ years. However, when she adopted a more subtle qualitative measure of maternal "acceptance" in response to the infant's vocalization she did find a positive correlation with I.Q. scores. Nelson (1973) also found that the measure of acceptance in mothers' replies at 13 months correlated with the child's use of object words and object naming at 24 months.

Ainsworth has also attempted to relate individual differences in the child's language and cognitive development to differences in the qualities of his early relationship with his mother. She has suggested (Ainsworth *et al.*, 1974) that a relationship with a responsive and sensitive mother fosters communication skills during the first year.

Findings from a longitudinal study in which I am involved with Stephen

Wolkind and Fae Hall also show a relationship between maternal behaviour when the infant is four months old and the child's later linguistic competence at 27 months and his cognitive development at 3½ years (Pawlby and Hall, 1980). Both the frequency with which the mother engaged in activities such as touching, talking, smiling, looking and the contingency of the interaction upon the infant's own behaviour were found to be related to the child's later language and cognitive ability. However, further analysis by sex shows that these findings are true only for mothers and their daughters, and not for mothers and their sons. Thus, although significant positive correlations exist between the frequency and contingency of each of the four-month maternal interaction measures and girls' later language scores, this is not so for boys.

Yarrow *et al.* (1974) in a longitudinal study of adopted children related several dimensions of maternal care by adoptive parents at six months to the child's I.Q. score at ten years. They found that physical contact, appropriateness of stimulation and responsiveness of the mother to the infant's atttempts at communication were all related to I.Q. at ten years. However, although the correlations between the variables and I.Q. were positive for both boys and girls, they were significant only for boys.

A fuller discussion on the mechanisms which might be operative in bringing about sex differences in the relationship between early mother–infant interaction and later outcome for the child can be found in Pawlby and Hall (1980). What our findings illustrate, however, is that any longitudinal study examining the effects of the relationship between a mother and her infant on the child's later development must look at boys and girls separately.

Whether or not the findings presented so far have any long term predictive power is open to question. Most of the studies are unable to project beyond the pre-school period. More detailed microanalytic interaction studies along the lines described in the first part of this chapter with a follow-up from infancy into both early and later childhood and even beyond, may help to shed light on the precise nature of the qualities of the mother–infant relationship which are thought to be important for the emotional, social and intellectual needs of the child and adult. Until such studies are carried out we have to rely on the long-term data provided by the clinical literature in order to assess the importance of the mother–infant relationship.

Effects of disruption in mother-infant relationships

In 1951 Bowlby stated that it was essential for mental health that the infant should experience a warm, intimate and continuous relationship with his mother. Although his writings have often been provocative and controversial his statement in general is now widely believed to hold true. In the wake of

Bowlby's claim there has now emerged a substantial body of literature on the effects of "maternal deprivation". Rutter (1972) distinguishes various forms of maternal deprivation, each having different outcomes. He suggests that developmental retardation and intellectual impairment are both a consequence of a lack of environmental, including maternal, stimulation; acute distress and depression appear to be related to the disruption of a relationship already made, such as might occur in cases of separation where the mother or infant were admitted to hospital; antisocial behaviour and delinquency are associated with distortions in the relationship involving lack of affection, hostility or discord as might be the case where the home is broken; and finally psychopathy and emotional disturbance are the result of failure to make a relationship as might be the case for children reared in institutions from infancy.

I have already drawn attention to some of the studies which show that even among "normal" infants reared by their own mothers in their homes, paucity of appropriate interaction between a mother and her infant may lead to developmental retardation and intellectual impairment. There is a good deal of evidence to show that children of working-class mothers do less well when compared with children of middle-class mothers in linguistic competence and subsequent intellectual development and scholastic attainment (Bernstein, 1965; Davie *et al.*, 1972; Douglas, 1964; Douglas *et al.*, 1968). It is likely that these findings reflect differences in styles of maternal interaction.

Other studies of infants reared in institutions showed that they were delayed in vocal and verbal development (Provence and Lipton, 1962). Brodbeck and Irwin (1946) compared the frequency of and variety in the vocalizations of "well-mothered" babies with those of children in orphanages and found significant differences between the two groups. Interestingly, two studies by Tizard and Rees (1974, 1975) of children raised in residential nurseries have shown that at two years, children who had lived all their lives in nurseries were not significantly different in non-verbal intelligence from working-class children reared in their homes. They were behind in language development but by four years there were no differences in intellectual development, verbal or non-verbal I.Q. between the two groups. These findings tend to substantiate the claim that the *pattern* of interaction between a mother and her infant is important for the child's cognitive development.

Most human studies of infant distress following separation have been concerned with children admitted to hospital or to a residential nursery. The fact that distress following separation does not usually occur in infants under the age of six months when maternal attachment becomes firm (Schaffer and Emerson, 1964) suggests that the child probably needs to have developed a relationship before he shows an emotional response to a separation experience (Rutter, 1972). If the child is deprived of the relationship he has formed, he reacts by manifesting protest, despair and detachment (Robertson and Robertson, 1968). Important here is the question raised by Rutter (1972) of whether children who have built up a strong relationship suffer more from the loss of their mother than those already relatively deprived. What evidence there is seems to suggest that children with a good relationship are least affected by the deprivation and that those who have least to lose are those most affected when they lose even that little. Hinde's work with rhesus monkeys (Hinde and Spencer-Booth, 1970) supports the theory that it is the *quality* of the infant–mother relationship prior to separation that determines the outcome.

Further evidence comes from studies of children who have experienced separations as a result of family disharmony. Again it is thought to be the disturbed nature of intrafamilial relationships which may lead to antisocial behaviour and delinquency rather than the separation itself (Rutter and Madge, 1976). In our own study (Wolkind *et al.*, 1977) mothers who themselves came from broken homes were found to interact less frequently with their infants at four months and their interactions were less contingent upon the infant's own behaviour. This was not the case for the mothers who had experienced care away from home outside the context of family disruption (Hall *et al.*, 1979).

We have no empirical evidence that the mothers in our study were deprived in their own infancy. Whether the mother–infant relationship is all-important in determining later outcome to the exclusion of other relationships is doubtful. However, the fact remains that it is usually the relationship with his mother which is the first that the infant makes and I cannot help but share Ainsworth's belief (1977) that the way in which this early relationship is established is important for the child's cognitive, emotional and social development. The finding that the failure to form a relationship in infancy may lead to emotional disturbance and the inability to sustain future relationships in depth (Rutter, 1972) adds weight to the importance of the building of the first relationship. This view is not meant to deny the possibility of reversibility. Clarke and Clarke (1976) present a good deal of evidence which demonstrates favourable reversals of previously adverse behavioural trends among children reared in institutions and then adopted into normal homes. However, the majority of children remain within their family throughout their childhood. Rutter and Madge (1976) have demonstrated marked continuity in the quality of individual marriages from year to year and Hall and Pawlby (in preparation) have suggested that it would be surprising if the behaviour of children growing up within the context of such marriages did not also show continuity. Even Clarke and Clarke (1979) argue that enduring influences make an enduring impression. Thus, in cases where the mother and infant have difficulty in forming a relationship, we might predict continuing difficulties for the child unless these can be stemmed by offering appropriate support at the right moment.

Recent clinical research has been directed towards the examination of the early relationship between mothers and their infants in groups identified as being "at risk" of developmental problems due to handicapping conditions and/or unfavourable caretaking environments. Such studies have included mother–infant pairs where the infant has experienced pre- or perinatal complications or has been diagnosed as being handicapped, as in the case of Down's syndrome; others have focused on pairs where the mother has been identified as being "at risk" for difficulties in child-rearing such as those who have experienced disruption in their own family of origin or those who have a history of psychiatric disturbance. Several researchers have detected interaction patterns between mother–infant pairs in risk groups, such as those just mentioned, which are different from those of normal dyads, and have postulated a circular relationship between disturbances in early interactions and later problems (Field *et al.*, 1980).

A number of studies have examined the interaction patterns between mothers and infants who have been separated immediately after birth (Kennell *et al.*, 1975; Leiderman and Seashore, 1975; Whiten, 1977). Richards (1979; Richards and Robertson 1978) has reviewed this research in detail. In summary he concludes that in spite of differences in the samples studied, in the reasons for separation, and in the length of separation, the findings are similar. Most report initial differences in the patterns of interaction between the mothers and infants in the separated group compared with those of the non-separated group. The separated group engaged in less face-to-face interaction, including eye-to-eye contact, less affectionate holding, less kissing and talking, less smiling and laughing, were less likely to sustain turn-taking sequences and were less responsive to their infant's own behaviour. Similar differences between the separated and non-separated groups were *not* found in maternal responsiveness to the infant's "functional" behaviour nor to his "non-social" behaviour (Whiten, 1977). The differences seemed to exist only in the purely social aspects of their interactions. However, it is precisely these aspects which I have earlier described as being important in the formation of the mother–infant relationship.

There have been few studies which have provided long-term follow-ups of their separated groups and so it is difficult to assess the importance of the early differences in the interaction between the mother and her infant for the future development of the child. Douglas and Gear (1976), however, in a follow-up of the low birthweight (< 2000 g) children in the 1946 national cohort at 13 and 15 years, found that they tended to do worse in terms of social adjustment and cognitive development compared with matched control normal birthweight children. In a follow-up study from birth to eight years, of 160 babies of low birthweight ($<$ 1500 grams) who survived after perinatal intensive care, Blake *et al.* (1975) found that while most of the mothers subsequently formed adequate relationships, there was a tendency for them to be overprotective and anxious, and for their infants to be mildly overdependent, shy and anxious.

A number of retrospective studies of children who have suffered non-accidental injury (Lynch, 1975), or who have been diagnosed as "failure to thrive" (Fanaroff *et al.*, 1972) have shown that a higher proportion of such children than would be expected by chance have histories of perinatal complications involving early separation from the mother, which in turn may have resulted in the inability to form an adequate relationship.

Another group of studies have examined the consequences of allowing mothers of normal full-term infants prolonged contact in the immediate post-partum period. Both Kennell *et al.* (1975) and de Chateau (1979) found that the extra contact seemed to facilitate the synchronous development of the mother–infant relationship. Differences between the extra-contact group and those who had experienced routine care were found into the child's second year but again a proper, fuller understanding of the implications of such a procedure for the future development of the child is dependent upon long-term studies.

Early separation of mother and infant and the subsequent deprivation of contact is only one example illustrating how the development of a mutually satisfying relationship may be impeded. In cases where the infant is born with a handicapping disorder not necessitating special care, the mother and infant may be in continuous contact but still they are unable to develop a harmonious relationship with one another. The relative disorganization of the behaviour of a malformed infant may make it difficult for the mother to interact successfully with him. In a study of Down's syndrome infants and their mothers in the first two years of life, Jones (1979) has shown how it is not the quantity of interaction episodes which differentiates them from normal infant–mother pairs, but the structure of their interactive exchanges. The Down's syndrome infant demonstrated poor timing in his interactions with his mother, making it difficult for the mother to establish the pattern of turn-taking found in successful dialogues. It is as if the infant is failing to anticipate a response from his mother and as a consequence the mother is deprived of the opportunity of providing one. The infant, in turn, is denied the opportunity of mastering the rules of interaction and of gaining knowledge either of the consequences of his actions or of his partner in the interaction.

Another example of how disorder in the pattern of the infant's own activity may affect his emotional and cognitive development is provided by Kalveboer (1979). He found that apathy in the newborn period is related to the development of depressive symptoms in the preschool and school-age child. He suggests that the lack of responsiveness in infants with the apathy syndrome may affect the mother so that she not only provides less stimulation but she is also less adapted to the structure of the infant's own behaviour and, therefore, her activity is less contingent upon his. Non-contingent stimulation may interfere with learning and the development of initiative.

Even a "normal" infant can have behaviour patterns which play a disruptive role in the formation of a relationship with his mother. Thoman (1975) gives an example of an infant who, from birth through the first weeks of life, showed avoidance to being picked up and held. The infant's behaviour was a source of frustration and confusion to his mother, who found it difficult to respond appropriately to the infant's needs. The resulting interaction in turn affected the infant's developing behaviours in that it impeded perceptual learning. In his study of twins Stern (1971) also shows how the twin whose earliest gaze exchanges with his mother were mutually unsatisfying and difficult, continued to have difficulties in interpersonal relationships.

So far I have confined my attention to describing the interaction patterns of mother-infant pairs where the infant has been deemed to be "at risk" of difficulties in establishing a relationship with his mother. Our own study (Wolkind et al., 1977) has been aimed at identifying groups of mothers who may be "at risk" of failing to establish a relationship with their infants. I have already described how mothers who themselves came from broken homes interacted less frequently with their four-month-old infants and how their responses were less contingent upon their infants' own behaviour. The inadequacy of their interaction was in turn related to the child's later language and cognitive development, but in the case of girls only (Pawlby and Hall, 1980). Another group which has been identified as being "at risk" is that of mothers who have had a history of psychiatric disturbance prior to their pregnancy. We have found a significant association between women with a previous psychiatric history and a rating of the infant as "atypical" during the administration of the Brazelton Neonatal Assessment Scale at six days (Hall and Pawlby, in preparation). A rating of "atypical" at six days was also positively associated with "problem" behaviour at 27 months and at 3½ years. We have suggested that the infants experienced as showing "atypical" behaviour on the sixth day of life may have been a group of infants whose behaviour already reflected their contact with a mother with emotional difficulties. The "atypical" features of the infants' behaviour may in turn make it difficult for the mother to interact appropriately with her infant, thus impeding the development of a satisfactory relationship.

Conclusion

Throughout this chapter I have tried to emphasize the importance of the contributions of both the mother and the infant in the development of their relationship. Under normal circumstances both partners are well equipped to engage in the interactions which make up their relationship. All may not always go smoothly but endowed with the propensity to adapt (Bell, 1974; Dunn, 1976; Stern, 1977) the vast majority of mother-infant pairs are able to develop mutually satisfying relationships. In cases where the interactive patterns of one or both partners are impaired for some reason the mother and infant may find it difficult to establish a "successful" relationship.

The precise implications of the quality of the mother-infant relationship for the child in terms of his cognitive, social and emotional development are unclear, not least because of the lack of both normative and clinical long-term studies of the infants whose early interactions with their mothers have been traced in minute detail. Evidence does exist, however, particularly in the clinical literature, which suggests that the mother-infant relationship may sow the seeds of future interpersonal relationships, especially where the child remains with his mother throughout his childhood as is the case for the majority of children in Western societies. Only longitudinal studies from infancy into adulthood will provide clarification of the features of the relationship which are important for the child's development.

My attention in this chapter has been confined to the formation of the relationship between a *mother* and her infant. This is not meant to deny the importance of the infant's relationships with others. Evidence of sex differences in the outcome of mothers' early interactions with their infants may indicate the importance of the relationship between father and son in determining a boy's future development, for example. Recent research examining the infant's relationships within the context of the whole family (Lewis and Rosenblum, 1979) has begun to fill the gap which has long lain open.

It still remains true, however, that the mother will normally be one of the first people with whom the infant will make a relationship. How can the formation of this relationship be enhanced? Concern has been expressed in clinical circles over the possible deleterious effects of intervening in the normally spontaneous process of establishing a relationship between a mother and her infant (Dunn, 1976; Stern, 1977), especially when we are unsure of the long-term importance of the relationship. One area in which there seems to be overall agreement is that the infant is an active partner in the process of building the relationship. However, in spite of the increased awareness of the abilities of the newborn among researchers, this knowledge has still not filtered through to mothers themselves. Isolated efforts are being made to demonstrate to mothers the social behavioural repertoire of the newborn with amazing success. Brazelton (1979) describes how if new mothers are shown their infants' behavioural responses in the neonatal period, these mothers behave significantly differently from a control group one month later in a feeding situation, and in an interview, say that their attachment and their self-image as parents are significantly enhanced by having been encouraged to see their babies as "people". We have evidence that the mother's perception of her baby as a person is related to the later outcome for the child (Hall *et al.*, 1979). There is no reason why demonstration of the newborn's social repertoire should not be a normal part of post-natal training for mothers, in the same way as they are shown the physical caretaking procedures. We may then find that mothers are able to adapt their behaviour more finely to their infants' whom they see as active participants in the interaction, the infants in turn playing a fuller part in the dialoque. The process by which a mother and infant build up their relationship is dynamic, reciprocal and important for the future of the child.

Acknowledgements

I should like to thank Fae Hall and John Newson for their help and support during the time I have been studying mothers and their infants.

CHAPTER 6

Parent-Child Relationships in the Middle Years of Childhood

M. M. Shields

This chapter is focused on parent-child relationships in the middle years of childhood at a time when there is a very rapid growth and change as the child develops from a toddler to the onset of puberty. In some ways the growth is not as spectacular as that of the earlier stages or those which succeed as the pubertal spurt carries the developing human being on towards maturity, yet a ten-year-old is very different from a four-year-old, and the impression of slow and steady progress may be an artefact of the measures we use to calibrate it rather than any relative deceleration of development. It is, after all, during this period that the child enters the social world on his own, in schools and in the peer group, yet our measures of increasing social and psychological knowledge and skill are primitive. It is during this time that he or she becomes literate and begins to tap the store of socially acquired knowledge which forms the second endowment of human heredity.

It is during this period also that the dispositional traits of the child are beginning to be organized into more stable patterns of personality under the impact of social interaction in the family and the school and peer-group, though patterns are still very labile (Neubauer and Flapan 1976). At the same time the schoolchild acquires a greatly increased repertory of role behaviours and interaction patterns as his social knowledge and experience expands.

Parents often say that their child is "not the same person" when in a different social milieu, and this may be a reflection of a differentiated development of social repertory, the extent of which is masked by the habitual relationships of the home. Nevertheless it is still widely assumed that it is within the home in interaction with parents and siblings that the child's personality and style of coping are chiefly formed, both by the behaviours he has under observation and by the interactions that affect him or her directly.

Therefore, when I was asked to write a chapter on "Parent–Child Relationships in the Middle Years of Childhood", I expected to find a more systematic and through literature than in fact exists to deal with this important topic. In comparison to the number of papers on mother–infant interaction, the research literature in the present topic lacks weight, and yet recent criticisms of the wisdom of undue extrapolation from experience in infant relationships to the structure of adult ones should be taken to heart. Adult relationships are more likely to be prepared in the middle years of childhood than in infancy. I will therefore spend some time considering why this feature of relationships at a central time in development is so curiously under-researched.

Difficulties for Research

Parent–child interaction takes place within a family and the family group has some unique features when it is compared with other social groupings which make it difficult to study. It is, for one thing, the smallest and least accessible of social groups, especially in Western cultures where each family is considered entitled to its own front door, and those which fall below this standard are considered unusually deprived. Problems of entry into the family network are among the primary difficulties for research, but others are posed by the nature of the family itself.

Problems created by the nature of the family

The family is the only group which must at some time consist of two persons of opposite sexes and, in spite of the growth of one-parent families, the great majority of families continue to have both a mother and a father. The family is also unique among small groupings because of the age distance between its mature and immature members and the consequent asymmetry in their relations. Even a family of three has three dyadic and one triadic interaction frames and each of these relations can be viewed from the perspective of each member and each interaction may produce an effect in any or all of the other interaction frames (Lindsey, 1976; Klein *et al.*, 1978).

The parental pair have separate histories before they form their bond, but afterwards their relationship provides a joint history, one in which their own reciprocal behaviour and the perception of each by the other forms an inward-looking system. Into this system children are born and the system, in the majority of cases, adapts to take them in, though not without some stress as the husband and wife take on new parental roles (Clausen and Clausen, 1973; Hoffman and Manis, 1978).

The children, in turn, form bonds with the parents who dominate the early social scene, and with one another; so the family, as a unit, is emotionally turned inward, and its life, behind its front door, consists largely of transactions between its members. These transactions are so complex and multifarious that the family members themselves are often unable to recall them in any detail, and when researchers are admitted into the family circle with their questionnaires, the family members themselves tend to describe their interactions either by using typical events as paradigms, or by descriptions of emotionally outstanding instances. Family research which is based on reports from family members therefore is usually at a double remove, since the researchers are generalizing from the generalizations of their respondents, and often, even more remotely, generalizing from statistical manipulation of such generalizations. This is not to say that such reports have not some relationship with what actually goes on, but the human tendency to notice contrast rather than the commonplace may give undue prominence to emotionally charged incidents of clash and control, whereas day-by-day episode sampling of family routine might reveal the relative rarity of such episodes amid the continual and habitual "press" for adjustment within a given life style.

In addition to the inaccessibility and inwardness of families another difficulty is caused by the fact that family processes take place in both biological and real time. Members of the family grow and age. In the typical three-generation family of preadolescent school children, the parents may be passing into early middle age, and their parents may be going out of working life into retirement. Some of the grand-parental generation may be experiencing sickness and disability which may stress the parents of the middle generation by increasing their caretaking load. At the same time the pre-school child who has only a tiny segment of his life outside the family, will be progressing into the role of a school-child and then into puberty and on to a stage in his education where his success may affect his life chances in important ways. These changes have an institutional and as well as biological component, but the dynamic which drives them forward is the process of growing and ageing. As family members grow and age, their roles within the family interaction pattern also change. There is therefore no time in its history when it can be said that any one family is *typically* "a family" though there may be resemblances with other families at a similar stage.

An attempt to deal with the element of time and development within the family relationship is being made by a confluence of psychological and sociological thinking in terms of a life-span view of the family (Baltes and Schaie, 1973; Lerner and Spanier, 1978). This view has theoretical strength in the determination of its proponents to leave no variable in the life history of the individual and family out of account, and is a welcome corrective to the simplistic search for causal links between a set of typified interactions and another set of typified outcomes. The heroic nature of the research programmes required to produce data for a life-span view appears, however, to require more intellectual and interdisciplinary cooperation than has hitherto been in evidence among the academic community, if the theoretical bones are to be fleshed out with empirical results of more than a very general kind.

Problems of access to data

The characteristics of families in general which have been outlined above pose considerable problems for the researcher, and these problems are increased for the age range examined here. Mothers and young babies appear to be easier game, for the baby is portable and can fairly easily be brought into a laboratory setting. Young mothers are usually heavily invested in their mothering task and so provide interested cooperators. In any case, the interpersonal behaviours of the mother and young child, rich though they are, are probably more routinized and certainly less varied in content than those of the older child and his or her mother, and so more readily investigated by the currently fashionable close-focus ethological techniques, with their fixed schedule of behavioural categories.

Once the child enters pre-school or school proper, a substantial amount of time is spent away from the family home with the consequence that, although the child itself can be more closely observed and investigated because in an institutional "trap", studies of teacher–child and child–child interaction are more numerous than those of parent–child interaction from then on. The family simultaneously may become less accessible due to the dispersion of its members during working hours, and the child's relationship with his family becomes correspondingly less easy to monitor. For most of the year, the real-time interaction of parent and child will be concentrated into a few hours at the beginning and the later part of the day. This may have the effect of an interactional "crush", as the punctualities of institutional time are imposed upon the family timetable. Much more of the interaction will be shifted to times when father is present as well, and the ability of the mother to share her attention between spouse and child will be constrained, whereas prior to the child entering school it could be distributed over time. The notorious paucity of father–child interaction studies is in part due to the fact that fathers are out at work during normal working hours and may have natural reluctance to consent to "home time" with its psychological concomitants of relaxation and togetherness being invaded by academically curious researchers. Nowadays more than one-third of women with school-age children work outside the home, and are similarly less likely to welcome any very prolonged contact with research workers during the time they have to shoulder their family duties.

There also appears to be a sociocultural consensus between families and research workers that evenings and weekends are protected time and not to be disrupted without good reason. The direct observation of families going about their normal business is therefore likely to be severely constrained by the enhanced interest of family members in protecting family boundaries. This may be one of the main reasons why there is a minuscule amount of relationship research on normal families of school-children compared with the burgeoning of studies of mothers with babies and toddlers.

There are, of course, other reasons of a more theoretical nature for the concentration of work in the younger age range. Among them is the theory of critical periods in development which has orientated interventionist research towards the early years in the hope of anticipating and altering family behaviour which might result in intellectual or emotional difficulty later. As a consequence the pressure of social concern and egalitarian ideals has pushed the money for research to the early stages of development. The theories which held that early experience is not only irreversible but irretrievable, have now come under criticism, however, (Clarke and Clarke, 1976; Tizard and Hodge, 1978). The Clarkes cite many instances where quite extreme deprivation was retrieved by a more normal and supportive environment in the middle years. The six children from the Tereszin concentration camp, originally studied by Anna Freud and Sophy Dann (Freud and Dann, 1951) and who were adopted in the middle years of childhood all showed a normal adaptation in the later years (Dann, 1978). It is also in the ages 7, 8, and 9 that referral to the school psychological services in England appear to show a peak which may indicate that it is during this period that children develop, or fail to develop, important coping and adaptive behaviours for dealing with normal life (Wright and Payne, 1979). So it is possible that in the future more interest will be shown in what goes on between family members in the middle years. It is likely, however, that family boundary maintenance will always keep the amount of direct observation to a small proportion in relation to other forms of information gathering.

Theoretical problems in studying relationships

Access to the data is one difficulty, but the study of relationships also poses considerable theoretical problems. In the first place the term relationship is extremely vague because it is so all embracing. Parent and child can be related biologically, legally, transactionally, socially, cognitively and emotionally. One obligatory substrate of meaning is that in any human relationship at least two persons are involved. As it is characteristic of most relationships between persons that each is aware of the other and behaves in reciprocity to the behaviour of the other, then it would seem to follow that the study of a relationship should be based on mutual perception and mutual interaction. Another underlying meaning in the term "relationship" when applied to families is that of duration, development and change as family members live out their individual and common biographies. The elements of mutual perception, reciprocal interaction and common biography have not been a direct focus of research in the middle years and what we know about them is inferred from studies undertaken for other purposes, such as surveys of parenting practices or clinical studies with therapeutic objectives.

This is in part due to the fact that mainstream psychology and psychiatry have traditionally concentrated on the behaviour of individuals whether impelled by internal biologically based dynamic systems, or controlled by stimuli from without. Interaction between two or more individuals, each of whom affects the behaviour of the others, makes any causal relations between the acts of one and the acts of another within a successive chain of reciprocal actions extremely diffuse and multidirectional. This is the case even within restricted episodes, involving few interactional turns. When interaction takes place within a prolonged relationship spanning many years during which the participants age and change, and the situations in which they find themselves alter and extend, causes and effects become confounded, and it is necessary to adopt a more open-ended and systems-based view in which the behaviour of each is constantly modified to adapt to the behaviour of the others.

It has now become fashionable to point out the inadequacies of some of the theories and methods traditional in social psychology for dealing with human and social behaviour, and to demand a Kuhnian paradigm shift (Harré and Secord, 1972). Social psychology, however, has never had a single paradigm, and has always given free run to various theoretical positions, and contained fruitful strands of eclecticism and cross fertilization of ideas from other areas of psychology and other disciplines such as sociology and anthropology. Theories on role and on the functioning of groups are cases in point and both have a contribution to make in the study of interaction between parent and child.

Role theory

Role theory developed from the interface between social psychology and sociology proper and focused closely on the relationships between people in specific social networks. According to this view, what the child learns in the course of interaction within the family is a series of behaviours which can form role appropriate clusters attached to the various positions he or she holds.

Within families a considerable part of the role repertory is attached to age, gender and biological relationship. Husband roles are played out *vis-à-vis* wife roles, and son roles are played out between dyads such as father–son and the triads of father–mother–son so that there is a familial set of role behaviours learnt in interaction with other role players appropriately modified to the circumstances within which an interaction takes place. For example, gender role behaviours are not usually expected to differ with regard to meal times, bed times and interactions set within a parent–child or generation framework, whatever the sex stereotypes held by the parents, but they may differ considerably with regard to other activities (Lambert *et al.*, 1971).

Group dynamics and structuralism

After the last war there were a series of studies engendered by the Field Theory of Kurt Lewin (1951) and by the categorization systems developed by Bales (1950) and Carter and his colleagues (Carter *et al.*, 1951). These were extensively used for the study of the behaviour of groups brought together *ad hoc* and appeared to show that they developed a group dynamic and identity and a set of rules which regulated the attitudes and actions of group members. Ideas from this research have been and still are being used in clinical studies of family function. Bales went on to collaborate with Tallcott Parsons in an analysis of the family as a system which combined notions from sociological structuralism with ideas from group dynamics and Freudian theory. This theory conceived the family along two dimensions: that of power and that of gender, with its associated gender function (which was said to be "instrumental" for males and "expressive" for females). This highly schematized view showed the child identifying with the same-sex parent and extending his or her roles expressively or instrumentally, as the case may be, in reciprocity with the opposite-sex parent, and the parents themselves assisting this process with the leverage of their superior power (Parsons and Bales, 1956). This pattern is surprisingly persistent in studies of family interaction especially in studies of relative dominance between the father and mother (Hetherington *et al.*, 1978).

Symbolic interactionism

The ideas of symbolic interactionism derived from the work of George Mead constitute another long-standing trend within social psychology and provide a rich source of ideas about how personality and self identity are constructed in interpersonal social exchanges. The build-up of internal representations of the behaviour and attitudes of other persons provide conceptual systems which are likely to be powerful factors in motivating and guiding the behaviour of the developing human being and the parents to whom he is bound in a reciprocal exchange of meaning. This strand of ideas has not, however, been much used in the study of parent–child relationships but has had considerable influence in the area of the development of the child's self concept. According to this view, the child's definition of himself, his role potential, capability and worth are derived from his belief as to how others perceive them, especially significant others who form a reference group for his activities.

Growing Points for Research

The ecological viewpoint

The work of Barker and Wright (1954) has secured more praise than imitation. The data of one complete day's recording for each of only eight children in Midwest produced 7751 classifiable behaviour episodes, 85% of which entailed social interaction, though some of this was with the observing psychologists. Nevertheless the authors concluded that at least 60% of the episodes in which the child participated were social, and that an average of 80% of the social episodes were reciprocal. The disadvantage of being "drowned in data" has discouraged much replication of this enterprise. Barker identified more than 200 behavioural settings in the mid-West town which formed the base for his research and children entered about 60% of them. He also found that the children's behaviour was more similar in similar settings than each child's behaviour was in different settings.

This ecological approach differs from the situationism of a behaviourist viewpoint in that it assumes that the situation does not control behaviour in any causal sense, but that persons recognize situations as having certain meanings and that there are appropriate behavioural patterns which pertain to these meanings. This concept is not new in social psychology; both Gestalt theory and Lewin's field theory laid strong emphasis on the subjective understanding of the individual of his internal life space which contains the representation he has built up of the social world around him. There is a similar emphasis in the theories of Carl Rogers and George Kelly and their followers. The phenomenological emphasis on the importance of subjective under-standing was developing strongly in psychology before it began to produce new thinking in sociology. Social phenomenology and ethnomethodology which have inspired the microsociology of Goffman and Garfinkel has now produced renewed stress on the analysis of interactional episodes. Tape- and video-recording has also provided a technology which can "freeze" such episodes for detailed examination.

Unfortunately and surprisingly these ideas have barely begun to permeate the study of parent-child relationships outside infancy. Even in studies of the early interactions of mother and child, the use of the broad spectrum of ideas available in social psychology has only recently begun to overthrow the blocking concept of early childhood egocentricity which prevented a study of the child's developing social consciousness and understanding, and with it the reciprocal nature of the relationships entered into by the child.

Recently Bronfenbrenner (1979b) has attempted to bring these ideas together and to provide an organised theoretical basis for a developmental social psychology. He advocates a systems approach to the study of the development of children and gives prominence to the network of settings which surround the interactional field of the developing child. These he grades by distance from immediate face-to-face interaction, which he calls the micro-system. This in turn is enveloped by a meso-system of linked settings within which various microsystems of interaction can take place. Bronfenbrenner also postulates an exosystem which a particular person may never enter but within which events occur which will affect what happens in his or her immediate environment. These are in turn embedded in the overall macro-system of institutions, beliefs and values which are common to a par-ticular culture or subculture (Bronfenbrenner, 1979b).

Not only, then, has the child to learn the rules and presuppositions con-cerning interpersonal behaviours, he also has to learn the appropriate setting for each. Differing settings evoke a different repertoire of behaviours even within the microcosm of the family. The behaviours expected of family members at getting up, at breakfast, at evening meals, at school, and at play time, all have their scenarios, scripts and order of performance although there are always individual variations. The child therefore must master the situation as a cue for sets of behaviours, and each situation is both inter-personal and embedded in the ecology of family and other settings of the meso-system. Furthermore, the child has to learn to vary his repertoire as he grows and the family style modifies to cope with changing relations between its members as the children grow older.

Bronfenbrenner's work is at the moment programmatic rather than empirical, though some empirical studies would fit comfortably within the framework he suggests. Empirical work on parent–child relationships which makes use of the spectrum of ideas recently developed within social and inter-actional psychology are yet to come.

Language and cognition in the study of relationships

Cognitive psychology has established a dominant position in the study of child development, but unfortunately both the bias of interest in Piaget's work and the practical manipulative element in the laboratory procedures which are used in cognitive experiments have placed emphasis on the logical and mathematical understanding of the impersonal world. The child's development of a cognitive model of persons and their interpersonal activi-ties has only recently begun to receive attention, although Flavell urged that this should become a central focus of developmental research some years ago (Flavell, 1974; Shields, 1978).

It is through the study of the child's development of communication skills that most progress has been made in the study of interaction. The first wave of language acquisition studies in the seventies was based upon the gram-matical theories of Chomsky and emphasized the acquisition of rules (Brown, 1973). Recently the emphasis has shifted away from syntax towards a functional and pragmatic approach. Ethological techniques used in the analysis of non-verbal communication have set the study of early communi-cation within a strongly interactional framework (Susan Pawlby, Chapter 5, this Volume).

As the exchange of meaning becomes more complex, it becomes increas-ingly necessary to call on work in pragmatics and sociolinguistics where the examination of turn-taking, semantic cohesion, cohesion of adjacent speech acts, shared presupposition and inter-subjectivity have emerged from the study of interactional episodes (Speier, 1971; Sacks *et al.*, 1974; Labov and Fanshel, 1977). Attempts are being made to relate this work to the com-munication skills of young children, but as yet the necessary cognitive abilities which underlie the child's skill in exchanging meaning with others are imperfectly understood, and without such understanding the analysis of interactions is likely to remain near the surface (Ervin-Tripp and Mitchell-Kernan, 1977; Shields, 1978).

Very few studies of spoken language exist for children over the age of four, and this reflects the general paucity of studies of social interaction in the middle years. Some data on the relation between various parameters in parent–child communication within the home and the child's subsequent progress at school are, however, emerging from the Bristol study which has collected examples of the child's linguistic interactions in the home by microtransmitter, and later investigated the child's development at school. The analysis of these naturalistic records of language development and parent-child communication highlight several important elements in the parent-child relationship. Those parents who have children who develop rapidly linguistically not only talk more to their children, but talk more in a context of shared activity, particularly in common household tasks, the procedures of which may be encoded in instructions and commands which pick out what is to be done in contexts with which the child is familiar and which also form part of adult activity in which the child is interested. They also take up the child's own focus of interest more frequently than the parents of children with slower linguistic development. In short, the interaction between these parents and their children has more mutualization of activities and interests than is the case in families of less rapidly developing children (Wells, 1979).

Methodology in the Study of Parent-Child Relationships

The intrinsic complexity of the parent-child relationship and the evolution of theoretical constructs designed to take account of this complexity has generated a proliferation of investigative instruments and procedures. Strauss and Brown (1978) list no less than 813 measures of parent-parent or parent-child relationships, 494 of these were added in the 10 years between 1964 and 1974 and many more have undoubtedly been added since their book went to press. They comment on the constant proliferation of these instruments some of which have close similarities and only minor alterations to embody slightly different ways of conceptualizing the data sought or the problems to be solved. There also appears to be a marked indifference of many of the authors to problems of reliability. Some of the instruments have a long history and have been widely used such as the Parent Attitude Research Instrument (PARI), the Maternal Behaviour Research Instrument (Schaefer *et al.*, 1959) and the Fels Parent Behaviour Rating Scale (Baldwin *et al.*, 1949).

These are the base materials from which many subsequent scales have been quarried and they are in some form or another still in use today (Baumrind, 1971). Their longevity is due partly to ecological constancies in the data investigated and partly to the academic affiliations of subsequent users and partly, as well, to continued sociocultural normative ideas about the idealized family in Western industrial democracies. The emphasis on dimensions such as authoritarian/democratic, dependent/independent, dominant/subordinate, masculine/feminine have an obvious cultural component whether they are used in the initial construction of the instrument or "emerge" as a result of factorial analysis.

For all their variety the instruments and procedures fall into a few main categories.

(a) Survey instruments, usually questionnaires, based on ecological variables and behavioural inventories and the elicitation of attitudes and beliefs about child-rearing, most often a mixture of more than one of these.

(b) Rating scales which are similarly based but in which the items are graded. These include self-administered rating scales, mainly designed to elicit attitudes but sometimes including behavioural descriptions.

(c) Observational schedules based on inventories of behaviour which may be ethologically derived from pilot observations or pre-categorized from behaviours deemed to be interesting for the research in question. These can be used in naturalistic settings, either unobtrusively with the observed being unaware of the observation, or in natural settings with the observer known to be present, or in laboratory or clinical settings. These can include continuous observation, time scheduling or episode sampling. Modern audio-visual recording techniques can be used and these facilitate post-categorizations of the data.

(d) Naturalistic experiments in which data from two or more contrasting ecological settings is compared, e.g. institutional versus home rearing, Kibbutz versus Western family life.

(e) Contrived experiments either in the home or laboratory where the subjects are asked to interact over a prescribed task or in a problem solving situation.

(f) Case studies and clinical records of deviant families.

(g) The use of standardized instruments of all sorts such as the TAT, the MMPI and all the well-known tests of intellectual performance.

(h) A variety of other instruments and other procedures such as sentence completion, story completion, *ad hoc* projective tests, doll play and games, etc.

Observational studies

In contrast to the proliferation of observational studies of mothers and young babies and toddlers, there is a relative paucity of observational material on parent-child interaction in the middle years. The ethological techniques which have been used in the study of the mother-infant dyad need considerable modification before they can encompass the more complex exchanges of meaning as the child matures. There are problems of what behaviour segments to choose as significant and also problems of how to reduce the immense burden of data, without draining it of meaning. Many of these problems are raised in a collection of studies of methodological issues in social interaction analysis edited by Michael Lamb and his colleagues (Lamb *et al.*, 1979).

A considerable number of observational studies are carried out for clinical purposes in order to look at the sequential contingencies of deviant behaviour in children (Patterson, 1977; Snyder, 1977; Taplin and Reid, 1977). In many ways the observational study of deviant behaviour is easier than that of normal behaviour because it is closely focused. Normal interaction is more difficult to get to grips with because it is more ordinary, multifaceted, more diffuse and more ambiguous. However, without close focus studies of normal interaction between parent and child, it is not possible to give a reasonable account of their relationship or of the transmission of the characteristic behaviours acquired by members of particular cultural groups and sub-groups.

Clinical studies

There are, of course, a great many clinical studies of the interaction patterns of families where one member has been referred for troubling behaviour of some kind. The reporting of these studies shows some developments of clinical methods such as the use of video tapes of family interaction with family members to elicit accounts of their action. By and large, however, the reports are heavily soaked in the preconceptions arising from the clinical or academic affiliations of the psychologists and psychiatrists concerned. There is an exhaustive review of such techniques by Cromwell *et al.* (1976) and some evaluations by Riskin and Faunce (1972), and Gurman and Kniskern (1978).

Experimental studies

Experimental studies of interaction within normal families are thin on the ground, though these are sometimes used as controls for malfunctioning families. In addition, they seem to be focused on younger or older age groups than the one considered here. It is difficult to study naturalistic behaviour in a laboratory setting, for the tasks often seems to be artificial and the older members of the family cannot help being conscious of the setting. It is also not easy to control the interaction of family members in order to isolate the effect that any one member is producing on the others. Osofsky (1971) was driven to use role playing children in order to discover whether mothers adapted their teaching style in accordance with the behaviour of a pre-instructed child who was not their own. She found that mothers did in fact vary their behaviour, both between tasks, and towards the differing roles played by the child accomplice. Bell and Harper (1977) have summarized a number of studies showing this bidirectionality of interactional effects. They postulate that parents have a complex repertory of parenting behaviours rather than a dominant parenting style, and that these are evoked differentially by the behaviour and perceived state of the child, its age, sex, birth-order, and the current circumstances of the family.

One of the experiments suggested by Bell has recently been carried out by Humphries and his colleagues. This tested out whether the well known restrictive and controlling behaviours of mothers of hyperactive children were a contributing or reactive factor to the child's hyperactivity. Humphries conducted a double blind test of the unidirectional hypothesis by setting a cooperative task to 26 mother-child pairs in which the child was hyperactive. The task was set in a double blind design both before and after the administration either of methylphenidate or a placebo. It was found that the amount of controlling behaviour by the mothers was reduced, the number of the child's directions to the mother increased, and the amount of praise given by the mother also increased in the medicated condition (Humphries *et al.*, 1978).

Interactional behaviour not only shows reciprocal adaptation between persons, but it is also affected by situation. Parents of different backgrounds may act very differently in unfamiliar settings. Schlieper (1975) looking at mother-infant pairs found that when recorded in their own homes there seemed to be only minor differences between mothers of lower and higher SES and she contrasted this with many studies in which quite marked differences in behaviour were found between mothers of different SES when observed in laboratories. O'Rourke (1965) observed 24 family triads at home and in the laboratory and found that the laboratory conditions increased both interpersonal activity and stress. There was a fairly marked sex effect as fathers of boys became more negative in the laboratory and mothers of girls became more positive and supporting towards their daughters (O'Rourke, 1965). Laboratories are perceived in a different way by people from different backgrounds and the experiments will be interpreted differently in different individuals. It is therefore unwise to extrapolate the differences found in laboratory conditions to ecological settings of another kind (Bronfenbrenner, 1979b).

Survey data on parent-child relationships

Most of the data that we have on the inter-relations of parent and child in the middle years are based on surveys using inventories, questionnaires and rating scales and often a combination of all three. The data are almost exclusively supplied by one parent, viz. the mother. This method has the advantage of being an economical way of obtaining a large amount of data from a large sample. The survey either has to deal with a narrow age band or to overlap parent cohorts to allow a wider age spectrum of the child-rearing community to be sampled. This can of course introduce cohort effects because the older parents may differ in their views on child-rearing from the younger parents owing to a different exposure to cultural value systems.

The Sears, Maccoby and Levin (1957) investigation of 379 mothers of five-year-olds was a trend-setting study not only because of the wide ranging questionnaire and rating scale but also in its use of factor analysis to extract abstract global factors in parenting behaviour headed by the famous permissiveness/strictness dimension. The finding that families of lower socio-economic status (who were incidentally not equally represented in the sample with mothers of middle and higher status) were less permissive, less warm, more likely to punish aggression against parents severely, and less likely to induce conscience-based behaviours, all contributed to the image of the poor family which emerges time and again in the research on deprivation in the middle 'sixties. Seminal though this study has been in the study of parenting, it can serve as a source of data only for one partner in the parent–child relationship, the mother, and all other family relations are seen through her eyes. It was based on a five-year span recalled at one moment in the joint biography, and uses a method of data reduction which picks out quite general affective and attitudinal categories as overall descriptors of parenting style, as though this was invariant over context, circumstance and time.

Longitudinal surveys

Longitudinal surveys allow a repeated sampling of the same cohort of parents at different stages in the family life-cycle, though even intermittent visiting from a research team may change the behaviour of the host families in some way (Campbell and Stanley, 1963). These also have the advantage that the parents do not have to stretch their memories too far back to give information but can answer from current practice. Memory is a notoriously unreliable tool, fatally prone to reconstruction in the very act of recall (Yarrow *et al.*, 1970; Hindley, 1979).

A group of studies which have exercised considerable influence were the Fels Institute Longitudinal Study (Baldwin *et al.*, 1949) and the series of developmental studies at the Institute of Human Development at Berkeley (Schaefer and Bayley 1963; Baumrind, 1971). In these, the samples were smaller, the study of both parents and children more intensive. The children's and parents' behaviours were independently observed and the children were also tested. Both groups of studies clearly show an attenuation of the relationship of the original factors extracted from parent behaviour ratings to the child's behaviour with the passage of time. Another finding was the differential effect of parent behaviours on boys and girls. For example, in the 1963 study by Schaefer and Bayley, boys', but not girls', performances were related to maternal warmth. In the cross-sectional study of middle-class families of children in their fourth year by Baumrind, the category of parent labelled "authoritative" i.e. firm, controlling, self-confident, but encouraging of individuality and independence in the child, produced socially responsible boys, but, on the other hand, "non-conforming" parents had high-achieving boys. High achievement in girls was associated with parental permissiveness, which was negatively associated with socially responsible behaviour in boys (Baumrind, 1971). Unfortunately, as in most studies the sample was small and socially selected and the sibling group was not studied to see if same- or different-sex siblings reacted differently to the parents' style or whether the parents reacted differently to them.

The attenuation of long-term effects in the longitudinal studies is not surprising. It is likely that parents' treatment of their children would vary with age, sex, the development of the child and its changed activities within and outside the home. Changes in family life-style due to life-span or ecological factors would also produce an effect. The search for simplistic global parenting factors as antecedents for subsequent measures of children's performance has so far been defeated by time and change.

One thing which emerges in the early studies and has persisted all through is the pervasive influence of father's occupation and ethnic subculture variables. The second is the different treatment and reactions of boys and girls. In the cohort of 700 children being studied longitudinally at Nottingham by John and Elizabeth Newson both sex and social class are associated significantly with different child rearing practices, though the increasing maturity of the child is also an important variable (Newson and Newson, 1976).

The Nottingham longitudinal survey

The Newsons' study differs from its American counterparts in several important areas. It is, of course, a survey based on a questionnaire eliciting information exclusively from mothers but the Newsons believe that the questionnaire's main value is as a guide to conversation because they believe that:

> Conversation is by far the most economical means in terms of time and effort of arriving at a valid assessment of a situation (Newson and Newson, 1970, p. 17).

The mother's accounts of parenting practices are set alongside the parents' expressed attitudes and beliefs about various areas of child upbringing because the authors believe that in the long run it is these beliefs and attitudes which will have the most lasting effect on how the mother or the father interacts with the child.

The Newsons interviewed the mothers of their 700 target children when these children were 1, 4, 7, 11 and 15. The last two survey interviews are still unpublished. The Newsons have deliberately eschewed any elaborate statistical treatment because they believe that it will reduce information without producing any gain in insight. Hence, the mother's account is the central feature of the study.

Age, sex and social class emerge as the main source of overall variance in the reported parenting behaviours. Age tends to be underemphasized because of the way the data are presented but is implicit in the changes in children's and parents' behaviour which emerge between the ages of four and seven. The Newsons could find no social-status differences in the affection with which children were treated, though they noted that demonstrative behaviour had become more private between four and seven years, and some of the indulgences enjoyed by four-year-olds had lapsed with the child's increasing independence. They did, however, find that equally affectionate parenting was accompanied by a significantly different degree of consideration for the child's point of view, the higher socioeconomic status families being more child-centred.

The Newsons attach particular importance to certain differences in upbringing style. There are those families, predominantly middle class, who use verbal methods of control, make rules salient, use words with a regard for truth, keep verbal contracts such as threats and promises, answer questions straightforwardly, and think that disputes should be sorted out verbally and treated equitably in accordance with rules governing the interpersonal relations between siblings, peers and members of the family. At the other end of the scale there are a minority of families who exercise an authoritarian and mainly non-verbal means of control, use words to threaten and bamboozle the child into obedience rather than explain the underlying rules which matter in each interaction, and whose attitude to truth is eroded by expediency. Either by imitation or cognitive understanding the middle class pick up the system which can be used rationally in the wider context of life whatever the setting. A minority of children, however, learn distrust of verbal messages and more primitive survival skills.

Pointing out the gaps in our knowledge and the problematic nature of some of the research from which inferences are made about parent-child relationships is not necessarily a criticism of any particular piece of research taken on its own terms. Information about relationships derived from studies of parenting practices is necessarily one-sided, but can hardly be faulted for not dealing with something the research workers did not include in their brief. Research such as that of the Newsons has the merit of a longitudinal or life-span perspective, and it also holds a balance between familial variation, and common and subcultural variables by adopting a low-key statistical analysis. Like the majority of similar studies, however, it focuses on the parents' relationship with only one of their children, and this masks the within-family variation that one might expect, given the prominence that the Newsons' data give to children's sex and age differences as influences on parenting. The Berkeley longitudinal studies have the merit of including observations of parent-child interaction, but as a consequence of a more elaborate method have small sample sizes which can be heavily subject to sociocultural bias. Moreover, they mask the detail of interfamily variation by a search for overall causal links between parenting and measured child behaviour. The Barker and Wright study (1954) picks up the interplay between parent and child for a very small sample at a single point in time. It is, however, rich in situational information and thus highlights the sheer variety of experiences and interactions in which a child participates. In order to study the unique characteristic of the parent-child relationship it would have to be set within each member's total network of experiences. Without this it would be impossible to elucidate any special characteristic of what happens between members of a family who have a shared biography.

The parent-child relationship is often given the main credit for the transmission of the perceptions, knowledge and skills which go to the maintenance and re-creation of the everyday life of families, communities and societies. What interactions within the relationship are crucial to this process we are not in a position to say, nor, on the other hand, can we say whether it is rather accomplished in a cumulative press of many small everyday messages. We do not know the sequential agenda of the process as the child grows, nor how far it is carried on intentionally, nor are we in a position to differentiate what is transmitted in highly scripted and conventionalized interactions, and what is transmitted in interactions of a more free-wheeling kind. Perhaps a study similar to that of Barker and Wright which recorded information intensively for all members of a small sample of families at set intervals of time would provide more information of how the relationship between child and parent develops and what it does for each of the parties to it.

Conclusion

In conclusion, what this exploration of studies of relationships between parent and child appears to show is that there is need for much closer investigation of what goes on in normal families during the time they spend together. This investigation must have something of the same order of intensity as the current study of young children. It is not possible to infer from the mother's interaction with her toddler what she will be doing with her older school-child. Reliance on a few traits and tendencies in early mothering and fathering to produce a different but equivalent set of behaviours for their seven-year-old or ten-year-old would ignore the fact that the child–parent relationship is a function of *all* partners within a changing family system and not a linear causal system. Perhaps the best approach would be to combine an overlapping cohort-survey of parenting practices with intensive observational studies of families drawn from samples taken from a cohort. This is an unexplored field and it seems to be high time that research work was prised away from its obsession with the toddler to dealing more adequately with the relationships of families at later stages in their life history.

CHAPTER 7
Children's Friendships

John J. La Gaipa

Social development during the elementary school years has generated surprisingly little research interest. Indeed the years from six to 13 have been treated almost as a latency period in which not much of anything happens, whilst the surrounding preschool and adolescent years are viewed as more provocative. Perhaps, during these childhood years not much does go on that is of interest to the developmental theorist, but this should be a conclusion drawn after the research has been done instead of an assumption diverting research effort away from this life period.

Accordingly, the present chapter will review developmental studies of children's friendship, focusing on theoretical orientations rather than on empirical findings. A large part of the chapter will be devoted to areas of neglect and areas of promise in the field of children's friendship research and the chapter will show that there are not only many important areas for future work in this field, but many that are theoretically challenging.

There are many evident excuses that can be given for the neglect of social development during childhood (see Preface, this volume) but among the most important are those based on the firmly held, but empirically unsupported, prejudgement that the preschool period is a more central transitional period for various aspects of cognitive development. Moreover, the emphasis on cognitive development has been at the cost of neglecting the impact of the social environment on development. In my view a further important but

161

often unstated reason has been the lack of effective or sophisticated procedures for studying social development — particularly in children's friendships — and, for this reason, methodological considerations will be of special concern in this chapter.

This chapter will also emphasize cognitive-developmental approaches to children's friendships. Such attention does not represent my assessment of its merits, but rather its popularity with developmental psychologists, and the emphasis of the work that I have done with my colleagues. Other stage approaches include Sullivan's (1953) "developmental epochs"; the Loevinger and Wessler (1970) "ego-development model"; Kohlberg's (1969) "moral development model", and Erikson's (1950) "eight stages of man". These models have generated little research bearing directly on children's friendships and somewhat more research has been done on adolescent friendships, which is an area outside the scope of this chapter (but see Chapter 8).

These developmental models, be they cognitive, ego or moral were not designed to explain changes in children's friendships, but the stage approaches to friendship described in this chapter have been influenced by these models, since it is typically assumed that changes in friendship parallel changes in one of these domains. For example, La Gaipa and Bigelow (1972) found that the kinds of notions about friendship emerging at different periods during childhood closely paralleled Kohlberg's stages of moral development. Such analogies are sometimes useful and interesting; but more conclusive evidence depends on independent measures of level of stage development, and Duck (1977 a, b) in his review of stage theory approaches, has noted some of their other limitations in this context. There are inherent value judgements implicit in such theories; for instance, the implication that people who do not achieve the highest level, or who move through levels at a slower rate than people, are somehow deficient. Such theories also imply that people who are fixated at an early stage are less likely to be able to form meaningly relationships as adults. Duck also cautions that stage-related hypotheses have not been clearly formulated or demonstrated by research, and since children's friendships are exceedingly complex, it is too early to say precisely how such friendships relate to development in any of the above domains. A further objective of this chapter, then, is to assess the validity of this position.

The Structure of Social Knowledge: Age-related Changes

The search for structure

What do we know about the nature and organization of the conceptual networks or "cognitive maps" that children form of their particular worlds? Kuhn (1978) argues that we know almost nothing about them, but our scanty knowledge does suggest one characteristic — that they are organized, or structured. The search for structure is a major characteristic assumption of the cognitive developmental approach. To deny structure is to imply that as children grow older they merely accumulate isolated bits of information and psychologically unconnected cognitive entities (Flavell, 1977). A structural approach to children's conceptions of friendship involves, instead, a search for some underlying organizing principle, that is, the structural core that shapes the knowledge and gives it coherence and regularity. It should be noted that structural analysis is more than just a procedure for studying social development; structural analysis can be applied to the whole spectrum of personal relations (see La Gaipa, 1981).

Selman and Jaquette (1977) describe structural analysis as a process of moving back and forth between a theoretical model involving explanatory constructs and surface data such as conceptions of friendship. The specific explanatory model that is posited is essentially what differentiates one approach from another. Selman (1976) highlights social perspective as the explanatory construct; drawing on Piagetian theory, Youniss (1978) focuses on such constructs as reciprocity; whereas, Bigelow and La Gaipa (1980) focus on equilibration. What these three approaches have in common is the use of verbal reports which provide the surface data regarding what children think about friendship. The investigator needs, however, to go below the surface and make inferences regarding how children think about friendship.

Social cognitions

During the last ten years much interest has been shown in the development of social knowledge, under such rubrics as social cognition, social perception and person perception. Because of the availability of several literature reviews, no attempt will be made here to summarize the findings (see Rogers, 1978; Youniss, 1978; Duck et al., 1980).

A major approach to developmental studies of person perception is based on the notion that the social behaviour of children cannot be comprehended without knowing how children seek to understand other people's behaviour. Age-related changes have been identified in the way children describe others, as well as how they learn to understand the psychological causes of behaviour. Few controversies have been generated by this body of research; the results have been quite clear cut.

Somewhat more controversial have been attempts to relate cognitive development to social development. The cognitive skill of role taking has received considerable interest and attempts have been made to determine if cognitive performance correlates with social performance. Investigations have been made of the relationship between social cognition and peer relations based, in part, on Piaget's writings on the role of social experience on cognitive development. Esquilin (1979) found that cognitive abilities were unrelated to peer success. Similar research by Lehr (1978) found no relationship between role-taking ability and either the quality or quantity of peer exposure. Bartholomew (1979) compared emotionally disturbed children with normal children and found that disturbed children were behind on cognitive tasks but there was no difference on role-taking performance. Selman (1976) compared normal and disturbed preadolescent boys and found that disturbed boys were at a lower interpersonal level regarding notions of friendship, but did not differ from normal children in their perspective-taking ability. A variety of explanations have been suggested for such contradictory or non-supportive results (Shantz, 1975) and Rubin (1978) suggests that one problem lies in the methods themselves, particularly the unreliability of the procedures used.

Social perspective

A major explanatory construct in theories of social knowledge is that of perspective taking. A somewhat narrow definition of this construct can be made in terms of role taking or the ability of the child to understand the point of view of Other in relation to that of Self. Selman has shifted recently from viewing social perspective as a developmental ability showing quantitative change to an interpretation of social perspective as a relational concept undergoing qualitative change (Selman and Jaquette, 1977). The attempt is to move away from role taking as an ability that involves gathering data about the content of another's mind and, instead, the relational quality of perspective taking is stressed; that is, with regard to the relation between the perspective of Self and Other, with particular emphasis on the form that it undergoes with changes in development.

This construct of perspective taking is a crucial one in Selman's structural analysis. Perspective taking provides the structural basis for the child's knowledge of interpersonal relations, and mediates stages of development. In support of Selman's notion of social perspective taking, Damon (1977) argues that this process has much significance for the development of social knowledge. Through perspective taking, the child comes to understand the relations between persons and the factors that lead to the growth and termination of relationships. A child learns to recognize, anticipate and possibly resolve conflicts. There is an appreciation for the needs and desires of other persons in relations to those of the self and through perspective taking, the child learns to reason about fairness, friendship and the society itself.

Relational theory

Youniss (1978) has taken a strong stand against the cognitive approach to social development that emphasizes role-taking as crucial in the acquisition of social knowledge. A different conceptual framework is proposed based on interpretations of Piaget's (1932) writings, in particular, the definition of knowledge as a relation between two actors. Social knowledge is treated as made up of conceptions of interpersonal relations. Youniss argues that one person does not get to know another person by penetrating his/her inner, psychological workings: instead, persons are known in terms of relations rather than as objects *per se*. Social cognition does not imply knowledge of "persons" but knowledge gained through social collaboration with other persons.

A relational theory is proposed in which the development of the self is taken to be simultaneous with the development of understanding of interpersonal relations (Youniss and Volpe, 1978). This approach derives from notions of Piaget (1932) and Sullivan (1953) that interpersonal relations form the basic unit of analysis for social science rather than the entities of "self" and "other". The individual, then, is viewed as subordinate to the relationship, with the eventual goal being to describe the structure of relationships giving rise to the characteristics of the individual (Youniss, 1980).

Social understanding begins with interpersonal relations in which each person compares, contrasts and confronts each other with their own thinking (Piaget, 1932; Youniss, 1980). What each person takes away from the interaction is a thought that is not a private construction but is a result of collaboration. Thus, social knowledge about interpersonal relations is constructed by both parties who enter the interaction, and is achieved by putting oneself into an orderly interaction with another.

Social knowledge of social relations is acquired as the child seeks some order and regularity in the social world. The child is exposed to an ever-changing array of interactions, and, in the search for order, the child turns to the exchange arena, looks first to his/her own actions, and then realizes the need to take into account the actions of others. Reciprocity occurs when allowances are made for differences of opinion, and each child submits his/her respective rules for mutual inspection. Order is imposed by constructing rule systems or relations in collaboration with each other.

Youniss (1978) argues that the understanding of interpersonal relations involves knowledge as to the effects of interaction on a relation, such as may be used to maintain, intensify, repair or terminate it. For instance, a child learns that self-disclosure makes people feel closer to one another, and that name-calling disrupts a relationship. However, except for verbal reports, there are few data available on how children negotiate and collaborate regarding the possible effects of different kinds of interaction on the quality of a relationship. Certainly, differences among children on such matters may generate quarrels, and the resolution of conflicts may provide a useful learning experience. Seven-year-old children, for example, have been described by their mothers as often quarrelling with their friends. Of interest is the observation made by these mothers that if children did not quarrel, they would never learn the techniques of getting on with people (Newson and Newson, 1978).

It should be clear from the above that such approaches, whilst mostly new and sophisticated, deal, nonetheless, with only one side of friendship in children and that it is predicated on an understanding of parallelism between cognitive development and sociality. Even so, little of the work described so far has concerned specifically the development of children's beliefs or cognitions *about* friendships, and it is to this that we now turn.

A Multidimensional Approach to Children's Friendships

Many of the data on friendship about to be described are a product of a research programme on adult and children's friendships (see La Gaipa, 1977a, for a summary). The most critical feature of this programme is the assumption that to understand the nature of friendship it is necessary to follow a multidimensional approach, and a primary task has been to identify and quantify friendship dimensions.

The initial step in this research programme involved interviewing close to 1000 young adults on the meaning of friendship to them. After a content analysis of the interview data, a series of factor analytic studies yielded seven dimensions of friendship expectations (FEs) that were incorporated into a friendship inventory. Subsequently, individual differences in conceptions of friendship were studied by relating scores on self-report inventories and projective tests to these friendship scales. Longitudinal studies later showed that the scales constructed on the bases of factor loadings were predictive of the growth of friendship.

This research strategy used with adults was extended with some modification to investigate children's friendships. If friendship is conceptualized as a multistructured thing, then certain strategies are suggested; for instance, there is a need to develop procedures for identifying some of the basic dimensions; there is a concern with the nature of the organization of friendship concepts; and there is an interest in the genesis, emergence and changes along such dimensions during the childhood years.

The isolation and measurement of friendship dimensions in adults provided us with a useful frame of reference: the experience of looking for patterns in adult thinking about friendship sensitized us to the kinds of things to look for in children's notions of friendship. Actually, a number of dimensions isolated in the adult research were found to be quite useful in studying children's friendships.

Two areas of research on children's friendships will now be described. The first area, involving Bigelow as a colleague, centred on the construction and validation of a developmental scale of friendship. This scale was a product of research showing the sequential nature of the onset of dimensions of friendship. The second area, involving Wood as a colleague, more closely parallels the psychometric approach useful in research on adults. The factor analytic studies culminated in the Children's Friendship Expectancy Inventory, an instrument for studying individual differences in conceptions of friendship.

The developmental scale of friendship

A cognitive-developmental orientation

As applied to friendship conceptions, a structural approach posits a hierarchical structure in the emergence of such cognitive entities as friendship expectations. The earlier emerging concepts are assumed to have different properties from later emerging concepts; for instance, the more abstract dimensions have a later onset than the more concrete dimensions. The notion of sequential invariance is one aspect of hierarchical structure and is a notion that pertains to the order of progression of the developmental sequence. Structural invariance posits that the order of emergence does not change; for instance, sharing always appears in children's thinking before the notion of intimate disclosure. The rate of development may vary with children but not the order of onset of the basic conceptions of friendship.

Why would a developmental scale be useful? Since children of the same age vary in their conceptions of friendship, it was necessary to construct a developmental scale of friendship that could be used to classify children according to their dominant developmental level.

The developmental scale was constructed on the basis of content analysis of children's essays. Children in grades one through eight (ages six to 14) were instructed to write an essay about their expectations of best friends. The coding system contained 21 dimensions and identified nine dimensions or variables that showed developmental change in both Canadian and Scottish samples. Cluster analysis provided some support for a stage conception of development (Bigelow, 1977) and dimensions within a stage correlated more with those in the same class and correlated less or inversely with dimensions in other classes.

The stages and the developmental position of each dimension are as follows: *Stage 1*: Common activities (1), Evaluations (2), Propinquity (3); *Stage II*: Character admiration (4); *Stage III*: Acceptance (5), Loyalty and commitment (6), Genuineness (7), Common interests (8), and Intimacy potential (9) (see Bigelow and La Gaipa, 1980). Some support, then, was obtained for the notion that the FE dimensions would fall into three distinct sets representing developmental stages: reward–costs; normative; and empathy.

Several studies have been done to extend the age range of the Bigelow and La Gaipa developmental findings or to test the feasibility of modification of the basic research strategy. Hayes (1978) demonstrated that the developmental scale can be extended down to pre-school children. These children were interviewed and asked to give reasons for liking or disliking specific other children: the liked children were described in terms of common activities, general play and propinquity, whilst the disliked children were described as high on aggression, aberrant behaviour and rule violation.

Gamer (1978) also used the interview technique, instead of written descriptions, with children ranging in age from six to 13 years. The older children mentioned more often the importance of the reliability of a friend, the support provided and the sharing of confidences. The statement most descriptive of friendship was "Someone who understands your feelings". No sex differences were found. These results are highly consistent with the Bigelow and La Gaipa data and another study provides evidence, extending beyond the original age range of the Bigelow and La Gaipa (1975) study. Reisman and Shorr (1978) found a developmental progression with age up to about the eighth grade, but with no changes after that along the dimensions of Intimacy Potential, Common Activities and Loyalty–Commitment. These findings also replicated the Bigelow and La Gaipa (1975) study based on the same age groups. When we extend the age range, we obtain the same results for common activities and loyalty–commitment, but not for intimacy potential. In late adolescence, intimacy is emphasized much more than in early adolescence (50% versus 16%). Reisman and Shorr (1978) also found that though talking about a problem with a friend increased with age, even at the youngest age (7–8 years), more than half of the children reported this behaviour. Evidently, discussing problems with friends is not uncommon among children but we found few instances where such young children mentioned talking over problems with a friend as an expectation. Perhaps, this disparity indicates that such behaviours occur prior to the time that they become valued, as such, as indicators of friendship.

The identification of a developmental sequence of friendship expectations (FE) is meaningful if it can be shown that the classification of children by this procedure has some functional value in friendship formation. The validity of the developmental scale, then, was examined, in the attempt to bridge the gap between thought and action. Two studies were conducted (reported in Bigelow and La Gaipa, 1980), the first asking whether children prefer friends at the same or different levels of development. Children were exposed to tapes of hypothetical friends expressing conceptions of friendship at different developmental levels and the task was to choose the most preferred friend. Overall, it was found that the preferred best friend was at a level higher than the child's dominant level whilst peers with the same level of development were the least preferred. Some age differences were found, however: among the 8–9-year-olds, as many showed a preference for friends at one level below or one level above as at the same level; but the 11–12-year-olds showed the most preference for others that were at one level above their own.

The second study was concerned with the relationship between children's developmental level and their sociometrically best friend. Children were asked to name their best friends and comparisons were made between each child's dominant FE level and the level of the person so named. A relationship was found, but it varied according to age: among the 8–9-year-olds, 60% named friends with the same FE level; but of the 10–11-year-olds, only 26% named a best friend who was at the same level. It should be noted that whether or not the person chosen as a best friend reciprocated the choice made no difference in the degree of correspondence of FE.

Why children often do not prefer or choose as friends person who are at the same conceptual level is not self-evident. One possible explanation is in terms of the Piagetian notion of equilibration: exposure to discrepancies in conception of friendship may generate disequilibrium that may serve as an impetus to growth. The social development of the 11-year-old child, then, may be facilitated by contact with children who are more advanced — but it is not clear why eight-year-old children do not show a similar pattern. Another interpretation can be made in terms of differences in onset of thought and action: behaviour may precede the ability to conceptualize it and perhaps the child preferred as a friend is at a higher cognitive level, but not at a higher behavioural level.

Insofar as real differences exist in friendship choice regarding developmental level, there is a source of tension inherent in childhood friendships. It is impossible, of course, for all children to interact with those at more advanced levels but in terms of Youniss' (1980) approach to friendship, such disparities are almost inevitable. A basic task of friendship formation is the cooperation and negotiation to resolve such differences, and in the very process of working them out, the relationship is enhanced.

The Bigelow–La Gaipa scale was designed to assess developmental levels of children's thinking about friendship, not to study individual differences. The developmental scale permits finer discriminations than existing procedures, focusing on the more global stage levels, but the classification system in this scale is based on a relatively small number of spontaneous responses. Quantitative distinctions along any specific dimension are limited. Moreover, the basic intent is the level of development instead of the content of the dimension used to classify the child.

A supplementary technique was seen as necessary when there is more of an interest in individual differences along specific content dimensions. In the second phase of research on children's friendships, a series of studies was completed in collaboration with Wood (La Gaipa and Wood, 1973, 1976, 1981; Wood and La Gaipa, 1978). These studies were designed to construct an inventory useful in measuring more precisely friendship expectations of children using more traditional psychometric techniques.

The children's friendship expectancy inventory (CFEI)

More than 500 children's friendship essays collected earlier by La Gaipa and Bigelow were used in the construction of this inventory. Two overlapping forms were constructed, one for middle childhood and the other for pre-adolescence. The items in each inventory were presented in groups of seven or eight along with a ladder-type rating scale with instructions to rate each item in terms of its importance for a best friend of the same sex. After a series of pretests, the inventories were administered to nearly 1000 children in grades three to eight (ages eight to 14). Separate factor analyses were conducted by grade level and by the two broader age groups. A varimax procedure was used in rotating the factors.

The factors isolated using the middle childhood group of children did not appear to be sufficiently clear to warrant the development of friendship scales for this age group, but the analyses were highly useful in illuminating changing conceptions of friendship. A 28-item inventory was developed for research on preadolescents. The factor analysis of the final form of the CFEI isolated four independent factors, listed with their alpha reliability: Conventional Morality (0.74); Mutual Activities (0.63); Empathic Understanding (0.70); and Loyalty and Commitment (0.70). The average intercorrelation of the four scales was 0.25 (La Gaipa and Wood, 1976).

Conventional Morality

Of the four factors isolated by factor analysis, this was the strongest and most reliable. This dimension emerges in middle childhood and continues on for the next five years or so, with only minor changes in content. It is similar to Character Admiration, the second stage (normative) in the Bigelow–La Gaipa three-stage model. The items making up this factor call attention to the tendency for children to assess their peers as potential friends on the basis of character and personality traits instead of qualities intrinsic to friendship. There is also a moralistic overtone to these traits, particularly in middle childhood: Do not lie or cheat; Do not fight with me; Never get me into trouble; Do not talk about me behind my back. Children are concerned in the conventional stage of moral development with gaining approval, and this is done by conforming (Kohlberg, 1969). There is a preoccupation in this stage with being a "good boy" or a "good girl".

There is little developmental change between middle childhood and the preadolescent years. A few traits are added during preadolescence that are suggestive of an emerging dimension of genuineness. Such items include: Do not pretend to like me; and Do not take advantage of me. During the childhood years, then, it appears as if "phoniness" is an issue of character with moral implications, rather than a separate dimension, as such. Factor analytic studies of adolescents and adult conceptions of friendship have identified a dimension labelled "Strength of Character" (La Gaipa, 1977a; 1979). This dimension is highly reliable, but not particularly valid in predicting the growth of friendship.

Mutual Activities

This factor, the second most important, has two major themes: common activities and stimulation value. The items include: Enjoy playing the same games and sports; Have fun together; Have good ideas about things to do. This dimension shows little developmental change during the childhood or adolescent years, and represents a Stage 1 orientation to friendship. Some of the items are captured in the similarity dimension of the Friendship Expectancy Inventory, used to study adolescent and adulthood friendships.

Empathic Understanding

This dimension emerges in the preadolescent years, and henceforth shows strong developmental trends. The content of this dimension is similar to the Third Stage (empathic) in the Bigelow and La Gaipa (1980) model. The major items include: Can be myself with them; Help me when I'm in trouble; Feel secure and relaxed with them; Can trust and rely upon them. Items also pertain to the disclosure of intimate information.

Statistically, this dimension is highly reliable, as is evident from the internal consistency of the items; conceptually, however, the content area is rather heterogeneous. During the adolescent years, this factor differentiates into several dimensions, including authenticity, self disclosure and empathy (La Gaipa, 1977a). The meaning, then, shows developmental change and after preadolescence, empathic understanding is defined to a greater extent in terms of the accurate interpretation of another person's thoughts and feelings. In spite of its heterogeneity, subsequent research indicated that this dimension has higher validity than the other three dimensions.

Loyalty and Commitment

This is the weakest of the four factors. It emerges during the preadolescent years, and shows strong developmental trends. The equivalent dimension of the same name in the developmental scale is level number six and is part of stage three. The items include: Are loyal to me; Stand by me through anything; and Do not forget me for someone else. This factor is rather complex and does not appear to be unidimensional in preadolescence or in any subsequent life stage. Research on preadolescent subjects, however, has demonstrated the validity of this dimension (Wood and La Gaipa, 1978).

Summary of age-related changes

The pattern of change can be described in terms of Werner's (1957) stage-free orthogenetic principle. Werner posits: "Whenever development occurs, it proceeds from a state of relative globability, a lack of differentiation, to a state of increasing differentiation, articulation, and hierarchic integration" (p. 126).

During the middle childhood years, it is possible to detect the broad outline or emerging pattern of several dimensions of friendship. Friendship concepts are still rather global: only the dimensions of Conventional Morality and Mutual Activities are clearly identifiable. Few dramatic shifts occur during these childhood years: the most striking changes seem to occur between the ages of eight and nine, which represents, perhaps, a transitional period. In the Selman and Jaquette (1977) stage theory, this involves a change from Stage 2 (Fairweather Cooperation) to Stage 3 (Mutual Sharing). Striking differences in mean increases occur at this time, particularly in terms of four items; do not forget me for someone else; do not talk about me behind my back; do not get me into trouble; and, can fight and still be friends.

The preadolescent period appears to be characterized by a consolidation of notions of friendship. Four dimensions of friendship are quite discernible, though it is apparent that there is considerable room for refinement of friendship concepts. The major change that occurs from the middle to the preadolescent years occurs along the dimension of Empathic Understanding around the ages of 11–12 years.

Differentiation of notions of friends does not occur until the early adolescent years. At this time there is restructuring of concepts of friendship, and an increase in number of dimensions from four to seven dimensions. Little change occurs after this age period in the number of dimensions or in the relationship among the dimensions (La Gaipa, 1979).

Functions of dimensions

The four relatively independent dimensions of friendships isolated during the childhood years appear to serve different functions: filtering, reinforcement, testing and growth. Conventional Morality appears to serve a filtering or screening function in that children are avoided if they possess negative qualities. Mutual Activities made up of common activities and stimulation serve a reinforcement function in so far as pleasant associations facilitate bonding. Loyalty and Commitment may serve a testing function regarding the limits or intensity of the relationship, since the actual existence of a relationship may be defined in terms of demonstrations of commitment (cf. Morton and Douglas, Chapter 1, this Volume). Empathic Understanding serves a growth function: a shared perspective and mutual understanding are likely to facilitate the movement of a relationship toward greater intensity.

Thus growth in beliefs about friendship are apparent in various complex ways. However, one of the intriguing areas that remains for future investigation concerns the causes of these developments and their social effects. We turn now, therefore, to these and other neglected, but promising, areas for future research.

Areas of Neglect and Areas of Promise

Thought versus action

A continuing problem in social science research is the difficulty in demonstrating a relationship between cognitive activity and "real-life" performance. For instance, Krasnor and Rubin (1978) have indicated that verbal assessments of social-problem solving abilities are very poor predictors of children's behavioural solutions to the same problems in natural settings. This problem of prediction has implications in the choice of research strategy preferred: to some social scientists only behaviour is valid; whereas to others, behaviour has little significance apart from its meaning to the person involved. This question of "words" versus "deeds" is a real one in research on children's friendships and I shall review some of the explanations given for the observed disparities, focusing, in particular, on prosocial behaviour.

Prosocial behaviour has multiple cognitive antecedents. Damon (1977) states that information regarding a child's conceptual network is vital in predicting prosocial behaviour. The attempt to predict social performance from data only in one concept domain is not likely to be successful: for example, an act of sharing can be influenced both by concepts of positive justice and by friendship. Moreover, a child may be at different developmental levels regarding different social concepts and prosocial behaviour may have a developmental course different from the value associated with it, or its verbal expression. In a literature review on cooperation, Bryan (1975) cites a number of studies showing little or no relationship between words and deeds at different ages. Bryan suggests this may be explained in terms of the differential onset of verbal and overt behaviour since children can do certain things before they can verbalize them. Laboratory studies indicate that perspective-taking skills appear at an earlier age in children than indicated by the use of clinical interviews (Rubin and Pepler, 1980).

A further reason may be that actual prosocial behaviour may receive less reinforcement than the verbal expression of its underlying values. Children are often exposed to inconsistent models; parents or friends may be inconsistent in their words and deeds and the observation of inconsistency in socialization agents may lead to the development of children who themselves voice altruism but practise selfishness (Bryan, 1975). Children, then, may learn to articulate the dominant values in our society without always implementing the implied behaviour.

Prosocial behaviour is learned and cannot be understood apart from a hierarchy of learning paradigm. There is hierarchical order that includes such steps as discrimination, concepts, rules, higher-order rules and cognitive strategies. Each step is a prerequisite of the next (Gagne, 1977). The social skill of maintaining and intensifying a close relationship is built on these earlier steps.

The prosocial behaviour found among friends is a product of efforts to establish methods and procedures for maintaining the relationship. The social processes leading to the emergence of such behaviours are of more critical interest than cognitive changes as such. Youniss (1980) suggests that prosocial behaviours emerge out of cooperation, collaboration and negotiation. What is critical to Youniss is children's understanding of the effects of interaction on a relation. Do they know how to repair or intensify a relation? Do they know the effects of certain interactions on the termination of a relationship? Youniss argues that children do know how to translate thought into action as is evident by their agreement about which interactions signify friendships. Children are also able to translate principles of the relation into interaction as is shown in their treatment of reciprocity with respect to the repair of relationships.

The role of reciprocity

Hartup (1978) has noted that friendship relations are reciprocal relations, and that research in this aspect of friendship is likely to be fruitful. The concept of reciprocity has become increasingly evident in the theorizing and data collection on children's friendship. Part of this reflects the attention being given to social exchange notions in research on the development of close relationships in adults.

The definition of reciprocity, however, depends on the particular theoretical orientation of the researcher: an economic approach defines reciprocity in terms of simple transactions of "giving" and "receiving"; a social exchange approach focuses on the rules of social exchange such as equity and equality (see La Gaipa, 1977b); a behavioural approach includes such concepts as behavioural interdependence or outcome dependence (see Huston and Burgess, 1979). Criteria used in assessing whether a relationship is truly reciprocal include the valuing of the exchange according to its effect on the quality of the relationship, instead of the rewards; and a relationship that is mutually beneficial, voluntary, spontaneous, among persons of equal status, and based on self identity and awareness of the other person (see DeVries, 1968), a description which clearly involves developmental aspects.

Selman and associates have described the development of children's friendship knowledge as one conceptual outgrowth of their social perspective taking. Stages are postulated in the development of perspective taking and for each stage there is a corresponding level of friendship awareness (see Dickens and Perlman, Chapter 4 in this Volume for description of stages). The stages of the development of friendship are essentially defined in terms of changes in children's reciprocal reasoning. In the Selman model, Stage 1 is one-way assistance; Stage 2 is fair-weather cooperation based on self-interest rather than mutuality; Stage 3 is intimate mutual sharing. The shift is from self interest to collaboration for mutual and common interests. "Trust in this stage is a sense of loyalty, of sticking together, and of sharing feelings, rather than sharing secrets (stage 2) or toys (stage 1)" (p. 168). Stage 4 is autonomous interdependence involving mutual sharing of the deeper aspects of self — of psychological meaning instead of common, but surface interests.

Youniss (1980) has proposed a two-stage description of the changes that occur in the form of reciprocity based on Piaget's (1932) earlier work. Youniss focuses on the content of the interaction, and on collaboration instead of perspective taking. *Symmetrical reciprocity* is characteristic of children of six to eight years old. The social exchange involves "giving" and "receiving" of equivalent amounts and is immediate rather than delayed. There is an element of low reliability in this form that is not conducive to enduring relationships. *Cooperative reciprocity* occurs when children are about nine years of age and is not something that occurs spontaneously, but is an act of deliberation: cooperative reciprocity is selective and mutually agreed upon by persons who want to be friends. The decision to be friends involves a willingness of the parties involved to cooperate on the methods and procedures for maintaining a relationship since procedures are necessary to maintain a relationship against forces working against it and friends must devise interaction procedures for enacting the principle of cooperation — accomplished only through a struggle.

How pervasive is the notion of reciprocity in children's conceptions of friendship? This depends, of course, on how the concept is defined. Several studies by Bigelow and La Gaipa, previously cited, have examined developmental trends in reciprocity of liking, reciprocity of exchange, and related notions of helping and sharing. Such friendship concepts have been found to show little if any developmental change but in particular, the notion of sharing appears in middle childhood, and is reported less and less as an element of friendship as the child grows older. Overall, less than one out of four children describe friendship using terms implying a concept of reciprocity and there is no dramatic increase in the use of this notion in adolescent descriptions of friendship.

Children's descriptions centre more on the amount received in a relationship than on the amount given or, more importantly, on the interaction between "giving" and "receiving". The method used to study friendship has some effect on the nature of the findings and verbal self-reports are not necessarily the most appropriate way to assess the importance of this notion. Reciprocity refers to the form of exchange rather than the content and is inferred from the data; it does not depend on its articulation in verbal reports.

Recent theorizing on the role of reciprocity in close relationships in research on adults could be extended to the study of children's friendship. For example, we know next to nothing regarding the effects on the development of friendship of moral obligation to reciprocate benefits received or the negotiation of reciprocity in children (see Scanzoni, 1979). There is an increasing emphasis on looking at the growth of relationships in terms of the notion of interdependency. Huston and Burgess (1979) have noted that in the early stages people experience " . . . the beginnings of dependency, accompanied by a sense of vulnerability, insecurity, and ambivalence" (p. 17). With their limited experience, this should be particularly characteristic of children as they start experimenting with closer relationships.

The nature of the social context in which reciprocity is learned is attracting some attention among advocates of a social network approach to developmental psychology since the learning of network-building and maintenance skills is said to be a major developmental task of childhood. A major skill is mastery of reciprocal exchange, that is, the ability to exchange goods, services, information and emotional support at increasingly sophisticated levels. Cochran and Brassard (1979) argue that the nuclear family provides limited opportunities for the child to observe or practise such skills. Furthermore, the peer group is not viewed as an adequate vehicle for learning about reciprocity. Cochran and Brassard suggest that it is through the exchanges between parents and members of their social network that the child is able to acquire notions of reciprocity. The adult members of the parent's social network, then, provide an important context for the development of reciprocal exchange skills and serve as observational models for the child to imitate.

The social management of relationships

Instability of children's friendships

If you ask children to name their best friends, and then ask the same question several weeks later, you will find low agreement in the names given. Such data are usually interpreted as indicating that friendships in children are quite unstable. It may be more accurate to describe children's friendships in terms of a carousel where children take turns going "up" and "down", returning again and again to be described as a best friend. The isolation of a stable pattern in this changing situation is a challenging task for future research (Duck *et al.*, 1980).

To comprehend instability of friendships, it is helpful to attend to its multidimensional character: in a typical day the child seeks friends to engage in mutual activities; issues of empathy and loyalty occur at less frequent intervals. The person who can be trusted is not always good at games; the friend who is loyal is not necessarily the person who is the most fun to be with — as one London preadolescent girl expressed it: "Staying with the same old friends can be awfully boring".

Children are open to the criticism that they are disloyal because of the changes in their friendships but this is an unnecessary value judgement since children have a sense of loyalty but are under pressures that they find difficult to articulate. When carried to extremes, loyalty can be dysfunctional to social development since it can limit the kind and degree of exposure that the child needs to increase his social understanding and interpersonal skills. Exposure to different persons contributes to learning about the effects of different interactions; and each new relationship reaccentuates the need for adjustment to another in ways not possible in sustained relationships.

Developmental trends

In interviewing children about their friendships, Youniss (1980) is sensitive to developmental trends in the social management of relationships. Youniss has found differences in children in the six- to eight-year group as compared to older children. The instability of friendships can be accounted for, in part, in terms of their limited knowledge: six- to eight-year-old children lack a concept of an enduring bond, as well as the collaborative procedures for maintaining relationships. Friends come and go as interactions change from positive to negative.

When children reach nine years of age, there is an increase in realism regarding the social management of relationships and an awareness that friendship is really a rather fragile thing: children come to understand that tolerance is required regarding the failure of others to live up to their ideals. Youriss has observed that the dilemma between the ideal and the real world is handled by looking at friendship as an enduring relationship, but one that has its "high and low points". The solution is to work out methods for building on the positive and initiating remedial actions to cope with the momentary breaks. Older children, then, understand that violations of friendship can be corrected, and they learn specific procedures for repairing relationships in the process of collaborating with others.

Selman (1976) conceptualizes such friendship parameters as selection, growth and termination of friendship as issues of friendship. In the clinical interview procedure used by Selman, questions are asked about these issues and children are assigned level of awareness scores depending on the developmental stage implicit in their responses. Selman is concerned with the developmental level of the child in dealing with each of these issues, to find out "how" the child thinks about friendship on such issues.

Bigelow and La Gaipa (1980) found that different developmental levels are expressed in the ideals of friendship and in the reasons given for the collapse of friendships. The relationship between ideals and breakup was nonsignificant: only a moderate consistency was found between how children describe their ideals about friendship and its growth or collapse. Common activities and helping are cited as important attributes of a best friend, and as instrumental in the growth of friendship, but the breakup of friendship is seldom described this way. Evaluation (global ratings of being "nice" or "good") is mentioned among the ideals, but seldom to describe either growth or decay. The character of a person is mentioned as one of the ideals, but few children said that this led to the growth of a friendships whereas the lack of character is often cited to account for the break-up of the relationship. Loyalty and commitment are seldom mentioned by children as among the ideals of friendship, nor is loyalty mentioned as promoting growth, but disloyalty is a major reason given for the collapse of friendships. Ego reinforcement (positive regard) is also mentioned infrequently as an ideal, but it does rank as rather important regarding the growth of friendship, whilst ego-degrading experiences, such as name-calling, are the most frequently cited reasons for termination. In general, children do not use the same conceptions of friendship to describe their ideal friend, on the one hand, and what specifically led to the growth or breakup of a specific friendship, on the other.

Social skills training

Can the management of social relations be taught in the classroom? Behavioural modification techniques are becoming increasingly popular and there is some evidence that shaping, modelling and coaching techniques can improve the social interaction of children with limited social skills (see Asher *et al.*, 1977). The manipulation of contextual elements has also been used. Hartup (1977), in a review of procedures for the social rehabilitation of the child, has observed that such changes in the context may modify the kind of feedback that the child receives. One procedure is to manipulate the composition of the peer group; for instance, by mixing children varying in age and social competency so that older children of less competence may learn from observing younger children with more competence, without experiencing "negative" feedback. The effectiveness of such programmes depends, in part, on the accurate assessment of children needing help. Wood and La Gaipa (1978) have developed a "Guess Who" sociometric test for this purpose, and have shown that withdrawn children have atypical conceptions of friendship, different from both popular and aggressive children. However, the potential impact of intervention techniques is still an open question and Duck *et al.* (1980) have noted the specific requirements of the better data base that is needed to structure such rehabilitation programmes.

The affective side of friendship

Children understand their social world in terms of what they experience in it, and the pleasures and pain they have encountered (Kuhn, 1978). The child's social world is not comprehended as made up of neutral objects of knowledge; the immediate social environment has both affective and informational components. Affect plays an important role in the organization of children's reasoning about friendship, as well as in their behaviour and there is more to children's friendship than cognitive development, as argued earlier.

The interdependence of cognitive and affective development is a key notion in Sullivan's (1953) interpersonal theory of psychiatry. Sullivan differs from some textbook writers in child psychology in not viewing the juvenile era as one of "peace and tranquillity". The middle childhood years are described, instead, as a time when there is a truly rather shocking insensitivity to the feelings of personal worth in others. During the elementary school years, children experience a degree of crudeness in interpersonal relations that is rarely paralleled in later life. The child is exposed to very direct and critical reactions from his peers and much of the learning that takes place relates to "competitive and compromising operations to preserve some measure of self-esteem, a feeling of self-worth" (p. 235). What is noteworthy about Sullivan's theory is the attention given to the role of anxiety in social development, and the effects of security operations implemented to minimize feeling of anxiety.

The groundwork for the subsequent development of interpersonal skills is laid in these childhood years. Let us take, for example, the skills of empathy and genuineness. Certain abilities are necessary for manifestations of such behaviours, in particular, the processing of information about self and others with a minimum of distortion. Security operations to handle anxiety may result in the reduction in the accuracy of information processing; discrepant information may be distorted to minimize anxiety (Sullivan, 1953). The nature of children's social experiences, then, may inhibit or facilitate higher-level manifestation of such behaviours.

Vulnerability

We have looked below the surface descriptions of friendship expectations in countless protocols searching for integrative concepts of a more affective nature. As noted earlier, the construct of reciprocity has attracted considerable attention as an organizing principle. We find the construct of vulnerability more compelling in the descriptions made by children of friendship: what appears over and over again is the concern of children over their potential to be "hurt" and a vulnerability to rejection, to ridicule, and to exploitation. Instead of the order and rationality of the market-place implied by the notion of reciprocity, we find instead much emotion and anxiety; indeed, there is an almost "jungle-like" quality to the way some children describe their social environment.

Kelvin (1977) assigns a high priority to this concept of vulnerability in his approach to interpersonal attraction. Kelvin argues that vulnerability is a basic aspect of interpersonal relations, but research on children's friendship has given far too little attention to the possible consequences of the fact that children are painfully aware of their vulnerability to "hurt". We know very little about the developmental aspects of this awareness of vulnerability and how it influences friendship formation.

Vulnerability has implications for several critical issues in friendship — selection, growth and termination. The potential to be "hurt" has an impact on the filtering stage in friendship formation since children seem to sense that friendship has a dialectic quality to it, and forming a friendship can serve to reduce as well as increase one's vulnerability. In choosing friends there appears to be an attempt to screen out those that increase one's potential to be hurt. This has some effect on information seeking. If a child fears being exploited, increased attention will be given to information relevant to such concerns.

The notion of vulnerability has relevance to the growth of friendship. We asked children to describe events that made them feel closer to another person (Bigelow and La Gaipa, 1980). The common denominator in their reports was the emotional context in which the prosocial behaviour occurred. There was little consensus on the kind of behaviour itself. Generally, the action took place during a critical event of a dramatic nature. "I got into trouble and he came to my aid." "I was sad because my dog was hit by a car and he cheered me up." A person who intervenes to reduce the other person's vulnerability is likely to be defined as a friend. The notion of vulnerability also has relevance to the break-up of friendships. Actions of a friend that increase one's vulnerability may lead to the dissolution of the relationship. The most frequently cited reason for the break-up of friendship in children was ego-degrading behaviour, particularly name-calling. "He said that no one likes me, and that I have no friends. I went home and cried."

Friendship can be viewed in terms of children's adaptation to their social world — as a way of coping with their sense of vulnerability. Friendship has an instrumental value; it provides an important means for navigating in a social world in which children feel unsure of themselves, where the routes are not clearly marked and the signs are not easy to read. What the child, then, looks for in a friend may tell us something about what the child perceives as having utility in making a safe voyage. When a ten-year old girl says she wants a friend who is "polite" and "nice", this could be interpreted as reflecting her stage of moral development. But such answers may also reflect her need for order, predictability and safety.

Levels of awareness

Different methods are necessary for capturing the full spectrum of friendship constructs and there are several levels of friendship concepts that the investigator needs to attend to. The first level involves purely visible self-presentation: a person may be quite vocal in expressing a particular notion of friendship, which may or may not reflect what he really feels. At the second level occurs the conscious self-description: a person may indicate by a self-report measure that loyalty, for instance, is important to him, and this expression may be an accurate one. The third level involves private symbolization: the meaning of a concept to a person can be detected only by indirect methods or prolonged interviews, and the person is unable to articulate the concept very readily. At the fourth level is encountered the conceptions that are anchored in unexpressed unconscious feelings that may or may not be consistent with what is expressed at higher levels. Verbal reports, then, provide only one aspect of concept assessment (Bigelow and La Gaipa, 1980).

Little use has been made of projective techniques to study children's friendships. The Thematic Apperception Test (TAT) has been used to study needs for affiliation in adults, but such research has had little impact on what is known about friendship. One problem is that such research has generally ignored the dyad as the unit of analysis. By way of contrast, Draper and La Gaipa (1980) found that fantasy productions on TAT were associated with the quality of friendship among college room-mates. The level of affiliative conflict was related to the tension level in the dyad. The greater the conflict, the less the trust expressed by the members, and the lower the level of friendship.

The concept of guilt may prove useful in understanding the limited friendships of socially withdrawn, preadolescent girls. Wood and La Gaipa (1978) found that the expression of guilt feelings in fantasy productions was associated with friendship expectations: the greater the guilt expressed, the lower the expectations of loyalty and empathy. No relationship was found, however, for popular or aggressive girls. The dynamic of guilt in withdrawn children is not sufficiently understood, as yet, to explain this finding; but, these data suggest the need to look below the surface descriptions of friendship if one is to understand interpersonal behaviour.

Fun and games

I suspect that fuller observations of the behaviour of friendships in their natural setting would quickly reveal the "lighter" side of friendship. There is more to friendship than manifestations of prosocial behaviour. This was aptly expressed on the wall of a school toilet: "A friend in need is a pest, indeed."

At all life stages people have a need for stimulation and cognitive arousal and the notion of "fun" as an essential ingredient in friendship is something that evokes the most consensus at all ages. Always near the top of the list of friendship values appears the statement "Have fun together . . . ." and in looking at the mean ratings of responses as measured by the Children's Friendship Expectancy, "fun" is given as high a rating as "loyalty" at all ages and for both sexes. The results using the method of spontaneous expression give even more dramatic differences: of the preadolescents, 55% gave remarks coded under "Stimulation Value" whereas 31% mentioned "Loyalty and Commitment".

It is a truism that children value "fun and games" because of the immediate satisfaction derived in the "here and now". We would conjecture that it is difficult to maintain a friendship that is devoid of fun and laughter: laughter is a measure of social responsiveness, and children highly differentiate the behaviour of friends from non-friends (Foot *et al.*, 1977). Humour and laughter are also important mechanisms in facilitating two-way interaction in children's groups (Foot *et al.*, 1980b).

The more serious side of "fun and games" is being studied in terms of its impact on the development of the child. Thematic or fantasy play encourages growth in perspective-taking skills. Social-cognitive growth is enhanced by play that forces the child to take on novel social roles; for instance, egocentric thought declines as a results of fantasy play and peer conflict (see Rubin and Pepler, 1980).

The ecology of social development

The child does not live in one social world, but in many worlds: the worlds of the home, the school and the peer group. Each of these worlds can be thought of as a social system. In highlighting this notion of "many-worlds", Hartup (1979) observed that attention has been given to intrasystem dynamics, such as parent-child relationships within the family. But less emphasis has been given to the impact of other social systems on the social dynamics within a family, or to the impact of the child's experience in one setting or system on his/her behaviour or development in another. The child acquires concepts and cognitive structures for dealing with interpersonal relations while part of a social network made up of such systems (Parke, 1979). In each of these interlocking systems, the child is exposed to different kinds of stresses and pressures, and subsequent social development is affected by how the child learns to cope with vulnerabilities. The nature of the interactions, stresses and supports encountered in these systems influences social-emotional development. It is necessary to analyse the nature of the interactions within the social systems in order to understand the growth of social competence of the child.

A theoretical framework is needed for analysing the environment in which children live. Because of the complexity of the problems, existing analytic and explanatory models are likely to be inadequate. New models are necessary that incorporate a variety of levels and systems, and the interactions necessary for such a theoretical framework. Bronfenbrenner (1979a) calls for a systems approach to the interaction of the developing person and the environment. Lerner (1979) uses such terms as "development-in-context" and the "dialectic context" of development. There is growing consensus, then, of the need to view the child as embedded in several interdependent support systems. There is also some awareness of the need to avoid limiting problem definition in terms of a cognitive-developmental approach. Instead, it is necessary to look at the interaction of the psychological, behavioural and cultural aspects of children's friendships.

This notion of support systems, and level of analysis, can be conceptualized as involving two different systems parameters. What seems necessary is a third system parameter, that is, the psychosocial resources provided by the support systems. La Gaipa (1981) has suggested a three-dimensional structural model that includes the support system, the level of analysis and the psychosocial resources. This model highlights the interdependencies within each of these systems parameters and across parameters.

What has received little attention in children's friendship and now requires serious consideration, is the interaction content of children's friendships, that is, the psychosocial dimensions. The nature of the rewards and benefits that motivate children to enter and leave friendships needs to be delineated more systematically. Theory building and testing will thus be aided by research on dimensions of friendship. A dimensional approach to friendship will also help in the study of the relationships between friendship and other support systems at each level of analysis and across levels; for instance, in tackling problems regarding the disparity between "ideal" and the "real".

Summary

An examination of children's "cognitive maps" of friendship reveals some broad trends. Friendship expectations "clock in" at different times during the school years, varying with the content or nature of the expectation, and changes in the pattern of dimensions are also apparent. In the middle childhood years, a rather global image of friendship exists, though the outline of subsequent patterns is discernible. In preadolescence, some restructuring and consolidation occurs; four dimensions can now be clearly identified. During the adolescent years, differentiation takes place, with little structural changes in subsequent years. Overall, there is a "stage-like" quality to the emergence and organization of friendship concepts, but the validity of a formal stage theory is, as yet, unclear. Rather, the research offers more support for a stage-free approach with emphasis on the sequential invariance notion of an orderly developmental progression in the emergence of friendship concepts, instead of the more abrupt, qualitative changes implied by a stage theory.

There is some evidence that cognitive developmental changes play a decreasing role after the child reaches eight or nine years of age. What merits further attention at this time is the study of individual differences, particularly, the impact of social experiences in different personal networks and support systems. I have suggested that the concept of "vulnerability" can play a major role in understanding the affective side of children's friendships but more research is needed on vulnerability, particularly its developmental aspects, as well as on the coping mechanisms used in the social management of relationships.

I have argued for a multidimensional approach to friendship. Support for this position is based on the isolation of four independent dimensions of friendship as measured by the Children's Friendship Expectancy Inventory: viz. Conventional Morality, Mutual Activities, Loyalty and Commitment, and Empathic Understanding. This orientation is compelling in view of the differential onset of these dimensions, and differences in content changes over time as well as regarding functions and consequences. Such a dimensional approach also implies a need for increasing emphasis on quantification. The development of reliable measures will facilitate a systems approach to the study of children's friendships.

CHAPTER 8

Adolescent Friendship: Some Unanswered Questions for Future Research

Igor S. Kon

Adolescent friendship (AF) had always had a prominent place in research literature on the developmental aspects of friendship; indeed there are more studies of AF than of any other life stage. Researchers unanimously emphasize the peculiar social and psychological status of AF, its ardent emotionality, social value etc. Nonetheless, we have to agree with Schaffer and Hargreaves (1978) that our scientific knowledge of AF is rather limited, and even more fundamental theoretical issues are not always clear. For example, some of the problems that I propose to discuss here in the light of available literature are:

1. Adolescent friendship is often associated with romanticism. But to say nothing of the vagueness of the term "romanticism" itself, it is not clear whether the "romantic syndrome" (the term belongs to W.T. Jones, 1961) is a specific trait of a particular life-stage, or of a certain historical epoch ("romantic movement"), or of a definite personality type ("romantic personality").

2. Psychological research on AF is particularly weak on the developmental aspect: how do the behavioural, cognitive, emotional and

187

axiological qualities of friendship change within the periods of childhood, adolescence (12–14), youth (15–18) and young adulthood (19–23)? To answer this question we need more longitudinal research work and clearer conceptualization of the life course.

3. The third question is concerned with sex differences: the particular characteristics of boy–boy, girl–girl and boy–girl friendship.

4. What are the interrelations between AF and sexuality? Can the emotional involvement of AF be interpreted as some form of sublimation of the awakening libido or does it fulfil some other psychological functions?

5. What are the connections between developmental, age-specific and personality factors of AF? Is it possible to determine the personality type by the friendship pattern and vice versa?

Adolescent Friendship and the Romantic Syndrome

Given the typical, assumed involvement of romanticism in AF, it is important to examine this supposed relationship more carefully and critically. Is AF universally, immanently romantic, that is, highly individualized, intimate and presupposing great emotional involvement, or are these traits normative only for a particular historical period with a definite sociocultural background? This problem is largely discussed in the context of sociology rather than in psychology. The widespread idea (e.g. Rosenmayr, 1963; Tenbruck, 1964; Toffler, 1970) is that contemporary AF is less intimate and exclusive than it used to be in the nineteenth century. This change is explained by several general societal trends: urbanization, growth of social mobility, weakening of traditional social and personal bonds, growth of alienation, extensivity and superficiality of interpersonal relationships. Some specific trends in adolescent socialization are also cited (see, for example, Wurzbacher, 1968): public education systems, facilitating interpersonal contacts and making individual friendships less exclusive and more similar to mere companionship; stronger educational pressures in the direction of group affiliation and solidarity at the expense of individual autonomy; coeducation, accompanied by earlier and more intensive heterosociality and the corresponding decrease in the social and emotional importance of traditional male pair-bonding which was the core of the romantic friendship ideal.

Empirical research data in many different countries — e.g. US and Denmark (Kandel and Lesser, 1972), West Germany (Wurzbacher, 1968), Austria (Kreutz, 1964; Rosenmayr, 1963), France (Zazzo, 1966), USSR (Kon and Losenkov, 1978); Hungary (Pataki, 1970) — agree that exclusive pair-friendship is really characteristic not of all but only of some modern adolescents. But there exist serious objections to this theory of emotional impoverishment and de-individualization of AF (see also Kon, 1979a, b), as follows.

1. It is methodologically inadequate to compare contemporary mass questionnaire data and average figures with classical examples of historical friendship. Those cases were probably normative for a definite cultural milieu but they are often strongly idealized and may not have been statistically typical even of their own epoch.

2. Complaints of the impoverishment of love and friendships are practically universal. Even in classical antiquity — which is represented today as the true kingdom of friendship — deep and lasting friendship was believed to be extremely rare and its examples were mostly attributed to the past.

3. These complaints may reflect and express not so much the objective changes in interpersonal relations (emotional coolness, etc.), but the growing individualization and "psychologization" of their criteria, the changes in the level and quality of aspirations, the degree of verbalization of intimate experiences and the like.

4. The romantic image of friendship both in art and psychology is contradictory in essence and in some aspects illusive.

5. The widening of the real circle of acquaintances, interpersonal contacts and interactions does not remove the psychological task of the choice of intimate friends; this selection may even become more problematic and difficult.

6. According to mass surveys, modern adolescents and youths distinguish the notions of friendship and comradeship (companionship) at least as well as did the earlier cohorts; the ideal of intimate friendship always has a prominent place among adolescents' social and personal values (Ikonnikova and Lissovsky, 1969; Yankelovich, 1972; Lutte et al., 1971).

7. The degree of psychological involvement and intimacy of AF both in the ideal case and in reality strongly depends on the ethnocultural and social milieu (Kandel and Lesser, 1972; Lutte et al., 1971). For example, the comparison of friendship-ideal and real friendship-relationships of Soviet urban and rural ninth graders (Kon and Losenkov, 1978) has shown that rural adolescents seem to feel less deficiency in intimacy. They express more satisfaction with their interpersonal relationships, including friendship. But their friendship seems to be less exclusive and less differentiated from their other interpersonal relationships; they put less value on understanding.

8. The theory of de-individualization of friendship is in itself implicitly romantic, that is, it takes the romantic friendship ideal as its starting point. However, the romantic notion of friendship cannot claim universal validity: it is closely connected with the fundamental processes of adolescent personality development, especially identity formation.

Developmental Aspects of Adolescent Friendship

The development of friendship from childhood to adolescence and from adolescence to adulthood can be considered in several different contexts.

1. *In connection with the changes in the structure of the individual adolescent's interpersonal relations:* for example reorientation from parents and other significant adults, towards peers; changes in the structure and function of peer groups and adolescent subculture; changes in the degree of selectivity and differentiation of interpersonal communication.

2. *As a function of cognitive development of the invididual:* e.g. the evolution of the language of friendship, that is, the nature of the conceptual system applied by the child to friendship and related topics, the content of children's description of their friends (Hartup, 1975).

3. *In connection with the development of emotions:* e.g. privileged objects of attraction, the degree of emotional involvement in friendship.

4. *As the function of development of interpersonal competence and capacities for communication:* e.g. friendship expectations (Bigelow and La Gaipa, 1975), the content and structure of verbal and nonverbal communication between friends, the degree and the means of self-disclosure

5. *In connection with Ego-development and growth of self-awareness,* which inevitably change the functions and axiological criteria of friendship.

Each of these separate lines of research is legitimate in itself but in most cases they are interwoven and little attempt has been made to establish causal relationships rather than mere correlations. Nonetheless, some substantive developmental trends seem to be firmly established.

The general background, and one of the causes of the growing importance of friendship in adolescence, is the reorientation from parents and educators towards peers. This trend is apparently cross-cultural and manifest everywhere: e.g. in the structure of adolescent activities and interactions, in the changing degrees of influence of various significant others, in the choice of ego ideals. But its magnitude and speed vary with different social and cultural milieus and with different spheres of adolescent activities. For example, Soviet high-school children in Crimea indicating whom they preferred for their leisure companions, almost unanimously rejected parents in favour of peers. On the other hand, answering a question about whom they would appeal to for advice in a complicated life situation adolescents named their mothers foremost. For boys the next choice to mother was their father, while girls chose their friends (Kon and Losenkov, 1978). Rodriguez Tome (1973) asked groups of French school-children aged 12–14 and 14–18 whom would they ask for help and who they thought would be most willing to help them in a difficult life situation. Three different situations were named involving moral, economic and emotional problems. In economic and moral questions the first place belonged to parents, though the importance of friends and peers increased with the age of the respondents. But where emotional support was needed the first place was reserved for one's friend, especially by older boys and by the girls.

To understand AF it is very important to distinguish three inter-related series of changes:

1. changes in relative significance of peers vs adults;
2. changes in friendship functions (roles) and expectations — friendship may be fused to other, more central roles, or be *a substitute for* major roles, or be *complementary to* or *competitive with* other roles (see Hess, 1972);
3. changes in the nature of individual friendship communication.

According to available data, the central position and importance of friendship is increasing in adolescence. For example, Soviet adolescents on the whole (Kon and Losenkov, 1978) rather positively estimate the degree of their being "understood" by people closest to them (parents, teachers, friends, etc.): in almost all cases their ratings are closer to the positive end of the scale. The overwhelming majority of adolescents do not feel loneliness, social or emotional isolation. Evidently, the romantic image of the adolescent as a lonely Child Harold is not statistically representative of today's youth (but was it ever representative?). But the best friend (the same-sex peer as a rule) is always seen as the most understanding and close person.

Another group of Moscow adolescents (fifth to tenth graders) were asked how well, in their own judgement, they were understood by their mother, father, friends and other significant persons and how important for them was their understanding (independent from the level of factual understanding). Answering these questions, boys considered their parents' understanding as more important than that of their friends (girls' answers were not unanimous). But when the level of real psychological proximity, understanding and confidence comes into question, the first place (in both Leningrad and rural samples) was assigned to friends. The level of understanding and confidence with mother (next to the friend), father, favourite teacher and other adults was rated not only lower, but dropped considerably, especially with 14–16 year olds, while the position of the friends remained stable and constant.

The growing selectivity of friendship choice is paralleled by the growing sophistication of the language of friendship (Douvan and Adelson, 1966; Zazzo, 1966). Older adolescents differentiate "friends" from mere "comrades" and "companions" more strongly than younger ones. In their definition of a friend's role ("A genuine friend is one who . . .") the exclusiveness, intimacy and stability of the relationship are stressed. School seniors and university students rather often believe that "genuine friendship" is very rare.

In the older children and adolescents, the friendship choice remains more stable and enduring (see Scopera *et al.*, 1963). This is connected apparently with the growing general stability of preferences (McKinney, 1968; Kon and Losenkov, 1978), which, in its turn, reflects the stabilization of personality structure. The establishing and maintaining of friendly relations in adolescence is less dependent on external, situational factors (as neighbourhood, coeducation, etc.) than it is with younger children (see Kreutz, 1964).

But the quantitative behavioural changes should be interpreted cautiously. The first thing is, that these conclusions are the results mainly of cross-sectional research, not necessarily reflecting the real process of development. Secondly, formal indicators, such as the stability of friendship, have no definite psychological meaning if we do not know the qualitative changes in the *criteria* of friendship choice and the values attributed to friendship and its psychological functions.

The type of the individual's interpersonal relations largely depends on his implicit personality theory. Judging from recent research data (Livesley and Bromley, 1973; Barenboim, 1977), the interpersonal cognitive system of a child undergoes considerable changes between the ages of seven and 12, when the child learns to draw "psychological" inferences from thoughts, feelings, personal qualities and general behavioural dispositions of other people. Later, between 12 and 16 years, generalized integrated models and representations are formed. "Preliminary results show that the major development after the age of 15 is a further increase in the 'psychological' content of impressions arising mainly from an increased awareness of the more covert determinants of behaviour" (Livesley and Bromley, 1973, p. 291).

The relation between these cognitive developments and adolescent friendship seems to be two-fold. On the other hand, the certain amount of cognitive complexity is a prerequisite of interpersonal competence and capacity for understanding. But on the other hand, children's friendship experiences may be considered as a means of anthropognostic learning. According to Peevers and Secord (1973), children usually describe at greater length those peers that they feel a sympathy for, giving more detailed characteristics than in descriptions of persons they dislike. Also, Duck (1975), using a personal construct methodology, analysed the personality similarities between friends of 12, 14 and 16 years old in a sample of British adolescents and found that the relevant similarities which predicted friendship choices were functionally related to the development of adolescent cognition. Twelve-year-olds chose as their friends those who were most similar to them in factual constructs; 14-year-old females were most similar to their friends in the "psychological" descriptive terms that they applied to people (but males did not develop this until later); whilst 16-year-olds showed a pattern of similarities akin to that manifest in adults. These similarities to friends actually occur precisely in those areas of personality that are undergoing growth and change, so the study confirms and specifies the real relationship between social attraction and cognitive development. With the growing complexity of personal constructs forming the basis of implicit personality theory, the criteria of friendship undergo psychological changes too.

Triger (1971) analysed 789 school compositions on "My friend" written according to the same plan by Soviet children of the third to sixth classes. The demands for sympathy and understanding, for common psychological experience and inner life with one's friend, increased with age (from 1% in the third to 12% in the sixth form). The same trend is evident in children's explanations of the deterioration or disruption of friendship: sixth graders mentioned this problem three times more often than the third graders, though this motive was still ten times less important than the breach of the unwritten "comradeship codex" where fidelity and capacity for keeping secrets, etc. were emphasized.

The study of friendship expectations among children aged from six to 14 in Canada and Scotland (Bigelow and La Gaipa, 1975; Bigelow, 1977) reveals three main developmental stages. Younger children understand friendship simply as behavioural relationship, based on joint activity and territorial proximity. Later, social and normative aspects of friendship become prominent: fidelity, mutual help, etc. are highly appreciated. The egocentric image of friendship gives place to the sociocentric. At the third stage empathy, understanding and self-disclosure are the dominant values. This certainly does not mean that earlier friendship was lacking affective components — emotional support and sympathy are important at every age — but younger children are as yet unaware of this need, while in adolescence it is of prominent importance.

The increasing focus on intimacy and expressive values is evident in Soviet research data (Kon and Losenkov, 1978). While completing an unfinished sentence: "A friend and a companion are not quite identical, since . . . .", about 37-65% of the respondents, depending on their age, emphasized the intimacy and confidence of friendship: "a friend knows everything about you . . . .", "a friend is much closer", "with a companion you never are as with a friend". Others emphasized greater stability of friendship, mutual aid and loyalty.

An even clearer picture is obtained from the analysis of answers to the incomplete sentence: "A friend is one who . . . .". In these definitions of friendship (without any preliminary schedule of reference), two leading motifs predominate: (1) the requirement for mutual aid and loyalty; and

(2) the expectations of sympathetic understanding.

It is noteworthy that the expectations of and requirements for understanding significantly increase with age (with boys — from 16% in the seventh to 40% in the tenth class; with girls — from 25% to 50% respectively) and that these expectations are stronger in girls than in boys.

Since both motivations are closely interconnected and presuppose one another, this partial reorientation from instrumental values (mutual aid and exchange) to expressive ones (understanding and sympathy) is undoubtedly connected with the development of self-awareness.

But to satisfy these more subtle psychological needs is very difficult for adolescents. This may account for a certain increase, with age, of doubts regarding the prevalence of "genuine friendship" and the widespread dissatisfaction of adolescents with their real friendships. It is also remarkable that adolescents' definitions of friendship are often more egocentric (emphasizing what a friend should do or feel for the individual) than allocentric (what the individual should do or feel for his friend).

Some essential clues to the psychological functions of AF can be derived from the study of images reflecting the "ideal friend" — his age, sex and other qualities. As an "ideal friend" Soviet adolescent boys definitely prefer their age-mate (75–85% of all choices), seldom is the choice fixed upon an older person (19% in the seventh class, 13% in the ninth class and 18% in the tenth class) and hardly ever on a younger individual (4% in the seventh and 1% in the tenth class). With girls the preference is also given to peers; however, girls more often than boys prefer an older friend (from 39% in the seventh to the half of all choices in the ninth to tenth classes) and practically never choose a younger person (Kon and Losenkov, 1978). Very similar orientations were discovered in French adolescents by Zazzo (1966). In her view, the age of an "ideal friend" reflects some, not always conscious, psychological craving. The orientation towards one's peer means the striving for a more or less equal relationship. This friendship is based on the principle of similarity and equality: ". . . it is easier to communicate with a boy of my own age, I can tell him everything . . . . .". The selection of an older friend expresses the longing for a model, for authority and guidance. In the latter cases these motives are mentioned: ". . . an older friend can serve as an example", "he can share an experience which I have not yet acquired", and the like.

But why is the orientation towards younger friends so rare? Intuitively it would seem that the relationships with a younger friend, giving the adolescent the possibility to guide, to be in charge of, to share experiences are highly gratifying and psychologically beneficial. Judging by some data (Kon and Losenkov, 1978), boys who have younger siblings possess higher self-evaluation than other boys when it comes to such qualities as courage, intelligence, kindness, independence. They also expect higher ratings for these qualities from their parents and peers (this correlation is not valid for girls). So it seems that friendly interaction with younger peers gives the adolescent the chance to display his positive qualities and hence to feel himself more mature and independent. But, however pleasing this may be, *friendship* with some younger individual doesn't quite meet the adolescent's ideal of the *alter ego*. Certain idealization of friends and friendship is very characteristic of adolescence. Research data on the relation between self-concept and the image of the friend are scarce. However, Thompson and Nishimura (1952) report that the average correlation between the individual's own ideal and his evaluation of his friend is significantly higher than the correlation between his ideal and his self-concept. In other words, one's friend is usually idealized. McKenna *et al.* (1956), experimenting in a girls' college with Q sorts, have found that persons chosen sociometrically or as friends are perceived by the chooser as more similar to their own ideal self than to their self-concept, except in cases of very high self-ideal congruence (see the discussion by Wylie, 1961).

Age differences are very important for adolescents: a younger person, being unequal in age, may be regarded as inadequate for the role of ego-ideal. This kind of friendship may apparently be conceived as being supplementary to friendship with an age-mate rather than as being the ideal situation. For adolescents who make friends solely with younger children the choice in most cases seems to be compulsory or compensatory. This may be the result of developmental retardation, when the interests and behavioural patterns of the subject are nearer to those of younger boys than to his age-mates. Sometimes it is the result of personality difficulties: excessive shyness, fear of competition, discordance between the level of aspirations and real performance, etc. Emotional attraction to younger children in these cases is compensatory.

The central and basic theoretical problem of AF is the developmental relation between identity and intimacy. According to Erikson (1968), the formation of identity necessarily precedes the need and the capacity for psychological intimacy. "It is only when identity formation is well on its way that true intimacy — which is really a counterpointing as well as a fusing of identities — is possible" (Erikson, 1968, p. 135).

Erikson's theory of identity formation has good empirical support. The egocentricity of AF, when passionate idealization of one's friend is often combined with insensitivity to his real individuality and the lack of real mutual understanding, has been more than once described in novels (one classical example: the friendship between Nicolas Irtenev and Dmitri Nechludov in Tolstoy's "Youth") as well as in psychological (see for example, Douvan and Adelson, 1966) and psychoanalytical literature (Blum, 1964). Several studies based on Eriksonian ideas do show that identity is really formed earlier than intimacy (see Orlofsky *et al.*, 1973; Marcia, 1976).

But identity is by no means a unitary construct. For example, the comparison of male and female concepts of identity shows that males give more importance to *intra*personal, and females to *inter*personal aspects of identity; identity formation and self-awareness in college females is more dependent on the previously achieved level of intimacy than in males (Matteson, 1977; Waterman and Nevid, 1977; Hodgson and Fischer, 1979). A female's identity and "her sense of self rests on the success with which she can resolve issues of getting along with others" (Hodgson and Fischer, 1979, p. 47). Hence, identity in this case will come after intimacy and not vice versa.

In the light of Eriksonian theory these problems are seen as exceptional or specific cases of the universal developmental succession — intimacy *after* identity. But there is an alternative reasoning. According to Sullivan (1953), the adolescent discovers his identity exactly on the basis and thanks to the experience of psychological intimacy and close communication with a friend. Hence, the crucial importance of preadolescent (between 8.5 and 10 years) chumship as the school of interpersonal sensitivity, altruism and intimacy.

This view has also some empirical support. Thus, the communicative traits of adult males, subjects of longitudinal research (Maas, 1968), did show significant correlations with their friendship patterns of childhood (around age 8) but not with their adolescent friendships. And according to Hoffman (1975), it is around this age that children become able to experience the sympathetic distress which is very important for intimate relationships. It is also noteworthy that the patterns of friendship and the degree of closeness between boys of that age significantly correlate with their level of altruism (Mannarino, 1976).

This controversy — whether identity formation precedes intimacy or vice versa — is to some extent the result of an inadequate conceptualization. Intimacy, like identity, is a multidimensional construct and its various levels or components are also formed at different times. In further research four dimensions at the least should be taken into account.

1. *The level of the Ego development*, including the degree of self-awareness.

2. *The privileged content of a friendly communication:* which aspects of one's self are most significant and intimate for the individual at a given stage of development (his bodily self, social ideals, personal traits, psychosexual experiences, etc.), both for self-evaluation and in the perception of others. The measurement of the level of intimacy is meaningless without preliminary knowledge of subjective criteria of intimacy and these criteria surely have many developmental, sexual and cultural determinants.

3. *The preferred type of partner ("ideal friend")*. In early adolescence the main confidant of boys is usually the same-sex friend: same-sex friendship

is more intimate than heterosexual. Later on, in the young adult males, the locus of intimacy moves towards heterosexual partners (Komarovsky, 1976).

4. *The privileged means of friendly intercourse* — it may be some kind of joint activity (play or work), verbal communication, non-verbal communication, including touching and sexual contact. Although different ways of communication are complementary and not exclusive, there may be some developmental trends too. It is well known, for example, that preadolescent chumship is usually based on intensive common activity, e.g. on making something together. Teenagers, on the contrary, associate friendship in the first place with verbal communication, argument, exchange of opinions and self-disclosure. A sizeable proportion of Soviet adolescents (20–40%) could not name any joint occupation with a friend apart from verbal communication (Kon and Losenkov, 1978). So here joint activity seems to be non-essential for friendship. The privileged manner of self-expression is always connected with the content of information one wishes to communicate and the *type of partner* needed for such an exchange.

If all these parameters are considered, the degree of intimacy of AF will probably appear both as the *function* of the previously achieved level of identity and as its *precondition*. In other words, identity and intimacy formation should be treated not as different *stages* of personality development but as different *aspects* of one and the same process.

Adolescent Friendship and Psychosexual Development

Sex differences in friendship patterns

Adolescent friendship is closely connected with the processes of psychosexual development. In the first place there is the problem of psychological sex differences in friendship patterns in boys and girls; what are these differences and can they be explained mainly by the different maturation rates of males and females, or by some immanent sex differences and or specific sex-role differentiation? It seems that all these factors are relevant (see Douvan and Adelson, 1966; Maccoby and Jacklin, 1974; Eder and Hallinan, 1978).

As a result of their earlier maturation, girls manifest earlier signs of more sophisticated self-awareness than boys. Girls' descriptions of another person, their friends included, are usually more sophisticated and differentiated than those of boys of the same age (see Livesley and Bromley, 1973; Kondratjeva, 1975). Females on the whole seem to be better at verbalizing their emotional states. The need for intimacy does emerge in girls earlier and their criteria of friendship are usually more "psychologistic" than those of boys (Douvan and Adelson, 1966). In their definition of a friend while completing the sentence "A friend is one who . . . . ." Soviet girls emphasized the "understanding" motif much more strongly than boys. With boys the emphasis on "mutual aid" outweighs "understanding" before they are in their twenties. In girls the motif of "understanding" is predominant already in the eighth class (Kon and Losenkov, 1978).

The word "understanding" has in itself different meaning for boys and girls. The answers of Moscow schoolchildren to the incomplete sentence "To understand a person means . . . .", classified by Mudrik (1975) fall into five categories: (1) to know this person well; (2) to experience and to feel like he does; (3) to share common interests and thoughts; (4) to help him, to be his friend; (5) to respect and love him. Boys' answers underlined mostly the first, cognitive meaning ("to understand somebody is to know him well") and the third aspect — intellectual similarity. Girls, beginning with the age 14, most frequently express the idea of sympathy and the sharing of emotions (category 2). This motif is already obvious in the third class girls aged nine.

Adolescent girls have a rather smaller number of same-sex friends than adolescent boys (Pataki, 1970; Kon and Losenkov, 1978). Girls having several close friends prefer to meet them not in a cluster but separately "*tête-à-tête*"; this was the preference of about two-thirds of Leningrad ninth-class girls and of only one-third of their male class-mates. In girls' conversations with their friends "personal" themes are more outstanding than among boys who more often discuss some "objective" topics. Girls more often than boys complain of loneliness, the lack of understanding by their friends, and the like.

So it seems that the need for intimate individualized friendship not only emerges in girls earlier than in boys but that female friendship itself is more strongly orientated towards emotional-expressive values than the more instrumental and group-orientated male friendship. In the light of these data the romantic ideal of "tender friendship" seems more feminine than masculine.

Does the greater emotional expressiveness of the adolescent female friendship make some impact on the stability and durability of a relationship? It is quite possible that the more intensive need for intimacy may be the potential source of misunderstanding and tension. The more restrained masculine friendship, where some emotional experiences are never verbalized nor compared — their similarity being silently taken for granted — may be somewhat easier to maintain.

But however proverbial the instability of female friendship, empirical evidence is scarce and contradictory. There are no longitudinal data on the relative stability and duration of boys' and girls' friendships. Young girls' microgroups seem to be more exclusive than those of boys (Eder and

Hallinan, 1978), and (contrary to the stereotype *"La donna è mobile . . . ."*)
girls' preferences, including the choice of friends, are more stable than the
preferences of the same-age boys (see McKinney, 1968; Kon and Losenkov,
1978).

Talking about friendship, adolescents mostly have in mind same-sex relationships. Although mutual interests and the range of interpersonal contacts
between boys and girls in adolescence are increasing in number, these
contacts are only infrequently symbolized as friendship. The adolescent
boy-girl friendship for the most part presupposes love or infatuation. Sometimes it is simply a question of labelling.

"Is true friendship between boy and girl possible without their being in
love?" — to this question more than 75% of Soviet seventh to tenth graders
answered affirmatively. As age increases, however, the doubts in this regard
also increase so that more than a half of male university students answered
the same question negatively (Kon and Losenkov, 1978). This is quite under-
standable. As a result of earlier physical, sexual and psychic maturation
adolescent girls are substantially different from their male age-mates. Erotic
feelings and experiences occupy a very important place in the adolescent's
inner world. To discuss such experiences with somebody of the opposite sex is
difficult and sometimes even impossible. All this makes communication and
relationships between adolescent boys and girls psychologically strained
(Broderick and Weaver, 1968; Zazzo, 1966), and less intimate than the same-
sex friendship.

Adolescent friendship and sexuality

The adolescent same-sex friendship means high emotional involvement and
phenomenologically is often very similar to love. This kind of experience is
described in many authentic diaries, autobiographies and novels. We can
mention, for instance, the friendship between Alexander Herzen and Nicolai
Ogariev in Herzen's "Past and Thoughts" and in Ogariev's "Confessions",
between Christophe and Otto in Romain Rolland's "Jean-Christophe" and
between Jacques and Daniel in Roger Martin du Gard's "The Thibaults".
These examples of friendship are almost impossible to distinguish from love
— hence, the problem of latent homosexuality as the possible source or at
least the background of adolescent friendship. This idea was explicitly
formulated by Freud (1921) and is often repeated in psychoanalytical literature, interpreting male homosociality in general and adolescent friendships in
particular as the manifestation of the unconscious "homosexual radical"
(Vanggaard, 1972). This problem seems really important, especially if we
take into account the amount of homosexual experimentation in adolescence

(for a review of data see Kon, 1978). But the reduction of friendship to sub-limated libido seems misleading both on theoretical and empirical grounds. Were the friendship only the expression of sublimated libido, this would be clearly evident in animals which have no need to suppress or sublimate their sexual drives. But close friendship and stable emotional attraction between same-sex animals in the natural milieu is only infrequently accompanied by homosexual contacts and only when the male animals in question were reared in isolation from females. According to Harlow (1971), in monkeys as well as in humans there are five relatively autonomous affectional systems — maternal love, infant love, peer or age-mate love, heterosexual love, and paternal love — none of which can be reduced to one another, each having its own developmental functions, including the preparation for more complicated social relationships.

Recent studies of peer relationship and friendship ties in monkeys and primates are especially illuminating (Rosenblum *et al.*, 1975; Suomi and Harlow, 1975; Suomi, 1977). Play-contacts not only help the animals to acquire necessary communication skills and rules of behaviour but are necessary also for their normal emotional development. Peer friendships help infants and adolescents to overcome the primary exclusive attachment to their mothers and to establish individual relationships of varying emotional intensity with other members of the troop. Animals reared in isolation from peers usually display serious communicative and emotional difficulties, including difficulties in the sexual sphere. All this shows the importance of the socializing functions of infant and adolescent friendships, their impact on the formation of the communicative patterns of the individual, including the *script* of his future sexual behaviour (on the concept of sexual script see Gagnon and Simon, 1973).

This problem has even wider methodological implications: have we to explain the social behaviour and personality of the individual from his psychosexual orientation or, on the contrary, is his sexual script to be explained as an aspect of his total personality? The reduction of friendship to sublimated sexual drive does not take into account the complexity of personality and interpersonal relations. Psychosexual identity of the individual on Kinsey scales of hetero/homosexuality (predominant type of sexual activity) and hetero/homoeroticism (preferred type of erotic object) does in no way determine personality traits on the axis of hetero/homosociality (predominant type of social interaction with people of same or opposite sex) and hetero/homophilia (preferred type of communication partner, whether he should rather be different — complementary — or similar to the individual). The inter-relationship of these four dimensions is by no means universal.

The well-known and apparently universal homosociality of adolescent males (which Tiger, 1969, has named the "male bonding") not only does not exclude the development of heterosexual interests and orientations, but seems to be a prerequisite for the formation of masculine character. Homophilia is an even broader attitudinal predisposition which is manifested not only in the preference for a same-sex friendship, but also in the choice and attribution of certain personal traits and qualities, e.g. the need to establish friendship with a person similar to one's ego. Maybe even the choice of the same-sex friend is only a special case of this general predisposition, resting on the presumption that the same-sex person tends to be more similar to oneself and hence more capable of understanding.

I shall not discuss here the very complicated question of the criteria of the presumed, perceived and objective similarity or complementarity of the friends and whether it is the result or the antecedent of attraction (see, for example, Duck, 1973a; 1975). But I wish to emphasize that such general dimensions as hetero/homosociality and hetero/homophilia cannot be explained by or reduced to specific psychosexual orientations, or preferences.

Empirical data on the interrelationship between the same-sex adolescent friendship, heterosexual bonding and love relations are scarce and contradictory. Among Austrian boys aged 15 and 17 studied by Kreutz (1964) the maximal level of affectional expectations (understanding, sympathy, common ideas, etc.) towards friendship were expressed by those adolescents who had not yet achieved successful and stable heterosexual contacts. For these boys, the emergence of a girl-friend seems to diminish the emotional involvement of the same-sex friendship; the friend becomes now merely a "good companion" (e.g. in answers to the uncompleted sentence "The friend I like the best is the one who . . . ."). So it seems that there is some contradiction between emotional involvement in friendship and in love.

But very much depends on the age of the subjects. Komarovsky (1976) has measured the level of self-disclosure of 62 American college seniors with their fathers, mothers, family members and close friends of the same and opposite sex. Female friends appeared to be preferred confidantes of the young males (age 20), whereas in adolescence the same-sex friendship is more intimate. The need of males for an intimate friendship with a female increases with age and the transference of psychological intimacy from a boy to a girl-friend is now accomplished at an earlier age than was normal in the 1950s. This trend runs parallel both with the earlier beginning of heterosexual activities *and* with the earlier reorientation of adolescents to the heterosocial type of communication (Kuhlen and Houlihan, 1965; Schlaegel *et al.*, 1975). But the increase in the tempo of this development does not change the order and succession of its phases. Young males, described by Komarovsky, achieved maximal self-disclosure with the females because their psychological contact was combined with a sexual relationship. On the contrary, the virgin males had the lowest overall level of self-disclosure, even with their male friends; their sexual inexperience made them feel shy and be more reserved. The same-sex friendship and heterosexual relationships may have different functions and value on different stages of the life course. In early adolescence, same-sex friendship may function as the preparation and partially as the substitute for heterosexual emotional ties. Later on, its functions in this respect diminish, and the deficiency in heterosexual contacts causes some strain even in the same-sex friendship.

But this depends also on some personal traits. One American study (Katz *et al.*, 1968) has found that students having close friends of the same sex were more likely than other students to have close friends with the opposite sex too. And this is quite comprehensible, for both types of relationships depend on certain communicative skills and personality traits.

The impact of modern social development (changes in sex roles differentiation, coeducation, etc.) makes the range of cross-sex social activity and communication broader and boy-girl interpersonal contacts easier. Many traditional barriers between adolescent boys and girls are diminished or have vanished altogether. This has attitudinal and behavioural consequences. Traditional adolescent homosociality, including friendship formation, is gradually giving way to heterosociality (see, for example, Schlaegel *et al.*, 1975).

But these historical changes should not be over-rated. Cross-sex friendship today, as well as formerly, is by no means easy; it is a rare phenomenon in adolescence. Almost 57% of Leningrad ninth-grade boys and 43% of girls, when asked to enumerate all their friends, did not mention persons of the opposite sex. Rarely, if at all, is a person of the opposite sex named among one's best friends (Kon and Losenkov, 1978). A similar picture has been recorded in France (Zazzo, 1966), West Germany (Wurzbacher, 1968), the United States (Katz *et al.*, 1968; Kandel, 1978) and in other countries.

It is noteworthy that boys and girls express different attitudes towards the idea of a cross-sex friendship. Answering the question "If you were given a choice, would you rather have a boy or a girl for your best friend?", almost all Soviet adolescent boys and a substantial number of girls gave preference to boys. But the proportion of girls choosing a cross-sex friend is always higher than that of boys. This difference increases with age. In the seventh to eighth classes a third of the respondents hesitated in their choice. In the ninth to tenth classes the returns were most definite: only 14% of boys chose a girl for an ideal friend, whereas the proportion of girls preferring boy-friends, increased from 56% in the ninth to 65% in the tenth class (Kon and Losenkov, 1978; compare Zazzo, 1966; Lutte *et al.*, 1971).

These sex differences may have various explanations. Firstly, an overall preference by both sexes for the male as an ideal friend may reflect the traditional higher evaluation of masculinity. Such preference is revealed in many different choice situations (see, for example, Musgrave and Reid, 1971). And friendship is traditionally believed to be a male institution. Many adolescent girls believe that boys in general are more loyal in friendship, etc. (Zazzo, 1966).

Secondly, it may be the result of sex differences in the rate of development. Friendship is a kind of model school for psychological intimacy, which is primarily achieved in communication with a person of the same sex and only afterwards with one of the opposite sex. Girls enter and finish this phase earlier than boys do. An adolescent girl's dream of friendship is already a dream of love: hence, her preference for cross-sex friendship, her insatiable craving for intimacy at an age when boys are still absorbed in their group-life and not ready for genuine intimacy.

Thirdly, it may be the result of the difference between male and female sexuality. The girls' early loves have only a weak erotic flavour and can sincerely be taken for friendship. Stronger and more open male eroticism, on the contrary, makes boys more sensitive to the difference between friendship and sexual attraction.

In any case, cross-sex AF has qualitative differences from same-sex friendship: different age proportions between friends, different privileged places of friendly meetings, different subjects of conversation, etc. In several languages the cross-sex friendship has even its particular name: a *boy-friend* or a *girl-friend* means something different from a *friend*, simply.

Concluding Observations

Further research on AF demands broader and more effective interdisciplinary cooperation and progress in methodology:

1. Alongside the experimental research of interpersonal attraction more studies of AF in its natural setting, taking into account socioeconomical conditions, the cultural milieu and the adolescent subculture itself, are needed (this has been emphasized also by Schaffer and Hargreaves, 1978);
2. Comparative cross-cultural research on AF among non-European nations is badly needed;
3. In psychological research on AF more attention should be given to longitudinal studies;
4. A central place in developmental psychological studies of AF should be given to personality factors and different types of adolescent

development; some important insights may come from adolescent psychiatry (see, for example, Kreisman, 1970),

5. Because AF is closely connected with ego development and self-awareness, more emphasis should be laid on the research of personality constructs and implicit personality theories.

CHAPTER 9
Adult Friendships

John M. Reisman

This chapter deals with friendships in adulthood, the most lengthy period in the life-span and the one which has inspired philosophers to wax eloquently about the desirability of this human relationship. For the purposes of this discussion, the adult years will be said to begin in the twenties with the assumption of vocational (career) and marital responsibilities and will be allowed to come gracefully to a close with the individual in the sixth decade of life, when old age looms. Thus adulthood extends over 40 years, from youth or young adulthood (20-30) to maturity (30-40) and middle age (40-60 or 65) to old age (65 +) (Neugarten, 1968), and might reasonably be expected to have changes in friendship related to the changes associated with adult development.

Features of Adult Friendship

What is meant by friendship frequently has an arbitrary quality, though people do have an agreement in general about what a friend is. During courtship it is common to hear references to one's "boy-friend" or "girl-friend," but after marriage a spouse may or may not be regarded as a friend, even when the relationship is quite friendly and intimate. Researchers have too readily accepted this personal understanding of friendship, and it has resulted in some reluctance on their part to impose their perhaps more rigorous definitions upon those they interview; the deplorable consequence has been that it is usually difficult to know in what sense respondents are answering questions about their friendly relations.

For our immediate purposes we shall define a friend as *"someone who likes and wishes to do well by someone else and who believes those feelings and good intentions are reciprocated"* (Reisman, 1979, p. 108), and it is hoped that this definition or some other can be agreed upon to facilitate communication and research in this area. It is particularly important in the context of research on the development of relationships in adulthood, for instance, that a number of crucial distinctions are recognized between different uses of the term "friendship" and between different types or aspects of relationships between adults. Thus, for example, if one wishes to trace the changes in relationships during the 40 years of adulthood, it is critical that one is alert to possible differences in the kinds of friendship studied, the variations in number of friends and the assumed functions of friendship at different ages since these differences may not be developmental changes so much as conceptual differences between the approaches of the different investigators. For this reason I will consider kinds of friendship, numbers of friends, and functions of friendship separately before attempting to incorporate them into one style of approach.

Kinds of friendship

People and social scientists ordinarily divide friendly relations into those that are close and those that are casual or acquaintances. Close friends are characterized by mutual feelings of affection, loyalty, and frankness. They enjoy each other's company and arrange to spend their leisure time together (Hartup, 1975). Peters (1974), in his discussion of what constitutes a friend added that it was essential that the involved persons acknowledge that they have a friendly relationship, both to themselves and to others; this stipulation effectively excludes from the conceptual domain of "friendship" such things as popularity or the relationship of a public figure to admirers.

McCall (1970) has suggested that close friendships are based upon the identities or personal qualities of the individuals concerned. In contrast, those friendly relations which are casual or superficial are frequently based upon the positions or activities of the parties. Acquaintanceship is an early stage of any dual personal interaction that may never progress beyond superficial recognition or that may lead to a close friendship.

What McCall meant by saying that casual friendly relations are based on activities or statuses is that in these relationships the people interact not because of fondness or choice, but because they have some task, function, or role relation that compels their interaction. People who work in the same office, for example, or who may be members of the same profession, try to be on friendly terms because it makes things go more smoothly than would the hostile alternative. However, the friendliness is extended not so much to the person as to whoever it is who occupies the position. Naturally such relationships will predictably change as developing adulthood brings the individual to different jobs, status, and roles.

I have proposed that superficial friendliness and casual friendships be termed *associative friendships* (Reisman, 1979); these friendly relations are distinguished by the absence of loyalty or a sense of commitment to seeing that the friendship endures much beyond the circumstances that bring the parties together. The relationship lasts so long as the persons work in the same place or live in the same neighbourhood or belong to the same organization — which may be for quite some time. Yet should one of the friends move or depart, there is little or no effort to keep in touch. Many adult friendships appear to be of this kind.

Reciprocal friendships is a term that I have used to describe what have been called intimate, close, ideal, "true" friendly relationships. A reciprocal friendship is characterized by loyalty and commitment between friends who regard one another as equals. So intense and consuming have some persons found this relationship that despite its many ennobling and inspirational features, they despair of ever having the vitality or good fortune to endure it again (Montaigne, quoted in Hutchins, 1952). "One friend in a lifetime is much; two are many; three are hardly possible" (Adams, 1931). One would hope that reciprocal friendships are not truly rare but as yet there is no definitive answer that can be given to that question. The research that addresses it simply has not been done.

A third type of friendship, *receptive*, is a relationship in which one of the members is primarily a giver to the other; it is distinguished by the difference in statuses recognized by the members. This would be the case when one person seeks the friendship of a mentor or patron, or in friendly relations between employer-employee, teacher-pupil, leader-follower, master-apprentice, supervisor-supervisee, and so on.

Freud (1959) in speculating about the emotional bases for interpersonal relationships theorized that they could be attributed to narcissism and our fondness for those qualities in others that remind us of ourselves. In receptive friendships, he might have argued, persons of superior or advanced status feel fondness toward underlings who have characteristics that remind them of how they used to be; while the students or underlings form their emotional attachments because those superiors have attributes that they would like to see in themselves. Many of the adult friendships between Freud and his colleagues — Rank, Jung, Jones, Ferenczi — were of this kind; that is, receptive.

It seems imperative in conducting descriptive research in this area that definitions of friendship be provided to respondents, especially when they are adults and might reasonably be expected to profit from such definitions in giving their answers. As we shall see in the studies that follow, the behaviours associated with close friendship appear to change through adulthood, so it becomes increasingly important to assess *how people identify their relationships* instead of depending solely upon objective indicators, such as frequency of contacts. Moreover, what constitutes "a friend" or "a close friend" differs from one person to another, and it is incumbent upon researchers not to perpetuate ambiguity and confusion by leaving those terms vague and idiosyncratic. Associative, reciprocal and receptive friendships have been proposed as one set of descriptive terms to clarify our understanding of friendly relations, and it is suggested that these concepts be presented to respondents so that there may be some basis for assuring reliable and valid communication.

Numbers of friends

The number of friends that people have is of interest empirically and phenomenologically. McCandless (1970) asserted that the influence of peers declines after adolescence and is at its greatest during that stage of life. While it is not possible to equate number with influence, his statement leads to the hypothesis that the number of friendships that are reciprocal declines during the adult years. At the same time it would seem that the number of friendly acquaintances, a network of friends, would expand as we get to know more and more people. Thus it might by hypothesized that the number of associative friendships increases during adulthood.

The number of friends that people appear to have is of interest since people make judgments about their own social desirability and acceptance on that basis. Many people wonder if they have enough friends and whether they are popular, and have little but their own impressions to draw upon to tell them. Feelings of loneliness, rejection, and alienation — and ultimately feelings about oneself — are dependent upon discrepancies noted between the friendly relations one has and those one would like to have (Peplau and Perlman, 1979; Perlman and Peplau, 1981; Reisman, 1979, pp. 181–199).

Ideally, to determine how many friends people have, a representative sample of progressive ages of males and females would be questioned about their friendly relations and relatively clearly defined terms of friendly relations would be employed. This could be done for members of different cultures and societies, and the samples would be followed over the years. Moreover, there would be routine checks on the validity of the reports. Unfortunately, we do not have this information, and it is questionable whether we have anything that comes close to approximating to it.

What we do have are two studies done recently in the United States that are at best suggestive. Reisman and Shorr (1978), as part of a larger study of friendship, interviewed children and adults and asked merely how many friends they had. As a simple check on the validity of these claims, the respondents were then asked to give the first names of their friends, and these names were counted.

TABLE I   Numbers of friends

Mean age ($N = 30$/level)	Claimed M	Claimed SD	Named M	Named SD
16.9	19	21	14	14
28.3	12	18	10	8
44.5	16	22	11	10
59.6	15	22	8	9

Note: The differences between numbers of friends claimed at different ages were, contrary to popular belief, not significant (see text).

M = Mean
SD = Standard deviation

The numbers of friends claimed was not significantly different from one age level to another. While it would be assumed that the numbers of people we know increase with increasing age, there was no evidence from these data to indicate that people see the numbers of their friends increasing. Adults reported having anything from one or two to 30 or more friends, with a mean of about 15.

Not surprisingly the number of friends named was less than the number claimed; this discrepancy usually came about when someone claimed to have a large number of friends and found it difficult to recall all of them. No adult who claimed to have a few friends had a problem in reporting the number of names required. With both sets of data at all age levels the variability was considerable, indicating that there may be no relatively specific number of friends that can be said to characterize the young or middle-aged or older adult.

To shed some light on how their respondents interpreted the question, Reisman and Shorr asked a class of young adults taking an evening course in business the number of friends they had and the number of close friends they had. Only one respondent gave the same figure to both questions. The number of close friends ranged from one to 27, with a mean of six, and for most respondents was less than the number of friends claimed. Therefore the number of friends claimed probably represented to most respondents both casual and close friendships.

The second study, though based on substantially greater data than the first, has findings that are in essential agreement with it. A questionnaire about friendship was published by the magazine *Psychology Today* which drew 40 000 responses. In analysing this wealth of data, 4000 of the completed questionnaires were randomly selected and tabulated. This sample, though probably representative of the population of respondents, did not typify the adult population of the US; it was 72% female and 78% college educated. Means and standard deviations were not reported (Parlee, 1979). However, it was found that 68% of the respondents claimed to have one to five close friends and 55% claimed to have 15 or more casual friendships. The mercurial nature of people's understanding of the term "friendship", perhaps depending upon the context in which the word is used, was illustrated by the finding that somewhere else in the questionnaire most respondents reported they had *more* close friendships than casual ones!

Functions of friendships

If one is willing to stretch matters a bit, it can be argued that every human relationship involves getting or giving something, or the expectation that one will receive something from the interaction. From that point of view, friendships are initiated and maintained when something valued comes to the participants; if that something is no longer delivered or if its value seems no longer commensurate with the cost or effort, friendships are terminated. Evidently few people perceive their friendships in so business-like and dispassionate a fashion (Phillips and Metzger, 1976).

When Aristotle (1952 edition) turned his attention to the subject of adult friendships, over two thousand years ago, he recognized that most of these relationships were based upon what the parties gained. Some people wanted only friends who would be useful to them, who had influence, power, skills, or material resources that they could draw upon for their own benefit; these were friendships of *utility*.

Many other friendships, Aristotle observed, were based upon the pleasurable stimulation they provided. Friends who got together mainly for sports, games, entertaining activities, amusing chit-chat, and stimulating conversation were involved in friendships of *pleasure*. Aristotle supposed that pleasure was probably the major function served by the friendships of children, and that it diminished in importance in adulthood when utility became the major consideration.

Both the friendships of pleasure and utility involve giving and getting, and therefore Aristotle judged them imperfect. Since they were rooted in gain and selfishness, he thought them likely to involve resentments, bickering, and complaints, with the parties trying to maximize what they wanted. The course of these friendships was erratic and they were apt to be quite limited in duration.

Far better than these two, in Aristotle's opinion, is the friendship based on *virtue*. In this relationship the parties are attracted to each other, not by what they can get, but by their admirable qualities, by the good or virtuous characteristics they admire and possess. Since these characteristics are enduring, these friendships are also enduring — at least so Aristotle thought. Of course, even in friendships of virtue the functions of utility and pleasure might be served; however, utility and pleasure were secondary considerations to those friends who were bound by an appreciation of their personalities.

Aristotle's analysis of friendship leads to a number of testable hypotheses — children's friendships are based on pleasure, while the friendships of adulthood are more often those of utility. Friendships of pleasure and utility are not as lasting as those of virtue. Friendships of pleasure and utility are more quarrelsome than those of virtue. Friendships of virtue are more satisfying than those of pleasure and utility. Thus far, few of these hypotheses have been tested, though there have been studies supportive of Aristotle's descriptive analysis.

In a study by Murstein and Spitz (1973–74) 120 female college students were presented with an 80-item bipolar check list. Among others, they were asked to rate their best friend, their most admired friend, their most useful friend, and their most enjoyable friend. The items on the list consisted of traits judged to represent pleasure, utility, and virtue.

Factor analyses of the ratings were in keeping with Aristotle's position: best friends were described mainly with traits of virtue; most useful friends were described mainly with traits of utility; but most admired friends were described primarily with traits of utility, suggesting that thoroughness and efficiency may also be virtues, while most enjoyable friends were rated mostly with characteristics of goodness. In short, the findings were somewhat mixed. Traits descriptive of virtue, utility, and pleasure were present to some extent in the various friends rated, though Murstein and Spitz believed their findings were for the most part consistent with Aristotle's concepts.

Reisman and Shorr (1978) asked children and adults: "Why is it nice to have friends? What do you like about having a friend?" The responses, which are regarded as indicative of expectations that people have about friendship (Bigelow and La Gaipa, 1975), were categorized according to the Aristotelian system. Of interest were that responses or expectations indicative of pleasure, virtue, and utility were found at every age from eight years through adulthood and that virtue expectations evidenced no developmental trend, being infrequently expressed by children and adults alike.

In keeping with Aristotle's hypotheses, younger respondents more often mentioned pleasure ("a friend is nice to play with"), and older respondents more often mentioned utility ("someone to talk to", "a help when you need help"). Thus the promotion and maintenance of friendly relationships at different age levels probably would be facilitated by addressing different expectations, those of entertainment for young children and those of usefulness for older children and adults.

A study by Crawford (1977) in England, where data were obtained from interviews with 306 middle-aged married couples, yielded results consistent with the above. The respondents were questioned about their closest friends, and only these most intimate of friendly relationships were investigated for their meanings. Two definitions were given most frequently: "A friend is someone I can talk to and trust." "A friend is someone I can call on for help." Although no statistical analysis of the data was reported, Crawford claimed that men, more so than women, cited the pleasure they derived from their friend's company, while women, more so than men, emphasized the importance of trust.

Phillips and Metzger (1976) also found that the largest proportion of their respondents defined friendship in terms of being able to discuss personal matters; not a majority, but enough to indicate that this is a specific function of friendship important to many adults. Similarly, in the *Psychology Today* survey (Parlee, 1979), the qualities of friends that appeared to be most valued were loyalty, warmth, and the ability to keep confidences. Accordingly, it would appear that one of the major ways in which a friend in adulthood is regarded as useful is by serving as a confidant.

Certain psychological benefits would seem to accrue to the person with friends, and these have yet to be documented adequately. One can argue that friends help to alleviate feelings of loneliness, bolster self-esteem, establish status, and enhance a sense of well-being (Huston and Levinger, 1978; Reisman, 1979). However, it is another matter to demonstrate these personal consequences. It is even difficult to establish what place of importance friendships occupy in adulthood, though there are any number of strong opinions about its significance. Let us consider this issue next.

Importance of Adult Friendships

Adulthood occupies such a long part of the life-span that it is more accurate to wonder what importance friendship may have to adults *at what time in their lives and under what conditions* than to ask a simple question about its significance. We have already noted the suggestion by McCandless (1970) that the importance of friendship diminishes after adolescence. Sheehy (1974), in her popular book "Passages", made a linear prediction about the significance of friendship in adulthood: "As age increases, there is a decreasing tendency to compare oneself with others. . . . In the process of moving toward this interiority, people find themselves beginning to enjoy a welcome detachment from others" (p. 349). These observations lead one to suppose that friendship becomes less and less important over the course of adulthood.

It should be stressed that McCandless and Sheehy were addressing their remarks to the situation in the United States, but that their remarks might conceivably be relevant to all industrialized societies. Even so, Huston and Levinger (1978) in their survey of the literature on interpersonal attraction concluded that friendships were probably important through young adulthood, decreased in significance during middle age, and became important again to the elderly. However, the relevant variable for this roller-coaster ride of friendship is not so much chronological age as it is the taking on of adult responsibilities, particularly career, marriage, and family obligations. Career and family duties usually take precedence over ties to friends.

Erikson's (1971) psychosocial theory of development sees human growth as a series of crises in which the individual acquires certain feelings of competence and trust. During early adulthood the person gains a sense of *intimacy*, a deep, enduring involvement with someone else, usually of the other sex, though it may be with a friend; this investment in a specific relationship is often accompanied by the termination of friendly relations that are no longer meaningful. Middle adulthood is concerned with the gaining of a sense of *generativity*, a feeling of accomplishment and extending one's influence to succeeding generations; and in the late adult years the person is supposed to acquire a feeling of *integrity*, a sense of self-satisfaction with life as it has been led.

The crises faced by adults in Sheehy's (1974) "Passages" are engagingly described versions of those mentioned by Erikson: "The Trying Twenties", "The Deadline Decade", "Renewal or Resignation". A task mentioned by Sheehy is that young adults seek a mentor, if possible, or seek to form a receptive friendship that will assist them in their careers. Young adulthood would thus be hypothesized to be a time when associative friendships are regarded as less important than they were in adolescence and when receptive friendships would be highly valued.

Neugarten and Datan (1974) have claimed that the adult years are viewed differently by those in the upper to middle classes and those who are "blue collar" or working class. Young adulthood is seen by the former as a period of exploration and groping for identity, intimacy, and a career; by the latter, it is regarded as a time to get married and settle down. Maturity, the years from 30 to 40, is seen as a time of accomplishment and establishing oneself by the middle class, but as a decade for getting older, quieter, and wiser by the working class. Middle age is the prime of life for the former, and a period of decline both physically and emotionally for the latter. Old age is perceived as a richly earned vacation by one group and a wretched time for making-do and battling illness by the other.

Little evidence is cited to support these views of adult development. One of the few studies conducted to test Erikson's theory, a follow-up of college graduates in middle age, was generally supportive of the theory and indicated that, if anything, career considerations may be of greater importance than had been supposed (Whitbourne and Waterman, 1979).

In general, empirical evidence indicates that friendly relations are important in adulthood, but they are less important, particularly to men, than career and family obligations. If should be emphasized that the preceding generalization refers mainly to middle-class adults in Western societies.

Brain (1976) has deplored this state of affairs and has pointed to cultures in which the relationship between friends is socially recognized and accorded great importance. He has advocated that our world would be a better place if we adopted similar practices, and has gone so far as to state: "The need for a permanent emotional outlet — for a strong love between two persons not based on sex or the social arrangements of marriage — is a real and basic one" (Brain, 1977).

Whether there is a *need* for reciprocal friendships outside marriage can be subjected to inquiry. Such a need would be indicated by harmful psychological consequences when it appears to be frustrated or not satisfied; less convincingly, it might be demonstrated by greater satisfaction and well-being among those who have reciprocal friendships than among those who do not, both groups consisting of married couples. Interestingly, Wright (1979) has informed me there are cultures (the Seri Indians of northern Mexico) in which friendly relations do not appear to be recognized at all and in which the word "friend" does not exist. This absence of friendship would not mean the need does not exist, but it would definitely imply that it is a low-priority need, as needs go.

I do not wish to imply or convey that friendships in adulthood are unimportant, but I do wish to state that the evidence makes clear that friendship are regarded by men as less important than their families and careers. A study emphasizing the importance of friendly relations has been reported by Valliant (1977, 1978). About 100 men who had graduated from Harvard were interviewed by Valliant and completed questionnaires. The men were about 54 years old at the time of the follow-up.

Valliant, who was influenced in his expectations by Erikson's theory, defined those adults who had good relations according to the following criteria: they were warm and open towards others and reported having friends; they had ten years of a stable marriage; they had fathered children or had adopted them; they engaged in activities, outside their work, with persons who were not members of their families. Those men who did have good relations tended to have been socially successful in adolescence as well. The major conclusion of the study was: "Good overall adult adjustment was highly correlated with good object relations, no matter how they were measured" (Valliant, 1978). In contrast, the men with poor relations tended to misuse drugs, to be an unhappy lot, and to suffer from many chronic physical ailments.

Note that a stable marriage was a criterion of good relations for men. For women, marriage may not have the same significance. A study by Gurin *et al.* (1960) found that single women were better educated and earned more money than single men. Furthermore, these women tended to feel happier, healthier, and more psychologically sound than unmarried males. It might well be supposed that among single females would be found those who are "liberated" and who see themselves placing careers and individual fulfilment above traditional mothering roles and family obligations. The same does not seem to be true for unmarried men, who have always been free to strive for vocational success while being expected eventually to marry and support families. Perhaps as greater latitude is given to male sex roles, the unmarried man will be found to be less disadvantaged than is now the case. At present it would seem that bachelorhood is a waste-basket into which drops a variety of social and physical misfits in greater proportion than is the case for spinsterhood.

In Western societies there appear to be definite differences in the friendly relations of adult men and adult women. Essentially, men are reported to have more associative friends than women, while women are reported to be more likely than males to have an intimate, reciprocal friendship. Why these findings occur, and what are the variables which influence them, has not been established, though one would suppose cultural role expectations and demands play some part. The male is expected to go out and work and be the primary support, "the breadwinner," of the family; to the extent that women may be expected to play a similar role, their friendship patterns may also be similar.

Differences between the friendly relations of the sexes appear evident by early adulthood. Yoon (1978) asked 80 male and 80 female college students, aged 17–25 years, to complete a questionnaire concerning friendship. Females, more so than males, claimed to value intimate, confidential relations with their friends. They desired friendships based upon affection and relationships that would endure and grow deeper with the years. Women sought reciprocal friendships. However, the males in this study emphasized friendships based upon shared activities and having fun together.

The value that women give to intimacy in friendship was also indicated by Davidson's (1978) study of 42 female college students. Here, too, women saw friendship as a means for helping them change their behaviours, be supported emotionally, and grow personally. Best friends were considered more valuable than associative friends in achieving these aims. With their best friends these women reported they felt more close and involved and better able to communicate and share feelings than they did with their casual friends.

Davidson's and Yoon's findings suggest that friendship may serve a different function for men than it does for women. This was also suggested by a factor analysis of the responses of 330 unmarried and married men and women to questionnaires about friendship (Lyness, 1978). There were two major variables in this study: friendship, which indicated the extent to which people were valued for their human qualities, and interactions with them were voluntarily sought; and intimacy, which suggested a wish for close, empathic, communicative relationships. Four clusterings of respondents were found: (1) single men were characterized by being low in friendship and low in intimacy; (2) married men tended to be high in friendship but low in intimacy; (3) single women were likely to be low in friendship and high in intimacy; and (4) married women were apt to be high in friendship and high in intimacy. Once again intimacy distinguished the friendly relations between the sexes.

In Crawford's (1977) study of close friendships of English middle-aged married couples, the results were remarkably consistent with the studies just discussed. Women were more likely than men to have a close friend, and this divergence increased as the men grew older, that is, as the men grew older, they were less likely to have a close friend than when they were younger. Strikingly, the majority of men (60%), when asked to name a close friend, mentioned a married couple, while their wives (63%) named a specific individual. And the women emphasized trust in the close friendship, but their husbands put the emphasis upon pleasurable activities and entertainment.

Levinson (1978) interviewed 40 middle-aged men, ten from each of four occupational groupings; industrial workers, to represent the working class; business executives; university biologists; and novelists. These occupations were intended to be a cross-section of social and intellectual groups in the United States, though the limitations of the sample are obvious and were readily conceded by Levinson. Nevertheless, his conclusion should by now come as no surprise: "In our interviews, friendship was largely noticeable by its absence. As a tentative generalization we would say that close friendship with a man or woman is rarely experienced by American men. . . . Most men do not have an intimate male friend of the kind that they recall fondly from boyhood or youth" (Levinson, 1978, p. 335).

We have already suggested several hypotheses that may be related to the lack of intimate and self-disclosing friendships among men. One is that career and marital responsibilities take precedence over reciprocal friendships, more so for men than for women. There is an old song ("Those Wedding Bells Are Breaking Up That Old Gang of Mine") that is consistent with that hypothesis. Moreover, it may be that the entertainment and pleasurable activities which are so valued in male friendships act against their continuance after marriage, but friendships based upon intimate communications are less apt to be disrupted.

Lewis (1978) has speculated that the competitiveness among men in Western societies acts to keep them apart and hinders them from entering into relationships where they are open about their weaknesses and concerns. The male role, with its praise for "manly" restraint and control over one's tender feelings, could also be a factor. This concept of manliness would lead men to fear vulnerability and openness since it might lead to questions about their own masculinity. A similar concern has been postulated in connection with being close to men, a fear of being thought to be homosexual. Another hypothesis offered by Lewis is that boys have fathers and role models of masculinity who infrequently demonstrate affection and intimate communication; this would lead to the hypothesis that boys and girls also value their friendships differently.

The implication, and declaration, is that men would be better, happier, lead a fuller life, if they had reciprocal friendships than if they did not. There can be no quarrel with the contention that lives would be more full and complete when something absent in them is provided. However, it remains to be determined whether men with reciprocal friendships differ from men without them, and if they do, the forms these differences take.

Associative friendships, that is the sheer number of friendly relations, have been seen as affording a number of advantages to those who have many of them. Through a network of friends, one can be informed about news in one's field, learn of advancement opportunities and be placed in consideration for promotion and positions of honour and responsibility. That studies have found men to have more associative friendships than women can, in part, be regarded as a function of men being more likely than women to have careers and jobs that bring them into contact with a number of other people. However, this does not appear to be a complete explanation.

Kaufman (1978) questioned 46 female and 32 male professors at a university in the United States about their friendships. The same pattern emerged — males had more associative friends than females. However, in this case Kaufman, a woman, saw the pattern working to the disadvantage of women, who had fewer friends than men among their professional colleagues and so might be less likely to receive the required number of votes for tenure and promotion. Of special significance was Kaufman's finding that this professional isolation was particularly pronounced for the unmarried women, indicating that marital and family responsibilities were not interfering with the formation of friendships at the university. A possible hypothesis is that unmarried women pursuing careers are seen by men as more deviant from their traditional sex roles and thus more competitive with them than married women, diminishing their attractiveness as associative friends.

A peripheral indication of the relative importance of friendship in adulthood comes from a study by Allan (1977) in Great Britain. The major comparison was in differences between the working and middle classes in friendship patterns. Friendliness in the middle class was signified by promoting interactions in settings other than work, such as by inviting people to a party in one's home. However, among the working class the tendency was to restrict friendly interactions to wherever it was that the persons were accustomed to meet. This may mean that members of the working class may never invite their associative friends to their homes, so Allan cautioned against using this as a criterion of friendship for members of this class.

Presumably working-class and middle-class children do not differ with respect to interacting with their friends in school and home settings. This aspect of childhood and youthful friendly relations appeared so prominent a feature of friendship that Hartup (1975) offered it as the major operational definitional characteristic: "Friends are people who spontaneously seek the company of one another; furthermore they seek proximity in the absence of strong social pressures to do so." On the basis of Allan's (1977) study and on the basis of what we have already mentioned about associative friendships, it would seem inappropriate to define adult friendly relations according to voluntary, "spontaneous" social contacts.

Related to Hartup's definition of friends is the frequency of contacts that people have; the more often people choose to interact with one another, the more friendly they are. Among children and adolescents, this relationship between number of contacts and the closeness of friendship seems to hold. Close friends in adolescence may see each other several times a week, and daily contacts between them are not unusual. Children and adolescents define friends in terms of personal contacts.

But beginning in young adulthood the frequency of contacts between close friends becomes quite variable (Reisman, 1979, pp. 124–140). A close friend may be someone who has been known for over 20 years (17% of Crawford's, 1977, respondents reported their closest friendship was formed in childhood and had endured for 40–50 years; similarly, it was most often reported by Parlee's, 1979, respondents that they had met their closest friends in childhood or in college) and who is seen as little as once or twice a year, or less. For adults, a friendship may be regarded as continuing and alive despite very infrequent contact.

To sum up these findings, they suggest that friendship is an important social relationship throughout adulthood, but that for many adults it is relatively less important than marital or family and career considerations. For males, friends appear to be valued as companions who share in mutually enjoyable activities and pastimes. For females, friends appear to be valued primarily as confidantes. For both sexes, many of their closest friendships have been formed by young adulthood and the frequency of their contacts with friends in adulthood has been appreciably reduced from what it was earlier in life.

Changes in Adult Friendships

Closely related to the previous discussion about the importance of friendship are changes in the ways adults feel about their friendly relations as they progress through adulthood. A major hypothesis in this regard is that friendship diminishes in importance during young adulthood and that it increases in importance during later adulthood when career and family responsibilities are reduced. A second major hypothesis, somewhat at variance with the first, is that of disengagement, which states that as adults grow older they become less involved in social relationships and activities (Cavan et al., 1963). Of course, ultimately everybody disengages, but the first hypothesis predicts a renewal of interest in friendly relations prior to senility, while the second predicts a steady decline in involvements with others.

Part of the difficulty in addressing these hypotheses (and, indeed, of making sense of the findings that close friendships are infrequent among American and British adult males), is how we define a friend. For children the problem is relatively simple. The differences between the sexes, between children who are separated in age from one another by a year or two, between youngsters and their relatives and parents, between those who live in one neighbourhood or community and another, are considerable. For adults these differences are far less pronounced and relationships are more heterogeneous. Are we willing to consider a wife a close friend to her husband? As sons and daughters grow into adulthood, can they be judged close friends of their parents? Is interpersonal contact a necessary condition for defining a friendship (Wright, 1978); and, if so, how frequent must these contacts be for the friendship to be regarded as viable? It would seem that social scientists have some obligation to come to some agreement about the answers to these questions so that the meaning of "friend" is similarly understood.

For purposes of exposition, we shall be discussing friendships in young adulthood (20–30 or so), middle age (30 or so to 60 or so), and later adulthood (60 or so to 65 or so). However, it should be understood that the changes discussed are not solely a function of time, but of the meeting of responsibilities and the alleviation of responsibilities associated with these periods. An adult who does not marry and have children, for example, is likely to have a friendship pattern that deviates markedly from those of married adults with offspring.

Young adulthood

The major developmental tasks in this period have to do with completing one's education and beginning one's career, growth of an intimate heterosexual relationship, the process of courtship, and marriage, and beginning one's family. Getting an education, marriage, and one's career may require going to communities far from home and being separated from family, friends, and neighbours, with consequent disruptions and subsequent losses of relationships. Moving was the reason most frequently given by the respondents to the *Psychology Today* questionnaire for terminations of their friendships (Parlee, 1979), and it is in young adulthood that moving about occurs quite frequently.

Packard (1972) supposed that the frequent moves of people in the United States was a major factor in producing alienation and a feeling of estrangement. However, his empirical assessment of this expectation provided it with no support. The number of friends claimed by adults in a stable New York community was not appreciably different from the number claimed in a suburb whose residents were being moved hither and thither by job transfers. Packard speculated that the process of friendship formation may be accelerated among people who find themselves in transition, since they share similar uncertainties, disruptions, and pressures to make friends quickly.

Certainly young adulthood could be regarded as a zestful, optimistic time of life. Opportunities and hopes for advancement and the similar problems of young married couples generate a certain degree of homogeneity. Fresh out of adolescence, there may be considerable interest and enthusiasm for making new friends compatible with their changing circumstances, friends who are similar in ages and in stages of the development of their families, such as newly married and no children, or married and with pre-school-aged children (Bischof, 1969).

Many of these friends are drawn from neighbours and co-workers (Newman and Newman, 1975), with the primary friendships drawn from places of employment and thus initiated by the husband (Bischof, 1969). Huston and Levinger (1978) stated, "Our own belief is that most adult friendships evolve from existing role relationships". This is akin to stating that most adult friendships are associative. Co-workers have much in common by virtue of their sharing experiences, conditions, and training in the same place of employment.

Which of these associative relationships are maintained and allowed to evolve into reciprocal friendships would seem to depend upon a number of factors. Duck (1973a, b) has proposed a filter hypothesis: "Individuals evaluate others on a progressively more specialized and specific set of criteria as a relationship progresses". In particular, Duck has postulated that subtle personality characteristics, such as similar attitudes, values, and beliefs, become decisive in determining whether an associative friendship grows into one that is lasting.

However, there is also the consideration of whether adults who start off sharing the same interests and values continue to do so. One married couple may have children and their friends may not, and thus they find they have significantly less in common. One person may advance in his position, while his friend does not; Verbrugge (1977) in a study of friendships among adults in the United States and Germany found that similarity in social status was a significant determinant of close friendships. Verbrugge's results document a rather commonplace observation, that those who move up the ladder of success frequently "forget" their friends.

Newman and Newman (1975) speculated that a husband and wife may differ in the kind of friendly relations they prefer:

> Some couples have only a few close friends, and others have a large circle of relatively distant acquaintances. . . . If one partner sought intimate friendship with other adults and the other partner preferred only distant acquaintances, there would certainly be a continuing source of conflict with regard to the planning of social activities (pp. 269-270).

Aside from the marital friction that might result, it seems conceivable that dissimilarity in friendship preferences may result in one spouse acting to influence or disrupt the friendly relations of the other.

Erikson (1971) has theorized that *intimacy* and *distancing* are required for satisfactory growth during young adulthood. In the former process, when individuals are sufficiently comfortable about who they are, they are capable of fusing their identities, that is, capable of accommodating themselves to one another without feeling personally threatened. In the latter process, the person allows relations to come to an end that are no longer compatible with the person he or she has become. Thus Erikson would seem to predict a reduction and greater selectivity in associative friendships in young adulthood than existed in adolescence.

This loss of friendships may be so extensive that the husband and wife have virtually no friendly relations outside themselves and the members of their immediate family. They become a "closed dyad". Although it has been alleged that, "So often a woman gives up her friends when she starts a family" (Sheehy, 1974, p. 148), the evidence indicates that this is more apt to occur for men (Crawford, 1977; Levinson, 1978). Whatever eventually may be determined to be the case, theoretically and empirically there are grounds to predict a narrowing of friendly relations among those who marry, as the marriage progresses.

Middle age

It seems reasonable to suppose that friendly relations in adulthood are more heterogeneous with respect to age than they are in childhood and adolescence. Receptive friendships and friendships between married couples who have a child of the same age are two examples of how friends may differ greatly in their ages and yet have much in common. Age, in fact, at least when restricted to the adult range, no longer seems to be a significant variable in determining friendship (Rosow, 1968).

Middle age is the period when people are "established". For the middle and upper classes, this is "the prime of life," the time when adults have achieved a certain success in their fields and before their physical condition has become a major concern. Of course, it is not necessarily such a positive time for everyone, even in the middle and upper classes. However, it does seem to be the time when, if adults are ever going to feel they have "arrived", or achieved success, this is most likely when they will be doing it.

Neugarten (1968) and Neugarten and Datan (1974) stressed that middle-aged professional people are, by and large, a secure and confident group. They have attained those positions of power and responsibility that they had been striving to reach through adolescence and young adulthood, and they are happy they got there. They constitute the age group which in most Western societies wields the most influence, and consequently they survey their domains with the assurance that they are in command of themselves, their destinies, and the lives of others.

Not wishing to make the middle-aged seem too overbearing, Neugarten and Datan (1974) did note that there were certain disquieting experiences. Some middle-aged people may assess their careers and lives and find they had fallen short of their goals and that their prospects for ever achieving them were not bright. Some may feel themselves separated from youth and alienated in a society that appears to value perpetual adolescence, both in appearance and psychological functioning. Already there may be declines in physical functioning (bifocals, illnesses) which cause uneasiness. There may be divorce, the death of a spouse, and other losses in human relationships. And the attitude toward time itself may shift in a significant fashion, from how much time one has lived from birth to how much time one still has left to live.

A sense of urgency, a feeling that if one is ever going to do something one had better do it now, may send people striking off in new directions, with new careers and new spouses. Hunt and Hunt (1975) argued that this may be the best time for adults to take stock of old friendships and eliminate those unsuited to the people they are or intend to become. They advocated a rather ruthless weeding out of "leftover" friends, the bores, and the ones who had outlived their usefulness.

If nothing else, this pop psychology with its enthusiastic prescriptions for what people should do can create conflicting expectations. On the one hand, adults are fed the sober conclusion from research that during middle age there begins a perceptible decline in social involvements (Bischof, 1969, p. 188), and they are tantalized by a number of hypotheses which have been advanced to explain this finding — The middle-aged have less energy for friendly relations? . . . Their interest in social activities declines? . . . Their interest in solitary activities increases? . . . Their time available for friendships decreases because of the time they have to devote to the increasing demands of their own immediate families? Accordingly, middle age is the time to husband one's resources and cherish and savour old friendships (Davitz and Davitz, 1976).

On the other hand, we have this bit of popular advice: "Middle age is, in fact, a particularly good time for making friends; sociological studies show that it is second only to adolescence as a period for forming new relationships. This is a result of the new activities, the new interests, and the new freedom typical of this time of life" (Hunt and Hunt, 1975, p. 141). It is also suggested that this social renewal is a function of the not-so-exhilarating new statuses in which people find themselves, such as the newly divorced and the newly widowed.

To make these discrepant expectations consistent, it would be hypothesized that middle age would be a period of declining social involvements or friendships for those content with or resigned to their personal adjustments.

However, middle age would be expected to be a time for forming new social relationships or friendships for those who sought or experienced significant disruptions in their personal adjustments, for examples, change of career, death of spouse, and divorce.

Middle age covers the longest span of years in adulthood, from 35 or 40 to 60 or 65, and it would seem necessary for researchers to divide this span into specific durations — 36–45, 46–55, 56–65 — so that the results from different studies can be readily compared. In Crawford's (1977) study, for example, the middle-aged ranged in age from 40 to over 60, and it would have been helpful if the results had been reported in connection with the ages of the respondents so that the findings could be related to the impressions of, for example, Hunt and Hunt (1975), where middle age was confined to the years 50–59.

Later adulthood

There are a number of situational variables that appear to enter into friendly relations in later middle age (56–65). The middle class is significantly more likely than the lower or working class to draw their friendships from a wider circle, both physically and psychologically. The middle class is less tied to a neighbourhood than the lower class, and thus the former maintains friendships with people who live some distance from their homes and who may be considerably younger than they are. Friendships are made more on the basis of similarities in sex, marital status, and social class, and less on the basis of age, narrowly defined (Rosow, 1968).

Proximity appears to have little to do with friendship. Crawford (1977) had very few respondents who considered their neighbours to be their close friends. In Rosow's (1968) study of 1,200 adults in Cleveland, there was no significant relationship between contacts with neighbours and whether people expressed a wish for more friends. Rosow concluded that people perceive the friendly contacts with their neighbours to be qualitatively different from their other friendships; these are associative friendships, in which people are friendly with the occupants of a house, whoever they might be. The question is raised whether, with time, associative friendships of long standing come to be regarded as empty and meaningless since they do not progress beyond superficiality.

The adults in Rosow's (1968) sample exhibited a variety of friendship patterns, and it should be understood that none of these was regarded by Rosow as especially pathological. Not every adult wanted more friends or more contacts with their neighbours, and whether they did or not had no significant relationship to their numbers of friends or neighbourly associations. In other words, some adults have very few friends and like it that way, while some adults have many friends and wish they had more.

A large group within Rosow's sample (32%) was composed of adults who led a very active and diversified social life. Most of their friends lived outside their neighbourhood, and they spent a considerable part of their time in going to and from their friends' homes. Physical and intellectual vigour and the financial resources to lead such an active social life would seem to have been important variables associated with this group. Rosow dubbed them the "cosmopolitans", claimed they were content with their friendships, and asserted that those with this pattern were mostly middle class.

Another large group, 23% of the sample, was composed of adults who had many contacts with friends and neighbours and who expressed satisfaction with their relationships. The members of this group did not indicate a wish for more friends and were composed of both the middle and the working classes. They differed from the "cosmopolitans" in that most of their social contacts were within their neighbourhoods.

The third largest group, 19% of the sample, was also made up of persons from the middle and the working classes. They were the "isolates" since they would have liked to have more friends, but kept to themselves and had a low number of social contacts.

Ten percent of Rosow's sample had high numbers of contacts with neighbours and friends, yet expressed the wish to have more friends. Rosow dubbed them "insatiable" and hypothesized that adults with this pattern of friendship are driven to maintain relationships in order to reduce their anxiety about being alone and their fear of alienation.

The smallest group, about 4% of the sample, was composed mainly of members of the working class and claimed to have no friends, few contacts with neighbours, and the wish to keep things that way. Rosow called the members of this group "phlegmatic". The remainder of his sample did not seem to fall neatly into any of the afore-mentioned categories.

If nothing else, Rosow's study demonstrated the variety of friendship patterns among adults, even a relatively homogeneous sample of adults of 62 or more years of age living in Cleveland, Ohio. Over half this sample led a fairly active social life and only a small minority had no friends. There would seem to be little support from these data for the disengagement hypothesis.

The names given by Rosow to the groups within his sample merit a moment's attention. "Phlegmatic" and "insatiable" are not neutral terms; it would have been possible to take the same descriptions and label them "self-sufficient" and "vibrant", which gives these friendship patterns a more positive cast. Until further research is done, it does not seem appropriate to regard any friendship pattern among satisfactorily functioning adults in late middle age as pathognomic.

Loneliness

No sooner having said the above, it is necessary to indicate that a growing body of evidence points to the relatively isolated individual, the person with few or no friends, as being more susceptible to the effects of physiological stress and breakdown (Lynch, 1977). Valliant's (1978) research found that men with poor social relationships demonstrated the effects of aging more so than men who had good social relations (defined as a stable marriage and a number of friendships); further, almost half of the poor social relationships group was found to be suffering from chronic physical ailments, which was a significantly higher proportion than found among the good social relationships group.

A study by Gore (1978) is even more dramatic since the sample consisted of 100 married men who were followed over a two-year period. These men were workers in a plant where employment was erratic due to frequent plant closings, and thus they experienced the stresses of unemployment, job insecurity, and economic uncertainties. Gore found that those married men who had social supports in the form of stable relations with wives, friends, and relatives had significantly fewer symptoms of illness and significantly lower levels of cholesterol than their married fellow workers who did not.

Thoresen in a discussion of research related to the Type A individual, the hard-driving, achievement-orientated person who is prone to coronaries, was reported to have said: "One of the things which characterizes Type A people is that they tend to have what epidemiologists call a low level of perceived social support. They have very few, if any, close friends and tend not to see others as caring" (*APA Monitor*, 1980).

These studies suggest that friends provide a means for the alleviation of stress. They indicate that a poverty of social relationships may be a stressor, which if prolonged can eventuate in physical ailments and disorders. They do not establish whether friendships are an essential ingredient for psychological well-being since they did not differentiate between various social support systems. To be specific, they did not determine if a person with a stable marriage and no close friendships outside the family was as much at risk as the person with no spouse and no close friendships. They did not determine whether close friendships can compensate for the absence of a marital partner, whether a marital partner can compensate for the absence of close friendships, or whether associative friendships can compensate for the absence of reciprocal friendships.

The literature directed to the public (Gordon, 1976), even those publications written by normally conservative psychologists, tends to abound in generalizations and assertions with a notable absence of documentation or evidence. For example:

> Loneliness — as experienced by the child, the adult, and the older person — is fast becoming increasingly prevalent, as more and more people are living alone or in ever-smaller families. Americans are marrying later, having fewer children, divorcing more often, and moving greater distances away from "home". . . . We are fast becoming not only a nation of strangers, but a nation of lonely strangers at that (Zimbardo, 1977, p. 48).

Loneliness is an issue of relevance to this discussion because it is frequently assumed there is a direct relation between feeling lonely and friendship; those who have many friends are less likely to feel lonely, and those who have few friends or none are more apt to experience bouts of loneliness. The experience of loneliness is, by definition, unpleasant, and thus it acts to motivate people to lessen its intensity and reduce its occurrence. It is also frequently assumed that loneliness is particularly troublesome to older adults, who are likely to endure the losses of spouses, relatives, and friends.

A moment's reflection is sufficient to demonstrate that there is no necessary relationship between being alone and feeling lonely. Certain activities, reading, writing, studying, are frequently accomplished without being accompanied by anyone else and without giving rise to loneliness. At other times solitude may be welcomed as a relief from interpersonal stimulation. Therefore it would seem that loneliness is dependent upon how the person perceives being alone, rather than the simple fact of being alone itself. Rosow's "phlegmatic" adults conceivably did not experience loneliness, despite their almost complete absence of friendly relations.

Peplau and Perlman (1979; Perlman and Peplau, 1981) have proposed an operational means for the identification of loneliness. They have defined it as a discrepancy between what people would like in the way of social relationships and what they believe their social circumstances to be: "loneliness exists to the extent that a person's network of social relationships is smaller or less satisfying than the person desires". Accordingly, loneliness would be predicted to occur more often among those who did not have the kinds of friendships they wished (associative, receptive, reciprocal) and among those who did not have the number of friendships they wished, as compared to those who expressed satisfaction about their friendly relations. The proposal by Peplau and Perlman is most constructive, and it is hoped that it will have its intended effect of stimulating research.

I have carried the notion of dissatisfaction in social relations a bit further by hypothesizing that feeling lonely becomes a source of personal concern when the individual feels unable to deal with it:

> By way of summary we might say that people welcome solitude when they feel they have chosen it. . . . They do not welcome being alone when they feel their solitude has been imposed upon them or they have little choice or control over their condition (Reisman, 1979, p. 175).

This would lead to the hypothesis that loneliness occurs more often among those who do not feel able to make friends than among those who do. Social skills training in making friends would appear to be an effective procedure for increasing one's feelings of being in control of one's friendly relations, and so for countering loneliness.

The evidence bearing upon loneliness in adult populations comes mainly from two surveys by questionnaire. One is the *Psychology Today* study, which was previously described. The other is by Rubenstein *et al.* (1979), which was unusual in that it was specifically concerned with loneliness.

Rubenstein *et al.* (1979) placed questionnaires in an unspecified number of newspapers on the East Coast of the United States and received about 25 000 replies. Only 6% of the respondents said they never experienced loneliness, suggesting that this is a rather common experience; and only 15% indicated they felt lonely most of the time or all of the time, which did not seem an extraordinary percentage when compared to the contentions that loneliness characterizes the US population (Gordon, 1976; Packard, 1972), though it certainly indicates a prevalent human problem.

One of the major findings of the survey was that loneliness was most common among adolescents and young adults and that it appeared to decrease in frequency with increasing age. This decrease was evident even among adults who were 70 or more years old. Rubenstein *et al.* (1979) explained this trend by hypothesizing that expectations about social inter-actions tend to be more pronounced and demanding, and thus discrepancies between what is desired and what exists are greater among younger than older age groups. With increasing age, they speculated, people either achieve the social relationships they desire or become reconciled to the ones they have. Another hypothesis, in view of the relationship between loneliness and physical well-being, is that with increasing age fewer lonely people survive or have the vitality and hopefulness to complete loneliness questionnaires. Evidence bearing upon any of these hypotheses is notable by its absence.

Although Rubenstein *et al.* (1979) found some relationships between lone-liness and demographic variables — lonely people tend to be more frequently found in the unemployed, the less educated, and the less well-to-do — they were most impressed by the phenomenal aspects related to this experience. Loneliness, they believed, is determined less by actual circumstances than it is by how people perceive those circumstances. Thus they discovered that those who move frequently are no more likely to feel lonely than those who are stable, and both groups appear to have about as many friends; this was also Packard's (1972) unexpected finding. Furthermore, people who had few friends might not be troubled by loneliness and people who had many friends might complain of frequent bouts with this feeling. The quality of relation-ships, they suspected, might have something to do with explaining this puzzling result; in this connection, the classification of friendly relations as associative, reciprocal, and receptive should be helpful.

The *Psychology Today* survey (Parlee, 1979) yielded results very much in agreement with the above. A majority of respondents, about 67% of both males and females, reported they felt lonely "often" or "sometimes". The complaints about loneliness decreased in frequency with age, and were more prevalent among those with lower incomes and the unmarried. Again, the phenomenal nature of loneliness and friendship was indicated by the finding that 97% of the respondents claimed to have friends that they did not often see, a result that challenges the validity of the stipulation that interpersonal contacts are a necessary condition for the maintenance of friendship (Wright, 1978).

In a previously unpublished study by the author of this chapter, 70 college undergraduates were given a friendship questionnaire and Rotter's measure of internal-external locus of control (I-E) (Phares, 1976). Rotter (1975) suggested that I-E differences would not be found in situations that are clearly defined and not ambiguous. If so, friendship would appear to be a clearly defined domain since no relationship was found between I-E scores and responses to the questionnaire.

To the question of how they would respond to being without friends, 10 internals indicated they would have an emotional response and 25 indicated they would simply try to make new friends; the corresponding figures for externals were 11 and 24. There was no significant difference between externals and internals in the frequency with which they claimed to experience loneliness. About one half of each group claimed to experience loneliness occasionally, about one quarter rarely, and about one quarter almost every day.

To a question of how they would relieve loneliness, 21 externals first mentioned trying to contact someone else, one said she would cry, and 13 stated they would engage in some solitary activity; for the internals, 20 first mentioned contacting others and 15 first mentioned doing something on their own. About half of each group expected to lose some of their close friends during their young adult years, and both groups employed outcome formulations of attribution (Miller and Arkowitz, 1977), that is, they attributed their success in keeping friends to their own efforts and attributed their losses of friends to external factors. Specifically, 31 internals and 30 externals attributed their success in keeping friends to their own actions or personality characteristics, such as trust and loyalty. In explaining why they expected to lose friends, 22 internals and 24 externals attributed losses to external factors, such as, "they'll move away," "those things just happen". This study indicated that young adults have definite opinions and expectations about friendship, which are unrelated to internal-external attributions as measured by Rotter's I–E Scale, but which are related to outcome formulations of attribution.

Summary

The scientific study of friendship in adulthood is in its infancy and consists largely of descriptive data derived from questionnaires and interviews with samples of unrepresentative adults. There are no normative data and limited information which would enable statistical and cross-cultural comparisons.

Many of the frequently expressed beliefs and opinions about adult friendships have received no support when they have been subjected to study. Though it is difficult to know what to make of these failures to support hypotheses, given the limitations of the studies, they at least conclusively demonstrate that loneliness and social isolation are not necessary correlates of advancing age, that mobility no more precludes friendships than stability assures them, and that the numbers of friends and the patterns of friendships among adults is quite diverse.

A number of intriguing findings have emerged, such as the differences between male and female friendships; and a number of suggestions have been offered for research and for improving the research in friendly relations, with the most pressing, in this reviewer's opinion, being the definition of friend.

CHAPTER 10
Friendship in Old Age

Sheila M. Chown

In the study of friendship in old age one is faced with some especially tantaliz-
ing problems, due in part to general features of research practice in the field
of personal relationships and in part to characteristic features of old age.
Those problems of definition of terms that afflict personal relationship
research in general are particularly troublesome in research on friendship in
old age since many but not all functions of "friends" tend to be performed by
relatives, as we shall see. Equally, many functions of friendship that depend
on mobility and frequent contact begin to become difficult or impossible for
persons of increasing age.

Many questions are raised for the gerontologist by any, even very brief,
attempt to describe the forms and functions of friendship, but the available
research does not even start to answer most of them. Reasons for this are, in
part, to be found in the special nature of the subjects of study. It is not easy to
obtain complicated information from very elderly people; information about
development of friendships is often regarded, especially by older people, as
private; memory is notoriously faulty, so that retrospective investigation may
simply provide most unreliable results. One other reason, however, is that
investigators have been more interested in the social condition of the elderly
than in the investigation of friendship *per se*.

One particularly intriguing issue in the available research concerns its general applicability, given the untypical historical circumstances surrounding the populations studied, which are almost exclusively residents in the USA. For example, as personality test norms show, America is an extravert culture compared with Britain. It has a tradition of geographical and social mobility, of greeting strangers and "first-naming" them at once. While there are many Americans who happen to have lived for most of their lives in one locality and many who have strong ties with their family or neighbourhood group, they do not expect their children to stay in the same place after them. It is not regarded as a hardship to have to move to a new area. Many of the elderly have themselves been immigrants or are the children of immigrants and few have the traditional European expectation of preserving friends from cradle or schooldays to grave. One might expect that in a less mobile society friendship formation would be slower, that more emphasis would be placed upon tried and tested friendship and that keeping up friendships during separations would be considered more important and worthwhile.

The predominant questions in the American research on friendship in the old so far have concentrated on the number of social contacts, the number of friends, and whether the person has any really close friends with whom confidential matters are discussed. Yet there are at least three distinct dimensions to the term "friendship" and their inter-relationship is by no means self evident in this context. These are frequency versus infrequency of contacts, transience versus long-term acquaintance, and superficiality versus depth of feeling about the other person. The last of these gets nearest the emotional core of friendship, but it appears in the literature only by inference, approached tangentially by enquiries as to who, if anyone, acts as a confidant to the old person. The length of friendship among the elderly has been ignored as a research variable, yet it may be very important since shared past experiences are likely to make bonds which are irreplaceable by links with newcomers. It seems at least plausible that one important feature of the change that takes place in friendship with increasing age may be a shift in emphasis among these three features of friendship.

Friendship may be presumed to provide benefits and obligations and some of these might well obtain whether the friend were to be physically present or in contact by telephone or letter. However, research on friendship in the old sheds little light on such matters. At its most superficial level, friendship gives opportunities for social interaction and amusement, shading over into serious discussions and exchanges of views. Face-to-face meetings are likely to be rather better than letters and telephone calls in satisfying this function of friendship. Friendship is also demonstrated by the giving or receiving of help; shopping, child-minding, gardening, helping with repairs and exchanging useful information are but a few examples of activities which friends often undertake and which might in other circumstances be carried out by members of an extended family or by paid help. Again, for many such exchanges, a friend must be physically present. A third activity of friendship is that of reminiscence. Reminiscers wish to keep the past vivid and do so by recalling shared experiences — a possibility only for long-term friends. This, though more easily accomplished in direct conversation, is not impossible by letter or by telephone. Perhaps the most central expression of friendship is the provision of emotional support. This is often accomplished by the exchange of confidences and giving or receiving personal advice or comfort. There is often a Rogerian element of unconditional positive regard between such friends which helps each to feel that they matter deeply to someone else. Physical presence makes this easier — but it is certainly not an essential to continuing an established relationship. The deeper the expression of friendship being undertaken, the more possible it would seem to substitute some communication at a distance; though whether this is as effective as physical presence remains a question for future research. Research workers, I believe, have attempted to avoid going into the functions of friendship, and concentrated merely upon the amount of social interaction, because most functions are more readily fulfilled by face-to-face interaction — and so the dubious assumption is implicitly made that amount of interaction provides a crude estimate of total friendship experienced.

If the activities of friendship are regarded as the variables for study, then anyone taking part in those activities can be called a friend. The literature on friendship in the old varies as to whether it limits its enquiries to non-relatives or whether it includes all social contacts. There is some evidence that family members are important sources of social interaction and of emotional support for the elderly, and omitting them from an investigation may give a false picture of the social situation of old people. Loss of relatives may in fact alter the friendship situation of the bereaved very considerably. Yet a distinction does need to be noted in case the old themselves have different expectations about the friendship activities of their friends and their relatives.

Problems Faced by the Elderly in Forming or Maintaining Friendships

Is old age any different from earlier times of life as far as friendship is concerned? Possibly so, because for friendship to develop there must be opportunities for social interaction and these tend to diminish with age.

Barker and Barker (1961) showed empirically that the number of social settings to which older people had access was low, in America and Britain, compared with those available to younger people. There are several reasons for this. *Retirement* from paid work is an obvious contributor; e.g., Booth and Hess (1974) point out that working together at a similar level is a useful source of friendships. *Illness* is another contributory factor. Many chronic conditions associated with old age such as rheumatism, bronchitis, and circulatory problems, result in lessened physical mobility, lowered ability to use public transport and decreased likelihood of driving a private car. Less specific ill health depletes general energy so that the chores of living take a greater proportion of time and leave the person unwilling or too weary to face "social" relaxation. Voluntary work is often given up as it becomes too much for the person doing it. Hearing losses occur, making social interaction difficult and reducing the pleasure of social occasions. A further reason is that as physical incapacity increases, elderly people are likely to *move house*, either to live with relatives or to accommodation more suited to their current needs, and very often such a move increases their physical distance from existing friends without providing opportunities to meet congenial substitutes. Even if an old person does stay in the same house or locality, many of his or her friends may well move away.

Finally, *bereavement* becomes a common occurrence in old age, reducing the actual number of living friends even for the physically well-preserved older person. The commonness of bereavement is illustrated by the figures for widowhood in the 75-plus age group in America — 70% of the women and 30% of the men have lost their spouse (Brotman, 1973). Since peers are all likely to be affected in one or more of these ways, the amount of interaction with current friends is highly likely to lessen, and the possibility of making new friends to decrease.

There is a school of thought which believes that lessened sociability is an intrinsic part of the aging process. Cumming and Henry (1961) suggested that, with age, "disengagement" sets in. They thought that people become by choice less interested in current issues, less involved in social activities, and more content to withdraw into themselves and contemplate the meaning of their lives by themselves. Their evidence was drawn from interview data in an American city, which showed that older people did interact less with others, and at a less involved level, than when they were middle-aged. On the other hand, later work (Lowenthal and Boler, 1965) showed that the cutting down of interactions was in many (though not all) cases forced on people by circumstances, and Carp (1968) showed that when disengagement does occur it is very selective, with less-preferred activities being abandoned first. For most people then, if not for all, disengagement is probably more a matter of deciding how to spend reduced energy rather than of having a real wish for fewer social interactions.

A further cause of a drop in social interaction with old age may have to do with the matter of reciprocity in friendship, which may be much harder for the old to achieve (Down, 1975). Friends may find that the "costs" of helping elderly friends are so great that they withdraw from the friendship, while the elderly person may feel so "in debt" to someone for help received that ending the friendship may seem preferable to the discomfort of the debt.

In a mobile society, members of younger age groups too are likely to find that they lose contact with many of their friends over the years; but they are not so handicapped by physical limitations and low energy when it comes to making new contacts, and they usually have ready-made a number of social settings, such as work groups, and parent-teacher associations which are not open to the old. Moreover, they are able to repay others for help received by giving similar or equivalent help in their turn, and can therefore maintain a feeling of equality in their relationships.

The Occurrence of Friendship in the Elderly

Attempts to measure the amount of social interaction in the elderly have concentrated on asking the old themselves to estimate the amount of their current interaction and also to compare that figure with the amount of social interaction they experienced when they were 45 years old. A ratio score of this kind has the advantage that it takes account of lifelong individual differences in sociability and concentrates upon the extent of remembered change in interaction.

It is, however, a very crude measure, not least because of its dependence upon the memory of the old person for what their life was like at age 45, and also because it fails to take into account anything about the quality of the interactions.

Typically, such interaction ratios fall off somewhat with age (Cumming and Henry, 1961), but with quite big individual differences in the extent of the fall off (Carp, 1968, 1974; Zborowski and Eyde, 1962). Disengagement theory (Cumming and Henry, 1961) was put forward to describe the process of voluntary withdrawal where this occurs. However, the development of complete social isolation appears to be comparatively rare. Pfeiffer (1977) recorded it in 9% of his North Carolina sample aged 65 and over, and he related it to a failure to develop any new relationships to replace lost ones.

The American elderly prefer existing friends to the prospect of having to make new ones. Langford (1962) noted that old people with social ties in a given neighbourhood were reluctant to move; and that the smaller the community the greater the proportion of friends who lived locally. Niebanck (1965) found that among elderly people who had been relocated to new areas from old urban areas, the most dissatisfied were those who had had, in the area that they had left, many friends with whom they were not able any more to keep in touch.

There are also social constraints to be considered. The American results show that friends tend to be similar with respect to age, sex, marital and social status. Retired people in particular seem to have most of their friends among their own age groups. Bultena (1968) found this in six Wisconsin towns of varying size, whilst Rose (1962) found that such age segregation became more marked after retirement, and that the elderly started to see the young as an "out-group" and those of their own age as an "in-group".

Blau (1961) compared patterns of friendship among the elderly in an area within New York City and in a small community outside the city. Overall, she noted, the total number of friends declined in old age; but this partly depended upon the closeness of the match between the individual's marital state and employment circumstances with those of the neighbours. A widow or widower, or a retired person, in an area full of married working people, suffered great loss of social life but did not do so where those around were also unmarried and retired. On the other hand, married or employed people tended to be ostracized in a district full of widowed, retired people.

There is a traditional pattern of relationships whereby married couples are friendly with married couples (Babchuk and Bates, 1963), although this friendship is quite often at only a superficial level. There is a strong tendency for husbands to be the leaders in initiating the friendships. Cross-sex friendships with other people are rare among the married (Booth, 1972). Thus the widowed person cannot easily be fitted into this pattern; nor the married couple into the pattern of widowed friendships.

Cross-sex friendships continue to be rare even among single and widowed elderly people; partly due to the shortage of men, no doubt, such friendships are more common for men than for women. Men are in fact much more likely to marry in old age than are women. For example, Cleveland and Giaturco (1976) found in North Carolina that 25% of men widowed after 65 remarried but only 5% of women did; and Treas and Van Hilst (1976) found for the USA as a whole that 1.7% of older single men married for the first time compared with only 0.03% of older women.

Nevertheless, it is common to find that elderly women have more friends outside the family than have elderly men (Itzin, 1970; Atchley, 1972; Booth, 1972), although occasionally results in the other direction are found (Powers and Bultena, 1976). Such factors as urban–rural populations and ease–difficulty of transport may play a part in these differences in results.

Booth (1972) noted in his sample, which was aged from 45 upwards, that women claimed more close kin relations than men and that friendship and kinship claims were positively correlated, suggesting that personal style plays a part in determining the number of a person's social relationships.

The existence of close friendships has been enquired into by several researchers. Arth (1962) found in several small samples of elderly men and women that close friendship was regarded as rare and that relatives were thought more likely than friends to be really interested in what happened to people. Booth (1972) reported a bias in his Nebraska sample towards more females than males having a confidant (53% versus 39%), which is very similar to the results of Powers and Bultena (1976) working in rural Iowa where 59 per cent of females and 41 per cent of males claimed to have a confidant. They also reported a marginally greater claim by women than men to have had a close friend or confidant at some time in the past (70% versus 68%). These intimate friends were usually of similar age and same sex as the respondent and in a third of the cases were relatives.

The development of friendship

On the question of how friendships are formed and how they develop, investigation has largely been confined to demographic and sociological variables. Getting to know other retired people seems best accomplished during informal interaction. Aldridge (1959) showed that, in a retirement community, although about half the inhabitants took part in formal activities, social cliques grew up as a result of informal activities.

This reflects the fact that physical proximity is the most important single variable in the determination of friendships in the elderly — but, as it is an important variable for young persons, too, this finding is not surprising (Festinger et al., 1950). Rosow (1967) has shown how the old people living in their own apartments in the community had more or fewer friends depending upon the number of elderly people living in the same apartment block. Lawton (1977) summarizing what is known of proximity effects pointed out that about 60% of the old claim to have friends, that these friends normally live nearby, and that these people usually see the friends frequently. Those claiming to have friends often live nearer to them, and see them more often, than they see their own offspring. Friendships between people of different ages, races or sex have been found to occur most often when people live in apartments very near to each other (Nahemow and Lawton, 1975). However, the effects of proximity and age-density seem more important among working class than middle class people (Rosow, 1967; Rosenberg, 1970), and it is possible that this may be bound up with the availability of private transport.

Where the environment is a specialized one, such as a retirement community or sheltered housing, the amount of social interaction goes up compared with that in an ordinary community (Messer, 1967; Carp, 1966, 1974;

Sherman, 1975b). This, it seems from Carp's study, is an actual change and not just a difference between different groups of people. Bultena (1969) found that in several retirement communities, proximity and to a lesser extent previous occupation seemed to determine friendship choices.

When people move into sheltered housing or institutions, proximity also seems to be a prime factor in determining with whom they will become friendly (Lawton and Simon, 1968; Friedman, 1966). However, factors of current social status also enter the equation. Thus in Moosehaven, Burgess (1954) found that a person's present status in the community influenced the extent of his social relationships — and present status was influenced by the visibility and usefulness of the way he spent his time. In a different old age home Friedman (1967) found that age and length of time in the institution influenced status and that people named those of similar status to themselves as friends.

Of course there is an element of personality at work in friendship choices, too. Davis (1962) analysed such choices obtained from institutional residents so that he was able to compare a group of popular residents with a group of unpopular ones. Not surprisingly the popular people were more contented and more positive in their outlook and had higher feelings of self-worth. (This could be a chicken and egg problem, but it agrees with personality characteristics of "stars" of sociograms obtained in studies on adolescents in which it usually seems to be the case that the personality characteristics predate the social success in the young people being studied.)

There does not seem to have been work charting the psychological development of friendships among the elderly. While Babchuk and Bates (1963) found many middle-aged couples' friendships remained superficial even when long-lasting, the actual development of the "confidant" relationship is still shrouded in mystery.

Exchange of goods and services

Little direct research appears to have been reported on exchanges of goods and services between aged friends, although investigators in the 1950s and 1960s showed that about 70% of families expected to help their aged members should need arise (Smith, 1954; Rosow, 1967). A series of papers by Albrecht (1953, 1954a, 1954b) found that, of a "grandparent generation", 85% claimed to have close interaction with their adult children, and 14% were in fact still giving rather than receiving help. Family members, then, could be seen as building up expectations of reciprocity for help obtained in the past.

There is some British evidence as to what happens in practice. Abrams

(1980) found that a third of his British sample aged 75 or above had no living children to provide them with help. Of those people in the sample who had some degree of difficulty with personal care, only just over one-quarter received any help. The help came from family members in two-thirds of the cases, and social workers, friends and neighbours provided the other third. The rest of the handicapped elderly had to manage for themselves. These were very often people living on their own. Such tasks as shopping and cooking attracted slightly more help, and this was nearly as often given by friends and neighbours as by family members.

In America, too, it seems that help between neighbours and friends does occur though it is by no means "expected". Sherman (1975a) showed that in the retirement housing she studied, some sites seemed to have a better record than others for neighbourly help; and that the help on some sites was greater and on other sites less than that given to her control group of old people living in ordinary housing. At the level of the individual she found big differences and these were extremely interesting. Some people received a great deal of assistance and others very little. The help came from both children of the elderly and neighbours in a positively correlated way. Old people who had no children received (and gave) least help. Such results suggest that some people grow to expect to be, and do remain, independent, while others expect to and do elicit help.

Does friendship matter?

Mitchell (1972), writing about retirement as a lay person, concluded that "health, income and friends, in that order of importance" led to a happy retirement (and he could have just as well written, to a happy old age). Many empirical results could be quoted to back up his statement. For example, Lebo (1953) found that people who claimed to be happier in their old age than they were before they became 60 had more close friends than did people who claimed to be less happy after 60 than they had been earlier; and Edwards and Klemmach (1973) found that the best predictors of high satisfaction with life in the second half of it was the number of informal social contacts with friends together with high socioeconomic class and good health. (Age itself was not a predictor.)

The exact type of social interaction found to be important has varied from study to study. Phillips (1969) reported that current happiness throughout adulthood was closely related to each of three separate measures of social participation — amounts of contact with friends, with neighbours, and with voluntary organizations. In contrast, Lemon et al., (1972) working within a middle-class retirement community of married people reported that satisfaction with their lives was positively correlated with current social activity with friends (but not with the amounts of interaction with neighbours, relatives or formal organizations). Bull and Aucoin (1975) also found that participation in voluntary organizations was a very weak predictor of life satisfaction. To complicate matters further, Graney (1975) carried out a four-year longitudinal study of 60 elderly women in which, at the beginning of the period, happiness was associated with amount of visiting of friends, relatives and neighbours, taking part in religious activities, attending various associations, and belonging to the associations. Over the four years, increments in visiting neighbours, attending associations and membership of associations all correlated with increases in assessments of happiness. Palmore and Kivett (1977) found that the best predictors of satisfaction with life after a four-year time interval were health at the beginning of that time and total amount of social activity. On the other hand, it has to be said that Palmore and Luikart (1972) found that health, organizational activity and belief that they could control their own lives (i.e. internal locus of control) related to satisfaction with life, but that such satisfaction did not relate to a measure of "total social contacts". Thus, there is some lack of concordance about the exact type of social interaction which leads to happiness or satisfaction with life, yet in nearly all studies some form of measure of it turns out to be a useful predictor, and this has particularly been the case when the emphasis has been on informal social activity.

In institutional settings a high degree of social involvement has been found to relate to high self-esteem (Anderson, 1967), positive mood-tone (Kahana and Coe, 1969), and not *feeling* old (Bell, 1967). Clearly, social involvement is a sign of the person having fitted in and found a successful niche in the particular environment. Marlowe's (1973) study of the effects of relocation of people in American state hospitals found that two factors influenced the well-being of the patients. One was the extent to which they were given some responsibility and opportunity for self-determination, and the other was the amount of social contact the person had. Thus, enforced or authoritarian sociability is not the answer — what is needed is provision of opportunities to be sociable, and then freedom for people to choose for themselves whether to be sociable or not.

Another way of examining the importance of friendship is to look at the state of those people who have very few or no social contacts and no deep friendships. When such social isolation has been a long-standing life pattern it may have very different effects from those associated with sudden isolation in old age.

Lowenthal (1964) has described how the mentally ill who are old tend also to be socially isolated (though she believes this is a result rather than a cause of the illness). She found that isolation can be a lifelong pattern, and in that case it did not seem to carry with it the same seeds of despair as for people not used to such isolation. The always-isolated people did not claim to be lonely. It has to be remembered that isolation can be used as a bulwark against interference with privacy and independence. Garside *et al.*, (1965) reported that in Newcastle-upon-Tyne, England, certain aggressive isolates were able to go on living in the community long after their mental and physical condition would have brought more accessible and compliant people into sheltered housing or geriatric care. Stephens (1975) recorded the reactions of the inhabitants of one large hotel for elderly people where most seemed to be suspicious and grudging about interpersonal relationships. It seemed as though they had chosen the way of life which suited their own personalities; and they were distrustful of friendly overtures because they would not have made any themselves without ulterior motive. This particular group did not seem to be depressed, though social isolation is more usually found to bring with it low morale (Rosow, 1968) and feelings of depression (Ellison, 1969). Surrounding such isolated individuals with people without providing a bridge for contact with those people was found to enhance their depression (Rosow, 1968). Munnichs (1964) reported that those people in Holland who felt lonely were in fact all socially neglected — though such neglect might not be the only factor contributing to loneliness. (Incidentally, it should be mentioned that Dean (1962) maintained that elderly men used "loneliness" to indicate that there was absence of activity, rather than absence of people; and she thought this backed up the theory of disengagement with which she is associated. However, such a change in the meaning of the word has not been reported by anyone else.)

In Britain today, 29% of 65- to 74-year-olds and the high figure of 47% of those aged 75 or more live alone (Abrams, 1978a, b). Abrams found that 23% of his total sample often felt depressed or very unhappy and 15% said they were often very lonely. Numerically, then, the problem of loneliness is a very large one and presents a practical reason for research interest.

A third approach to examining the effects of friendship upon the enjoyment of life is to look at those who have confiding relationships with at least one other person. In general, the possession of a confidant was found by Lowenthal and Haven (1968) to act as a buffer against social losses, and in particular to aid people through serious crises such as bereavement and retirement. The buffering effect of a confidant in cases of bereavement was noted also by Fromm–Reichman (1959). Schooler (1975) found that having a confidant helped people who were forced to move to a different social environment; morale was far less affected for those who had someone to confide in about their worries and problems. Payne's (1953) work on the effects of a wife's welcome or dislike of a man's retirement on his adjustment to it provides further evidence of the supportive role which an understanding companion can play.

Married couples rarely admitted to having confidants apart from each other (Babchuk and Bates, 1963); they often named each other, and especially husbands named wives (Lowenthal and Haven, 1968). Pineo (1961) noted that many married couples ceased to confide in each other during a long marriage; within the social conventions it may not be possible for such people to find a substitute confidant. However, Cumming and Schneider (1961) and Marney (1975) found that kinship relationships often became important to older people. Especially important were sibling relationships. These could come to matter more in terms of "closeness" than those between husbands and wives — and of course they are conventionally allowable. It was particularly sisters who mattered as confidantes. The importance of sisters in providing emotional support to both elderly men and women was also noted by Cicirelli (1977) in a study using special TAT pictures.

In these studies, the role of confidant was variously filled by a spouse, a sibling, an adult child or a friend of the same sex and age as the elderly person. It looks as though the choice of a confidant depends upon who is available, who seems trustable and is willing to undertake the role; but practically nothing is known of the process whereby confiding develops.

It is quite clear from the literature that friendship matters for morale and is related to satisfaction with life (except perhaps in those people who have had a lifelong history of isolation). Moreover, close, confiding relationships appear to offer some protection against and aid resilience to social losses and personal crises. This aspect of friendship in the elderly, far from being a peripheral topic for psychologists, seems to be one that, from many points of view, merits far more detailed study.

Friendship In The Elderly Compared To Other Age-groups

The study of friendship in the elderly has had a practical focus. The tendency has been to look at social activity to see how many people there are who think they have enough friends, and how many there are without any or with too few. The demographic, social and situational characteristics of those with friends and those without have been examined with a view to improving the lot of the friendless by manipulating those characteristics which prove relevant (e.g. as proximity is an important element and as "like calls to like" then one may be tempted to conclude that age-segregated housing for the elderly would be a sensible system to support). The further argument underlying this approach has been that high social activity can be shown to correlate well with high morale (e.g. Maddox, 1965); so an increase in the number of people with high social activity can be expected to lead to an increase in the number of people with high morale. This is a crude argument which ignores the extent to which the social activity of each individual satisfies his needs with respect to the functions of friendship, and fails to take into account his own evaluation of the worth to himself of his social interactions. Nevertheless, Carp's (1966) study of the effect of Victoria Plaza on the social life and happiness of its inmates is a demonstration that it can and does work. However, another way to describe this approach to the study of friendship is to say that there has been very little recourse to psychological concepts and variables; it has been a sociological approach.

Work on interpersonal attraction in other, usually student, age groups, has begun from a very different standpoint. It has used personal liking as the ultimate variable and has sought to examine what matching of characteristics, ideational constructs, attitudes and personality attributes in the liker and the liked lead to liking. The approach has ranged from practical (arranging dates and seeing how people get on together) to abstract (specially prepared similar-other and dissimilar-other attitude profiles for the subject to rate for attractiveness). There has been more intellectual and theoretical curiosity in this approach, and far less inclination to attempt to alter or interfere with personal life styles. The variables studied are harder to get at, harder to assess, and would be harder to use as a basis for "segregation". It is more to be compared with picking suitable donors and recipients for transplant surgery; whereas the social gerontologists would throw people together who have some background characteristics in common and hope that a few "grafts" would then occur naturally. (Presumably those few "grafts" would have been the selected pairs had they had interpersonal-attraction methods applied to them.)

The topic of friendship in elderly people is still very much in need of psychological study, and people interested in interpersonal attraction could with benefit specialize in it because there are practical reasons for supporting such study. Alternatively, those working with younger subjects might take a leaf from the gerontologists' book and pay some attention to the demographic background of their own subjects. It would be interesting to have some more information about numbers of friends, frequency of meetings and existence of confidants among young adults.

Future Directions for Research on Friendship in the Elderly

As the above review makes clear, work on friendship in the elderly needs expanding, and there would seem to be four major themes for exploration.

1. Cross-cultural research. The American findings on proximity and similarity should be used as a starting point for research in other societies. Do similar results hold good? Does cultural background influence people's expectations about the possible roles and functions of friendship? Do the aged from different cultures place different emphases upon age-similarity sex-similarity and similarity of psychological structure in their friends? Is proximity as overwhelming an influence in other societies as it is in America? Is friendship at a distance possible in one culture rather than another?

2. Work on functions of friendship and roles of friends. In all age groups attention should be given to the relative importance of the social, exchanging, experience-sharing and supportive aspects of friendship. The parts played by relatives as friends and non-kin friends should be further investigated. Studies are required to examine relationships between different levels of friendship, for example to see whether superficial levels have to precede deeper ones, to see whether length of friendship is an important prerequisite for deep friendship or whether perhaps some particular aspect of individual experience or personality is more important.

3. Age-group comparisons. The interpersonal attraction work with young adults could usefully be extended into the realms of gerontology — though some of the methods used might have to be simplified and made rather less abstract. Age group comparisons would be helpful in examining friendship behaviours. Do old and young people see themselves as giving and receiving the same sorts of thing in friendship? If so — or if not — does friendship between people of different ages present any special difficulties or any special characteristics? What are the "rewards" and "costs" of friendship with the very elderly, compared with those for young people?

4. The development of friendship. How do friendships develop for elderly persons, and for those in other age groups too? Where are potential friends first met, and what sort of contacts take place? For old people, can new friends replace old ones? Particularly from the gerontologists' point of view, the development of confiding relationships would repay study, to understand who is chosen as a confidant and why and in what circumstances. Jourard's (1971) work on self-disclosure might suggest that reciprocity would be involved, for example. The development of practical helping relationships also calls for more study; for example, whether help is received according to "need" or whether as in Sherman's (1975a) American study some people attract extra help even though they have help available, and others who need help do not get any. If this were found to hold in general, the question arises as to what makes the helped person attract that help.

While a start could usefully be made in almost any one of these four areas, the most important for gerontology would, in my opinion, involve an examination of the functions of friendship and the roles of friends. This is such a central topic, yet has been neglected by gerontologists and has not come within the purview of those interested in interpersonal attraction.

Summary

Friendship is defined in this paper as covering the wide spectrum of relationships from that of enjoyable colleague to one where such deep feelings exist that each person would put the welfare of the other above his own.

In considering friendship at least three dimensions would seem pertinent: the frequency of contact; length of time for which the person has been known; and superficiality or depth of the relationship. The first of these has been used as a measure in many studies of ageing, but the third is the one nearest the essence of friendship. Friendship activities to be investigated encompass social relaxation, exchanging goods and services, remembering the past and providing emotional support through confiding behaviour. Little distinction has been drawn between these in the literature, except for some separate enquiry into "confidants".

Most research has been American, and generalizations from existing results to cultures very different from the American pattern need caution. Most investigators have used very simple questions about the number of social contacts and frequency of interaction without exploring types of interaction, or the development of interaction.

Findings are that the number of social contacts decreases with age but there are individual differences in the extent of the decrease when it is entirely a matter of choice rather than induced by circumstances. Elderly women, according to most results, have more friends outside the family than have elderly men; and they are more likely to have a confidant. Influences on the formation of friendship seem to be physical proximity, similarity of circumstances, age, and sex, and opportunities for meeting informally. Friendly people with high self-esteem attract others to them. Little has been done on the exchange of goods and services in old-age friendships; relatives seem more likely than non-kin friends to provide help.

Friendships and social interaction are usually found to go with high morale and satisfaction with life; when people become socially isolated they become depressed. Having someone to confide in turns out to be of central importance in old age; it allows people to withstand much better the crises they have to face. Confidants are often sisters, or daughters, or friends of similar age and sex to the old person.

Whereas work on friendship in the elderly has concentrated upon demographic and sociological influences, interpersonal attraction research with young adults has looked in much more detail at psychological variables influencing liking. The gerontologists could with advantage look at some psychological variables. Directions for future work would seem to be four in number. Work on the functions of friendship and roles of friends should be undertaken. Cross-cultural comparisons are needed to confirm or amplify the American work. Comparisons between age groups of friendship functions and roles and psychological variables are needed. Last but not least, there is a need to study the growth of individual friendships, particularly of the way that confiding relationships develop.

References

ABRAMS, M. (1978a). The future of the old. Paper delivered at the meeting of the British Association for the Advancement of Science, September, 1978.

ABRAMS, M. (1978b). "Beyond Three Score Years and Ten, A First Report", Age Concern, London.

ABRAMS, M. (1980). "Beyond Three Score Years and Ten, A Second Report", Age Concern, London.

ADAMS, B.N. (1970). Isolation, function, and beyond: American kinship in the 1960s. *J. Marriage Family* **32**, 575-597.

ADAMS, H. (1931). "The Education of Henry Adams", Modern Library, New York.

ADLER, J. and CAREY, J. (1980). The science of love. *Newsweek* **95**, 49-50.

AINSWORTH, M.D.S. (1977). Social development in the first year of life: Maternal influences on infant-mother attachment. *In* "Development in Psychiatric Research", (Ed. J.M. Tanner), Hodder and Stoughton, London.

AINSWORTH, M.D.S., Bell, S.M. and STAYTON, D.J. (1974). Infant-mother attachment and social development. *In* "The Integration of a Child into a Social World", (Ed. M.P.M. Richards), Cambridge University Press, Cambridge.

ALBRECHT, R. (1953). Relationship of older people with their own parents. *Marriage Family Living* **15**, 296-298.

ALBRECHT, R. (1954a). The parental responsibilities of grandparents. *Marriage Family Living* **16**, 201-204.

ALBRECHT, R. (1954b). Relationship of older parents with their children. *Marriage Family Living* **16**, 32-35.

ALDRIDGE, G. (1959). Informal social relationships in a retirement community. *Marriage Family Living* **21**, 70-72.

ALLAN, G. (1977). Class variation in friendship patterns. *Br. J. Sociol.* **28**, 389-393.

ALTMAN, I. (1973). Reciprocity of interpersonal exchange. *J. Theory Soc. Behav.* **3**, 249-261.

ALTMAN, I. (1975). "The Environment and Social Behavior", Brooks/Cole, Monterey, California.

ALTMAN, I. and TAYLOR, D.A. (1973). "Social Penetration: The Development of Interpersonal Relationships", Holt, Rhinehart and Winston, New York.

247

ANDERSON, N.E. (1967). Effects of institutionalization on self esteem. *J. Gerontol.* **22**, 313–317.

ANDERSON, N.H. (1968). Likeability ratings of 555 personality-trait words. *J. Personality Soc. Psychol.* **9**, 272–279.

ANDERSSON, B.E. (1969). "Studies in Adolescent Behaviour", Almquist and Wiksell, Stockholm.

APA MONITOR. (1980). Taming type A's. *APA Monitor* **11**, 8, 33.

ARGYLE, M. (1979). Sequences in social behavior as a function of the situation. *In* "Emerging Strategies in Social Psychological Research", (Ed. G.P. Ginsburg), Wiley, New York.

ARISTOTLE (1952). Nichomachean ethics. *In* "Great Books of the Western World", Vol 9, (Ed. R.M. Hutchins), Encyclopaedia Britannica, Chicago.

ARLING, G. (1976). The elderly widow and her family, neighbors and friends. *J. Marriage Family* **38**, 757–768.

ARTH, M.J. (1962). American culture and the phenomenon of friendship in the aged. *In* "Social and Psychological Aspects of Aging", (Eds C. Tibbitts and W. Donahue), Columbia University Press, New York.

ASHER, S.R. and GOTTMAN, J. (Eds), (1981). "The Development of Friendship", Cambridge University Press, Cambridge.

ASHER, S.R., GOTTMAN, J.M. and ODEN, S.L. (1977). Children's friendships in school settings. *In* "Contemporary Readings in Child Psychology", (Eds E.M. Hetherington and R.D. Park), McGraw-Hill, New York.

ATCHLEY, R. (1972). "Social Forces in Later Life", Wadsworth, Belmont, California.

ATHANASIOU, R., SHAVER, P. and TAVRIS, C. (1970). Sex (A report to *Psychology Today* readers). *Psychology Today* **4**, 39–52.

BABCHUK, N. (1965). Primary friends and kin: a study of the associations of middle-class couples. *Social Forces* **43**, 483–493.

BABCHUK, N. and BATES, A.P. (1963). The primary relations of middle-class couples: A study in male dominance. *Am. Sociolog. Rev.* **28**, 377–384.

BACKMAN, C.W. and SECORD, P.F. (1959). The effect of perceived liking on interpersonal attraction. *Human Relations* **12**, 379–384.

BALDWIN, A.L., KALHORN, J. and BREESE, F.H. (1949). The appraisal of parent behaviour. *Psycholog. Monograph* **299**, 63 No. 4.

BALES, R.F. (1950). "Interaction Process Analysis : A Method for the Study of Small Groups", Addison Wesley, Cambridge, MA.

BALTES, P.B. and GOULET, L.R. (1971). Exploration of development variables by manipulation and simulation of age differences in behavior. *Human Dev.* **14**, 149–170.

BALTES, P.B. and SCHAIE, K.W. (1973). On life-span developmental research paradigms : retrospects and prospects. *In* "Life-span Developmental Psychology: Personality and Socialisation", (Eds P. Baltes and K.W. Schaie), Academic Press, New York and London.

BARENBOIM, C. (1977). Developmental changes in the interpersonal cognitive system from middle childhood to adolescence. *Child Dev.* **48**, 1467–1474.

BARKER, R.G. and WRIGHT, H.F. (1954). "Midwest and its Children: The Psychological Ecology of an American Town", Row Peterson, Evanston.

BARKER, R.R. and BARKER, L.S. (1961). The psychological ecology of old people in Midwest, Kansas, and Yoredale, Yorkshire. *J. Gerontol.* **16**, 144–149.

BARTHOLOMEW, K.L. (1979). Cognitive and social cognitive development as a function of social—emotional adjustment. Unpublished Doctoral Dissertation, Temple University.

BATESON, G., JACKSON, D.D., HALEY, J. and WEAKLAND, J. (1956). Toward a theory of schizophrenia. *Behav. Sci.* **1**, 251–264.

BAUM, M. (1972). Love, marriage, and the division of labor. *In* "Family, Marriage, and the Struggle of the Sexes", (Ed. H.P. Dreitzel), Macmillan, New York.

BAUMRIND, D. (1971). Current patterns of parental authority. *Dev. Psychol. Monographs* **4**, 1–103.

BECKER, J.M.T. (1977). A learning analysis of the development of peer-oriented behavior in nine-month-old infants. *Dev. Psychol.* **13**, 481–491.

BELL, R.Q. (1974). "Contributions of human infants to caregiving and social interaction". *In* "The Effect of the Infant on its Caregiver", (Eds M. Lewis and L. Rosenblum), Wiley, London.

BELL, R.Q. and HARPER, L.V. (1977). "Child Effects on Adults", Erlbaum, Hillsdale, New Jersey.

BELL, T. (1967). The relationship between social involvement and feeling old among residents in homes for the aged. *J. Gerontol.* **22**, 17–22.

BEM, D.J. (1972). Self-perception theory. *In* "Advances in Experimental Social Psychology", (Ed. L. Berkowitz) Vol. 6. Academic Press, New York and London.

BEM, D.J. and ALLEN, A. (1974). On predicting some of the people some of the time: the search for cross-situational consistencies in behavior. *Psycholog. Rev.* **81**, 506–520.

BEM, S.L. (1974). The measurement of psychological androgyny. *J. Consulting Clin. Psychol.* **42**, 155–162.

BENTLER, P.M. and HUBA, G.J. (1979). Simple minitheories of love. *J. Personality Soc. Psychol.* **37**, 124–130.

BENTLER, P.M. and NEWCOMB, M.D. (1978). Longitudinal study of marital success and failure. *J. Consulting Clin. Psychol.* **46**, 1053–1070.

BERKOWITZ, L. and WALSTER, E.H. (Eds), (1976). "Advances in Experimental Social Psychology", Vol. 9, Academic Press, New York and London.

BERMANN, E., and MILLER, D. (1967). The matching of mates. *In* "Cognition, Personality and Clinical Psychology", (Eds R. Jessor and S. Fishback), Jossey-Bass, San Francisco.

BERNARD, J. (1964). The adjustment of married mates. *In* "Handbook of Marriage and the Family", (Ed. H.C. Christensen), Rand McNally, Chicago.

BERNARD, J. (1972). "The Future of Marriage", World Publishers, New York.

BERNSTEIN, B. (1965). A sociolinguistic approach to social learning. *In* Penguin Survey of the Social Services", (Ed. J. Gould), Penguin, Baltimore, Maryland.

BERSCHEID, E. and WALSTER, E. (1978). "Interpersonal Attraction" (2nd edn), Addison- Wesley, Reading, MA.

BIGELOW, B.J. (1977). Children's friendship expectations: a cognitive—developmental study. *Child Dev.* **48**, 246–253.

BIGELOW, B.J. and LA GAIPA, J.J. (1975). Children's written descriptions of friendship: a multidimensional analysis. *Dev. Psychol.* **11**, 857–858.

BIGELOW, B.J. and LA GAIPA, J.J. (1980). The development of friendship values and choice. *In* "Friendship and Social Relations in Children", (Eds H.C. Foot, A.J. Chapman and J.R. Smith), Wiley, Chichester.

BISCHOF, L.J. (1969). "Adult Psychology", Harper and Row, New York.

BLACK, H. and ANGELIS, V.B. (1974). Interpersonal attraction : an empirical investigation of platonic and romantic love. *Psycholog. Reports* **34**, 1243–1246.

BLACK, H. and ANGELIS, V.B. (1975). Sex role differences in the patterning of love among college students. *Psychology* 12, 50-53.

BLAKE, A., STEWART, A. and TURCAN, D. (1975). Parents of babies of very low birth-weight : long term follow-up. *In* "Parent—Infant Interaction. CIBA symposium No. 33." (Ed. M.A. Hoffer) Associated Scientific Publishers, Amsterdam.

BLAU, P.M. (1964). "Exchange and Power in Social Life", Wiley, New York.

BLAU, Z.S. (1961). Structural constraints on friendships in old age. *Am. Sociolog. Rev.* 26, 429-439.

BLUM, C.S. (1964). "Psychoanalytic Theories of Personality", McGraw-Hill, New York.

BLURTON JONES, N., FERREIRA, M.C.R., BROWN, M. and MACDONALD, L. (1979). Aggression, crying and physical contact in one-to-three year-old children. *Aggressive Behav.* 5, 121-133.

BLURTON JONES, N., FERREIRA, M.C., BROWN, M.F. and MACDONALD, L. (in preparation). Language development and mother's response to child vocalisations: influences of child's simultaneous behaviour.

BOLTON, C.D. (1961). Mate selection as the development of a relationship. *Marriage Family Living* 23, 234-340.

BOOTH, A. (1972). Sex and social participation. *Am. Sociolog. Rev.* 37, 183-192.

BOOTH, A. and HESS, E. (1974). Cross-sex friendships. *J. Marriage Family* 36, 38-47.

BOTT, E. (1971). "Family and Social Networks", (2nd edn), Tavistock, London, 1971.

BOWER, T. (1974). Competent newborns. *New Scientist* 14th March, 1974.

BOWLBY, J. (1951). "Maternal Care and Mental Health", World Health Organization, Geneva.

BRAIKER-STAMBUL, H.B. (1975). Stages of courtship: The development of premarital relationships. Unpublished doctoral dissertation, University of California, Los Angeles.

BRAIKER, H.B. and KELLEY, H.H. (1979). Conflict in the development of close relationships. *In* "Social Exchange in Developing Relationships", (Eds R.L. Burgess and T.L. Huston), Academic Press, New York and London.

BRAIN, R. (1976). "Friends and Lovers", Basic Books, New York.

BRAIN, R. (1977). Somebody else should be your own best friend. *Psychol. Today* 11, 83-84, 120, 123.

BRAZELTON, T.B. (1979). Earliest parent—child interactions. *J. National Children's Bureau* Concern No. 33.

BRAZELTON, T.B., TRONICK, E., ADAMSON, L., ALS, H. and WEISE, S. (1975). Early mother—infant reciprocity. *In* "Parent–Infant Interaction. CIBA Foundation Symposium 33" (Ed. M.A. Hoffer), Associated Scientific Publishers, Amsterdam.

BRENNER, M. (1971). Caring, love, and selective memory. *Proc. 79th Annual Convention Am. Psycholog. Assn.* 275-276

BRENTON, M. (1975). "Friendship", Stein and Day, New York.

BRODBECK, A.J. and IRWIN, O.C. (1946). The speech behaviour of infants without families. *Child Dev.* 17, 145.

BRODERICK, C. and WEAVER, J. (1968). The perceptual context of boy—girl communication. *J. Marriage Family* 30, 618-627.

BRONFENBRENNER, U. (1979a). Contexts of child rearing: problems and prospects. *Am. Psychol.* 34, 844-850.

BRONFENBRENNER, U. (1979b). "The Ecology of Human Development: Experiments by Nature and Design", Harvard University Press, Cambridge, MA.

BROTMAN, H.B. (1973). Who are the aging? *In* "Mental Illness in Later Life", (Eds E.W. Busse and E. Pfeiffer), American Psychiatric Association, Washington, D.C.

BROWN, R. (1973). "A First Language", Allen and Unwin, London.

BRYAN, J.H. (1975). Children's cooperation and helping behaviors. *In* "Review of Child Development Research" (Vol. 5), (Eds E.M. Hetherington), The University of Chicago Press, Chicago.

BULL, C.C. and AUCOIN, J.B. (1975). Voluntary association, participation and life satisfaction: a replication note. *J. Gerontol.* **30**, 73-76.

BULTENA, G.L. (1968). Age grading in the social interaction of an elderly male population. *J. Gerontol.* **23**, 539-543.

BULTENA, G.L. (1969). The relationship of occupational status to friendship ties in three planned retirement communities. *J. Gerontol.* **24**, 461-464.

BURCHINAL, L.G. (1964). The premarital dyad and love involvement. *In* "Handbook of Marriage and the Family", (Ed. H.T. Christensen), Rand McNally, Chicago.

BURGESS, E.W. (1926). The romantic impulse and family disorganization. *Survey* **57**, 290-294.

BURGESS, E.W. (1954). Social relations, activities and personal adjustment. *Am. J. Sociol.* **59**, 352-360.

BURGESS, E.W. and COTTRELL, L.S. (1939). "Predicting Success and Failure in Marriage", Prentice-Hall, New York.

BURGESS, E.W. and LOCKE, H.J. (1945). "The Family from Institution to Companionship", American Book Company, New York.

BURGESS, E.W. and LOCKE, H.J. (1960). "The Family from Institution to Companionship", (2nd edn), American Book Company, New York.

BURGESS, E.W., LOCKE, H.J. and THOMES, M.M. (1963). "The Family" (3rd edn), American Book Company, New York.

BURGESS, E.W. and WALLIN, P. (1953). "Engagement and Marriage", Lippincott, Philadelphia.

BURGESS, R.L. and HUSTON, T.L. (Eds) (1979). "Social Exchange in Developing Relationships", Academic Press, New York and London.

BYRNE, D. (1971). "The Attraction Paradigm", Academic Press, New York and London.

BYRNE, D. and CLORE, G.L. (1970). A reinforcement model of evaluative responses. *Personality: An International Journal* **1**, 103-128.

BYRNE, D., ERVIN, C.R. and LAMBERTH, J. (1970). Continuity between the experimental study of attraction and real-life computer dating. *J. Personality Soc. Psychol.* **16**, 157-165.

BYRNE, D. and GRIFFITT, W. (1966). A developmental investigation of the law of attraction. *J. Personality Soc. Psychol.* **4**, 699-702.

BYRNE, D. and NELSON, D. (1965). Attraction as a linear function of proportion of positive reinforcements. *J. Personality Soc. Psychol.* **1**, 659-663.

CALDWELL, M.A. and PEPLAU, L.A. (in press). Sex differences in same-sex friendship. *Sex Roles.*

CAMPBELL, A., CONVERSE, P.E. and RODGERS, W.L. (1976). "The Quality of American Life: Perceptions, Evaluations, and Satisfactions", Russell Sage Foundation, New York.

CAMPBELL, D.T. and STANLEY, J.C. (1963). "Experimental and Quasi-experimental Designs for Research'', Rand-McNally, Chicago.

CARP, F.M. (1966). ''A Future for the Aged'', University of Texas Press, Austin, Texas.

CARP, F.M. (1968). Some components of disengagement. *J. Gerontol.* **23**, 382–386.

CARP, F.M. (1974). Short term and long term prediction of adjustment to a new environment. *J. Gerontol.* **29**, 44–453.

CARSON, R.C. (1979). Personality and exchange in developing relationships. *In* ''Social Exchange in Developing Relationships'', (Eds R.L. Burgess and T.L. Huston), Academic Press, New York and London.

CARTER, L.F., HAYTHORN, W., MEIROWITZ, B. and LANZETTA, J. (1951). The relation of categorisations and ratings in the observation of group behaviour. *Human Relations* **4**, 239–254.

CASLER, L. (1969). This thing called love is pathological. *Psychol. Today* **3**, 18–20, 74–76.

CATE, R. and HUSTON, T.L. (in press). Premarital relationships: toward a typology of pathways to marriage.

CAVAN, R.S., BURGESS, E.W., HAVIGHURST, R.J. and GOLDHAMER, H. (1963). ''Social participation and personal adjustment in old age''. *In* ''Psychological Studies of Human Development'', (Eds R.G. Kohlen and G. Thompson), Appleton-Century-Crofts, New York.

CENTERS, R. (1975). Attitude similarity—dissimilarity as a correlate of heterosexual attraction and love. *J. Marriage Family* **37**, 305–312.

CHALLMAN, R.C. (1932). Factors influencing friendship among preschool children. *Child Dev.* **3**, 146–158.

CHELUNE, G.J. *et al.* (Eds), (1979). ''Self-Disclosure'', Jossey-Bass, San Francisco.

CHRISTENSEN, H.T. and MEISSNER, H.H. (1953). Studies in child spacing: III-Premarital pregnancy as a factor in divorce. *Am. Sociolog. Rev.* **28**, 114–123.

CHRISTENSEN, H.T. and RUBINSTEIN, B.B. (1956). Premarital pregnancy and divorce: a follow-up study by the interview method. *Marriage Family Living* **28**, 114–123.

CICIRELLI, V.G. (1977). Relationship of siblings to elderly persons' feelings and concerns. *J. Geronto.* **32**, 317–322.

CIMBALO, R.S., FALING, V. and MOUSAW, P. (1976). The course of love: A cross-sectional design. *Psycholog. Reports* **38**, 1292–1294.

CLARKE, A.M. and CLARKE, A.D.B. (1976). ''Early Experience: Myth and Evidence'', Open Books, London.

CLARKE, A.M. and CLARKE, A.D.B. (1979). Early experience: its limited effect upon later development. *In* ''The First Year of Life'', (Eds D. Shaffer and J. Dunn), Wiley, London.

CLARKE-STEWART, A. (1973). Interactions between mothers and their young children: characteristics and consequences. *Monographs of the Society for Research in Child Development* **38**, Nos. 6–7.

CLAUSEN, J.S. and CLAUSEN, S.R. (1973). The effects of family size on parents and children. *In* ''Psychological Perspectives on Population'', (Ed. J. T. Fawcett), Basic Books, New York.

CLEVELAND, W. and GIATURCO, D.T. (1976). Remarriage probability after widowhood, a retrospective method. *J. Gerontol.* **31**, 99–103.

COCHRAN, M.M. and BRASSARD, J.A. (1979). Child development and personal social networks. *Child Dev.* **50**, 601–616.

COLEMAN, J. (1974). ''Relationships in Adolescence'', Routledge, London.

CONGALTON, A.A. (1969). "Status and Prestige in Australia", Cheshire, Melbourne.

COOMBS, R.H. (1966). Value consensus and partner satisfaction among dating couples. *J. Marriage Family* **28**, 166–173.

COZBY, P.C. (1973). Self-disclosure: A literature view. *Psycholog. Bull.* **79**, 73–91.

COZBY, P.C. and ROSENBLATT, P.C. (1971). Privacy, love, and in-law avoidance. *Proceedings of the 79th Annual Convention of the American Psychological Association*, 277–278.

CRAWFORD, M. (1977). What is a friend? *New Society* **42**, 116–177.

CRITELLI, J.W. and DUPRE, K.M. (1978). Self-disclosure and romantic attraction. *J. Soc. Psychol.* **106**, 127–128.

CROMWELL, R.E., OLSON, D.H. and FOURNIER, D.G. (1976). Tools and techniques for diagnosis and evaluation in marital and family therapy. *Family Process* **151**, 1–47.

CUBER, J.F. and HARROFF, P.B. (1965). "The Significant Americans: A Study of Sexual Behavior Among the Affluent", Appleton-Century-Crofts, New York.

CUMMING, E. and HENRY, W.E. (1961). "Growing Old", Basic Books, New York.

CUMMING, E. and SCHNEIDER, D.N. (1961). Sibling solidarity a property of American kinship. *Am. Anthropol.* **63**, 498–507.

DAMON, W. (1977). "The Social World of the Child", Jossey-Bass, San Francisco.

DANN, S. (1978). Personal communication to Maureen Shields.

DAVIDON, S.L. (1978). The therapeutic dimensions of friendship between women. *Dissertation Abstracts* **39**, (1-A), 192.

DAVIE, R., BUTLER, N. and GOLDSTEIN, H. (1972). "From Birth to Seven", Longmans (for National Children's Bureau), London.

DAVIS, H. (1978). A description of aspects of mother—infant vocal interaction. *J. Child Psychol. Psychiatry.* **19**, 379–86.

DAVIS, R.W. (1962). The relationship of social preferability to self concept in an aged population. *J. Gerontol.* **17**, 431–436.

DAVITZ, J. and DAVITZ, L. (1976). "Making it from 40 to 50", Random House, New York.

DEAN, D.D. (1961). Romanticism and emotional maturity: a preliminary study. *Marriage Family Living* **23**, 44–45.

DEAN, L.R. (1962). Aging and the decline of affect. *J. Gerontol.* **17**, 440–446.

DE CHATEAU, P. (1979). Long-term effects of early post-partum contact. Paper presented to ISSBD Conference, University of Lund, Sweden.

DERLEGA, V.J. and GRZELAK, J. (1979). Appropriateness of self-disclosure. *In* "Self-Disclosure", (Ed G.J. Chelune), Jossey-Bass, San Francisco.

DERLEGA, V.J., WILSON, M. and CHAIKIN, A.L. (1976). Friendship and disclosure reciprocity. *J. Personality Soc. Psychol.* **34**, 578–582.

DERMER, M. and PYSZCZYNSKI, T.A. (1978). Effects of erotica upon men's loving and liking responses for women they love. *J. Personality Soc. Psychol.* **36**, 1302–1309.

DE ROUGEMONT, D. (1940). "Love in the Western World", Harcourt, New York.

DE ROUGEMONT, D. (1949). The crisis of the modern couple. *In* "The Family: Its Function and Destiny", (Ed. R.N. Anshen), Harper Brothers, New York.

DEUTSCH, M. (1975). Equity, equality, and need : what determines which value will be used as the basis of distributive justice? *J. Soc. Issues* **31**, 137–149.

DE VRIES, E. (1968). Explorations into reciprocity. *In* "Essays on Reciprocity",

(Ed. E. De Vries), Mouton, The Hague.

DION, K.K. and BERSCHEID, E. (1974). Physical attractiveness and peer perception among children. *Sociometry* 37, 1–12.

DION, K.K., BERSCHEID, E. and WALSTER, E.H. (1972). What is beautiful is good. *J. Personality Soc. Psychol.* **24**, 285–290.

DION, K.K. and DION, K.L. (1975). Self-esteem and romantic love. *J. Personality* **43**, 39–57.

DION, K.L. and DION, K.K. (1973). Correlates of romantic love. *J. Consulting Clin. Psychol.* **41**, 51–56.

DION, K.L. and DION, K.K. (1976a). Love, liking, and trust in heterosexual relationships. *Personality Soc. Psychol. Bulletin* **2**, 187–190.

DION, K.L. and DION, K.K. (1976b). The Honi phenomenon revisited: factors underlying the resistance to perceptual distortion of one's partner. *J. Personality Soc. Psychol.* **33**, 170–177.

DION, K.L. and DION, K.K. (1979). Personality and behavioral correlates of romantic love. *In* "Love and Attraction", (Eds M. Cook and G. Wilson), Pergamon, Oxford.

DONELSON, E. and GULLAHORN, J. (1977). "Women: A Psychological Perspective", Wiley, New York.

DOUGLAS, J.W.B. (1964). "The Home and the School", MacGibbon and Kee, London.

DOUGLAS, J.W.B. and GEAR, R. (1976). Children of low birth-weight in the 1946 National Cohort. *Arch. Diseases Child* **51**, 820–827.

DOUGLAS, J.W.B., ROSS, J.M. and SIMPSON, H.R. (1968). "All Our Future", Peter Davies, London.

DOUGLAS, M.A. (1980). Contextual analysis of interaction processes of communication in conflict management. Unpublished Ph. D. dissertation, University of Utah.

DOUVAN, E. and ADELSON, J. (1966). "The Adolescent Experience", Wiley, New York.

DOWN, J.J. (1975). Ageing as exchange. *J. Gerontol.* **30**, 584–594.

DRAPER, M. and LA GAIPA, J.J. (1980). The role of need affiliation in the social exchange of friendship rewards. Unpublished MS.

DRISCOLL, R., DAVIS, K.E. and LIPETZ, M.E. (1972). Parental interference and romantic love: The Romeo and Juliet effect. *J. Personality Soc. Psychol.* **24**, 1–10.

DUCK, S.W. (1973a). "Personal Relationships and Personal Constructs: a Study of Friendship Formation", Wiley, Chichester.

DUCK, S.W. (1973b). Personality similarity and friendship choices: similarity of what, when? *J. Personality* **41**, 543–558.

DUCK, S.W. (1975). Personality similarity and friendship choices by adolescents. *European J. Soc. Psychol.* **5**, 351–365.

DUCK, S.W. (1976). Interpersonal communication in developing acquaintance. *In* "Explorations in Interpersonal Communication", (Ed. G.R. Miller), Sage, Beverly Hills, CA.

DUCK, S.W. (1977a). "The Study of Acquaintance", Teakfields (Saxon House), Farnborough.

DUCK, S.W. (1977b). Tell me where is fancy bred: some thoughts on the study of interpersonal attraction. *In* "Theory and Practice in Interpersonal Attraction", (Ed. S.W. Duck), Academic Press, New York and London.

DUCK, S.W. (1981). Towards a research map for the study of relationship breakdown. *In* "Personal Relationships. 3: Personal Relationships in Disorder", (Eds

R. Gilmour and S.W. Duck), Academic Press, London and New York.

DUCK, S.W. and CRAIG, R.G. (1978). The development of friendship: a longitudinal study. *Br. J. Soc. Clin. Psychol.* **17**, 237-242.

DUCK, S.W., MIELL, D.K. and GAEBLER, H.C. (1980). Attraction and communication in children's interactions. *In* "Friendship and Social Relations in Children", (Eds H.C. Foot, A.J. Chapman and J.R. Smith), Wiley, Chichester and New York.

DUNN, J. (1976). Early differences and later development. *In* "Growing Points in Ethology", (Eds P.P.G. Bateson and R.A. Hinde). Cambridge University Press, Cambridge.

DUNN, J.B. (1977). Patterns of early interaction: continuities and consequences. *In* "Studies in Mother—Infant Interaction", (Ed. H.R. Schaffer), Academic Press, London and New York.

DUNPHY, D.C. (1963). The social structures of urban adolescent peer groups. *Sociometry* **26**, 230-246.

DUVAL, S. and WICKLUND, R.A. (1972). "A Theory of Objective Self-Awareness", Academic Press, New York and London.

DYMOND, F., HUGHES, A.S. and RAABE, V.L. (1952). Measurable changes in empathy with age. *J. Consulting Psychol.* **16**, 202-206.

ECKERMAN, C.O., WHATLEY, J.L. and KUTZ, S.L. (1975). The growth of social play with peers during the second year of life. *Dev. Psychol.* **11**, 42-49.

EDER, D. and HALLINAN, M.T. (1978). Sex differences in children's friendships. *Am. Sociolog. Rev.* **43**, 237-250.

EDWARDS, J.N. and KLEMMACK, D.L. (1973). Correlates of life satisfaction. *J. Gerontol.* **28**, 497-502.

ELLISON, D. (1969). Alienation and the will to live. *J. Gerontol.* **24**, 361-267.

ERIKSON, E.H. (1950). "*Childhood and Society*", Norton, New York.

ERIKSON, E.H. (1968). "Identity, Youth and Crisis", Norton, New York.

ERIKSON, E.H. (1971). Growth and crises of the healthy personality. *In* "Personality in Nature, Society, and Culture", (Eds C. Kluckhohn, H.A. Murray and D.M. Schneider), Alfred A. Knopf, New York.

ERVIN-TRIPP, S. and MITCHELL-KERNAN, C. (1977). "Child Discourse", Academic Press, New York and London.

ESQUILIN, S.C. (1979). Social cognition and children's peer status. Unpublished Doctoral Dissertation, The University of Chicago.

FANAROFF, A., KENNELL, J.H. and KLAUS, M.H. (1972). Follow-up of low birthweight infants — the predictive value of maternal visiting patterns. *Paediatrics* **49**, 287-290.

FANTZ, R.L. (1961). The origin of form perception. *Sci. Am.* **204**, 66-72.

FANTZ, R.L. (1966). Pattern discrimination and selective attention as determinants of perceptual development from birth. *In* "Perceptual Development in Children", (Eds A.H. Kidd and J.L. Rivoire), International Universities Press.

FARBER, B. (1962). "Types of family organization: child-oriented, home-oriented, and parent-oriented. *In* Human Behavior and Social Process", (Ed. A.M. Rose), Houghton Mifflin, Boston.

FESTINGER, L. (1954). A theory of social comparison processes. *Human Relations* **7**, 117-140.

FESTINGER, L., SCHACHTER, S. and BACK, K. (1950). "Social Pressures in Informal Groups: A Study of Human Factors in Housing", Harper and Row, New York.

FIELD, T., GOLDBERG, S., STERN, D. and SOSTEK, A. (Eds), (1980). "High-risk

Infants and Children — Disturbances and Intervention", Academic Press, London and New York.

FINE, G.A. (1980). The natural history of preadolescent male friendship groups. *In* "Friendship and Social Relations in Children", (Eds H.C. Foot, A.J. Chapman and J.R. Smith), Wiley, Chichester.

FINE, G.A. (1981). Friends, impression management and preadolescent behavior. *In* "The Development of Friendship", (Eds S. R. Asher and J. Gottman), Cambridge University Press, Cambridge.

FIORE, A. and SWENSEN, C.H. (1977). Analysis of love relationships in functional and dysfunctional marriages. *Psycholog. Reports* **40**, 707–714.

FIRESTONE, S. (1970). "The Dialectic of Sex", Morrow, New York.

FISCHER, C.S. (1979). Friendship, gender and the life cycle. Unpublished manuscript. (Available from Institute of Urban and Regional Development, University of California, Berkeley, California.)

FISCHER, C.S. and PHILLIPS, S.L. (in press). Who is alone? Social characteristics of people with small networks. *In* "Loneliness: A Sourcebook of Current Theory Research and Therapy", (Eds L.A. Peplau and D. Perlman), Wiley Interscience, New York.

FLAVELL, J.H. (1974). The development of inference about others. *In* "Understanding Other Persons", (Ed. T. Mischel), Wiley, New York.

FLAVELL, J.H. (1977). "Cognitive Development", Prentice-Hall, Englewood Cliffs, New Jersey.

FOA, U.G. and FOA, F.B. (1971). Resource exchange: toward a structural theory of interpersonal communication. *In* "Studies in Dyadic Communication", (Eds A.K. Siegman and B. Pope), Pergamon, New York.

FOGEL, A. (1977). Temporal organisation in mother–infant face-to-face interaction. *In* "Studies in Mother–Infant Interaction", (Ed. H.R. Schaffer), Academic Press, London and New York.

FONTAINE, G. (1975). Causal attribution in simulation vs real situations: When are people logical, when are they not? *J. Personality and Social Psychol.* **32**, 1021–1029.

FOOT, H.C., CHAPMAN, A.J. and SMITH, J.R. (1977). Friendship and social responsiveness in boys and girls. *J. Personality Soc. Psychol.* **35**, 401–411.

FOOT, H.C., CHAPMAN, A.J. and SMITH, J.R. (1980a). "Friendship and Social Relations in Children", Wiley, London and New York.

FOOT, H.C., CHAPMAN, A.J. and SMITH, J.R. (1980b). Patterns of interaction in children's friendships. *In* "Friendship and Social Relations in Children", (Eds H.C. Foot, A.J. Chapman and J.R. Smith), Wiley, London and New York.

FRENCH, J.R.P. Jr and RAVEN, B.H. (1959). The bases of social power. *In* "Group Dynamics", (Eds D. Cartwright and A. Zander), Row, Peterson, Evanston, IL.

FREUD, S. (1921). "Massenpsychologie und Ich-Analyse", Wien.

FREUD, S. (1959). "Sigmund Freud: Collected Papers. Vol 4", Basic Books, New York.

FREUD, A. and DANN, S. (1951). An experiment in group upbringing. *Psychoanalytic Study of the Child* **6**, 127–168.

FRIEDMAN, E.P. (1966). Spatial proximity and social interaction in a home for the aged. *J. Gerontol.* **21**, 566–570.

FRIEDMAN, E.P. (1967). Age, length of institutionalization and social status in a home for the aged. *J. Gerontol.* **22**, 474–477.

FROMM-REICHMAN, F. (1959). Loneliness. *Psychiatry* **22**, 1–15.

FURFEY, P. (1929). Some factors influencing the selection of boys' "chums". *J. Appl. Psychol.* **11**, 47–51.

GAGNE, R. (1977). "The Conditions of Learning", (2nd edn)., Holt, Rinehart and Winston, New York.

GAGNON, J.H. and SIMON, W. (1973). "Sexual Conduct", Aldine, Chicago.

GALLAGHER, J.J. (1958). Social status of children related to intelligence, propinquity, and social perception. *Elementary School J.* **58**, 225–231.

GAMER, E.B. (1978). Children's reports of friendship criteria. Unpublished Doctoral Dissertation, Boston University Graduate School.

GAMER, E., THOMAS, J. and KENDALL, D. (1975). Determinants of friendship across the life-span. *In* "Life, the Continuing Process", (Ed. F. Rebelsky), Knopf, New York.

GARSIDE, R.F., KAY, D.W. and ROTH, M. (1965). Old-age mental disorders in Newcastle-upon-Tyne. A factorial study of medical, psychiatric and social characteristics. *Br. J. Psychiatr.* **111**, 939–946.

GINSBURG, G.P. (1979a). The effective use of role-playing in social psychological research. *In* "Emerging Strategies in Social Psychological Research", (Ed. G.P. Ginsburg), Wiley, New York.

GINSBURG, G.P. (Ed.), (1979b). "Emerging Strategies in Social Psychological Research", Wiley, New York.

GLASS, S.P. and WRIGHT, T.L. (1977). The relationship of extramarital sex, length of marriage, and sex differences on marital satisfaction and romanticism: Athanasiou's data reanalyzed. *J. Marriage Family* **39**, 691–703.

GOLDSTEIN, M.A., KILROY, M.C. and VAN DE VOORT, D. (1976). Gaze as a function of conversation and degree of love. *J. Psychol.* **92**, 227–234.

GOODRICH, D.W., RYDER, R.G. and RAUSH, H.L. (1968). Patterns of newly-wed marriage. *J. Marriage Family* **30**, 383–389.

GORDON, S. (1976). "Lonely in America", Simon and Schuster, New York.

GORE, S. (1978). The effect of social support in moderating the health consequences of unemployment. *J. Health Social Behavior* **19**, 157–165.

GOTTMAN, J.M. (1979). "Marital Interaction : Experimental Investigations", Academic Press, New York and London.

GOTTMAN, J., NOTARIUS, C., MARKMAN, H., BANK, S., YOPPI, B. and RUBIN, M.E. (1976). Behavioral exchange theory and marital decision making. *J. Personality Soc. Psychol.* **34**, 14–23.

GOULD, R., BROUNSTEIN, P. and TAYLOR, D.A. (1978). A re-examination of personalistic disclosure. Paper presented at the 86th Annual Meeting of the American Psychological Association, Toronto, Canada, August, 1971.

GRANEY, N.J. (1975). Happiness and social participation in aging. *J. Gerontol.* **30**, 701–706.

GREEN, E.H. (1933). Group play and quarreling among preschool children. *Child Dev.* **4**, 302–307.

GREENFIELD, S.M. (1965). Love and marriage in modern America: a functional analysis. *Sociolog. Q.* **6**, 361–377.

GROSS, L. (1944). A belief pattern scale for measuring attitudes toward romanticism. *Am. Sociolog. Rev.* **9**, 463–472.

GURIN, G., VEROFF, J. and FELD, S. (1960). "Americans View their Mental Health", Basic Books, New York.

GURMAN, A.S. and KNISKERN, D.P. (1978). Deterioration in marital and family therapy. Empirical, clinical and conceptual issues. *Family Process* **17**, 1, 319.

HALEY, J. (1963). "Strategies of Psychotherapy", Grune and Stratton, New York.

HALEY, J. (Ed.), (1971). "Changing Families: A Family Therapy Reader", Grune and Stratton, New York.

HALL, F., PAWLBY, S.J. and WOLKIND, S.N. (1979). Early life experiences and later mothering behaviour — a study of mothers and their 20-week-old babies. *In* "The First Year of Life", (Eds D. Schaffer and J.B. Dunn), Wiley, Chichester.

HALL, F. and PAWLBY, S.J. (in prep.). Continuity and discontinuity in the behaviour of British working-class mothers and their first-born children. Paper submitted to the ISSBD Conference, Lund, Sweden.

HAMBY, C.S. (1977). The relationship between extraversion and neuroticism and perception of romantic love. Unpublished doctoral dissertation, Virginia Commonwealth University.

HARLOW, H.F. (1971). "Learning to Love", Jossey-Bass, San-Francisco.

HARRÉ, R. and SECORD, P. (1972). "The Explanation of Social Behaviour", Blackwell, Oxford.

HARTUP, W.W. (1970). Peer interaction and social organization. *In* "Carmichael's Manual of Child Psychology", (Ed. P.H. Mussen), Vol 2. Wiley, New York.

HARTUP, W.W. (1975). "The origins of friendships." *In* "Friendship and Peer Relations", (Eds M. Lewis and L.A. Rosenblum), Wiley, New York.

HARTUP, W.W. (1977). Peer interaction and behavioral development of the individual child. *In* "Contemporary Readings in Child Psychology", (Eds E.M. Hetherington and R.D. Parke), McGraw-Hill, New York.

HARTUP, W.W. (1978). Children and their friends. *In* "Issues in Childhood Social Development", (Ed. H. McGurk), Methuen, London.

HARTUP, W.W. (1979). The social worlds of childhood. *Am. Psychol.* **34**, 944–950.

HARTUP, W.W., GLAZER, J.A. and CHARLESWORTH, R. (1967). Peer reinforcement and sociometric status. *Child Dev.* **38**, 1017–1024.

HATFIELD, E. and TRAUPMANN, J. (1981). Intimate relationships: a perspective from Equity Theory. *In* "Personal Relationships. 1: Studying Personal Relationships", (Eds S.W. Duck and R. Gilmour), Academic Press, London and New York.

HAYES, D.S. (1978). Cognitive bases for liking and disliking among preschool children. *Child Dev.* **49**, 906–909.

HEIDER, F. (1958). "The Psychology of Interpersonal Relations", Wiley, New York.

HENDRIX, L. (1979). Kinship, social class and migration. *J. Marriage Family* **41**, 399–407.

HESS, B. (1972). Friendship. *In* "Aging and Society, (vol. 3). A Sociology of Age Stratification", (Eds M.W. Riley, M. Johnson and A. Foner), Russel Sage Foundation, New York.

HETHERINGTON, E.M. COX, M. and COX, R. (1978). The aftermath of divorce. *In* "Mother-Child, Father-Child Relations", (Eds J.H. Stevens and M. Mathews), Nat. Assoc. Edvc. Young Children, Washington.

HILL, C.T., RUBIN, Z. and PEPLAU, L.A. (1976). Break-ups before marriage: the end of 103 affairs. *J. Soc. Issues* **32**, 147–168.

HINDE, R.A. (1976). On describing relationships. J. Child Psychol. Psychiatr. **17**, 1–19.

HINDE, R.A. (1979). "Towards Understanding Relationships", Academic Press, London and New York.

HINDE, R.A. (1981). The bases of a science of interpersonal relationships. *In*

"Personal Relationships. 1: Studying Personal Relationships", (Eds S.W. Duck and R. Gilmour), Academic Press, London and New York.

HINDE, R.A. and SIMPSON, M.J.A. (1975). Qualities of mother—infant relationships in monkeys. *In* "Parent—Infant Interaction", *CIBA Symposium No. 33* (Ed. M.A. Hoffer), Associated Scientific Publishers, Amsterdam.

HINDE, R.A. and SPENCER-BOOTH, M. (1970). Individual differences in the responses of rhesus monkeys to a period of separation from their mothers. *J. Child Psychol. Psychiatr.* **11**, 159–176.

HINDE, R.A. and STEVENSON-HINDE, J. (1976). Towards understanding relationships: dynamic stability. *In* "Growing Points in Ethology", (Eds P.P.G. Bateson and R.A. Hinde), Cambridge University Press, Cambridge.

HINDLEY, C.H. (1979). Problems of interviewing : obtaining retrospective information. *In* "The Recall Method in Social Surveys", (Eds L. Moss and H. Goldstein), University of London Institute of Education, London.

HOBART, C.W. (1958). The incidence of romanticism during courtship. *Social Forces* **36**, 362–67.

HODGSON, J.W. and FISCHER, J.L. (1979). Sex differences in identity and intimacy development in college youth. *J. Youth Adolescence* **8**, 37–50.

HOFFMAN, L.W. and MANIS, J.D. (1978). Influences of children on marital interaction and parental satisfactions and dissatisfactions. *In* "Child Influences on Marital and Family Interactions : a Life-span Perspective", (Eds R.M. Lerner and G.B. Spanier), Academic Press, New York and London.

HOFFMAN, M.L. (1975). Developmental synthesis of affect and cognition and its implications for altruistic motivation. *Dev. Psychol.* **11**, 607–622.

HOWITT, R. (1976). A self—other attributional model of friendship formation. Unpublished Doctoral dissertation, University of Windsor, Canada.

HUESMANN, L.T. and LEVINGER, G. (1976). Incremental exchange theory: A formal model for progression in dyadic interaction. *In* "Advances in Experimental Social Psychology", Vol. 9. (Eds L. Berkowitz and E.H. Walster), Academic Press, New York and London.

HUMPHRIES, T., KINSBOURNE, M. and SWANSON, J. (1978). Stimulant effects on cooperation and social interaction between hyperactive children and their mothers. *J. Child Psychol. Psychiatr.* **19**, 13–22.

HUNT, B. and HUNT, M. (1975). "Prime Time", Stein and Day, New York.

HURLOCK, E.B. (1973). "Adolescent Development" McGraw-Hill, Toronto.

HUSTON, T.L. (1974). A perspective on interpersonal attraction. *In* "Foundations of Interpersonal Attraction", (Ed. T.L. Huston), Academic Press, New York and London.

HUSTON, T.L. and BURGESS, R.L. (1979). Social exchange in developing relationships: an overview. *In* "Social Exchange in Developing Relationships", (Eds R.L. Burgess and T.L. Huston), Academic Press, New York and London.

HUSTON, T.L. and LEVINGER, G. (1978). Interpersonal attraction and relationships. *In* "Annual Review of Psychology", Vol 29. (Eds M.R. Rosensweig and L.W. Port), Annual Review, Palo Alto, California.

HUTT, S.J., HUTT, C., LENARD, H.G., BERNUTH, H.V. and MUNT-JEWERFF, W.J. (1968). Auditory responsivity in the human neonate. *Nature* (London) **218**, 888–890.

IKONNIKOVA, S.N. and LISSOVSKY, V.T. (1969). "Youth on Themselves and their Contemporaries", Leningrad.

ITZIN, F. (1970). Social relations. *In* "The Daily Needs and Interests of Older

People'', (Ed. A.M. Hoffman), C.C. Thomas, Springfield, Illinois.

JACKSON, D.D. (1965). Family rules: The marital *Quid Pro Quo. Arch. Gen. Psychiatr.* **12**, 589–594.

JACKSON, R.M. FISCHER, C.S. and JONES, L.M. (1977). The dimensions of social networks. *In* "Networks and Places: Social Relations in the Urban Setting", (Ed. C.S. Fischer), Free Press, New York.

JONES, E.E. (1964). "Ingratiation", Appleton-Century-Crofts, New York.

JONES, E.E. and ARCHER, R.L. (1976). Are there special effects of personalistic self disclosure? *J. Exp. Soc. Psychol.* **12**, 180–193.

JONES, E.E. and DAVIS, K.E. (1965). From acts to dispositions: The attribution process in person perception. *In* "Advances in Experimental Social Psychology", Vol 2. (Ed. L. Berkowitz), Academic Press, New York and London.

JONES, E.E. and NISBETT, R.E. (1972). The actor and the observer: divergent perceptions of the causes of behavior. *In* "Attribution: Perceiving the Causes of Behavior", (Eds E.E. Jones), General Learning Press, Morristown, N.J.

JONES, E.E. and WORTMAN, C. (1973). "Ingratiation: an Attributional Approach", General Learning Press, Morristown, N.J.

JONES, O.H.M. (1979). A comparative study of mother — child communication with Down's syndrome and normal infants. *In* "The First Year of Life", (Eds D. Shaffer and J. Dunn), Wiley, Chichester.

JONES, W.T. (1961). "The Romantic Syndrome", Martinus Nijhoff, The Hague.

JOURARD, S.M. (1959). Healthy personality and self disclosure. *Mental Hygiene* **44**, 449–507.

JOURARD, S.M. (1971). "Self Disclosure", Wiley, New York.

JOURARD, S.M. and LANDSMAN, M.J. (1960). Cognition, cathexis and the "dyadic effect" in men's self disclosing behavior. *Merrill-Palmer Q. Behavioural Dev.* **6**, 178–186.

KAHANA, E. and COE, R.M. (1969). Dimensions of conformity, a multidisciplinary view. *J. Gerontol.* **24**, 76–81.

KALVEBOER, A.F. (1979). Neurobehavioural findings in pre-school and school-aged children in relation to pre- and peri-natal complications. *In* "The First Year of Life", (Eds D. Shaffer and J. Dunn), Wiley, Chichester.

KANDEL, D.B. (1978). Similarity in real-life adolescent friendship pairs. *J. Personality Soc. Psychol.* **36**, 306–312.

KANDEL, D.B. and LESSER, G.S. (1972). "Youth in Two Worlds: United States and Denmark", Jossey-Bass, San Francisco.

KANIN, E.J., DAVIDSON, K.D. and SCHECK, S.R. (1970). A research note on male — female differentials in the experience of heterosexual love. *J. Sex Res.* **6**, 64–72.

KATZ, J. *et al.* (1968). "No Time for Youth: Growth and Constraint in College", San Francisco.

KAUFMAN, D.R. (1978). Associational ties in academe: some male and female differences. *Sex Roles* **4**, 9–21.

KAYE, K. (1977). Toward the origin of dialogue. *In* "Studies in Mother — Infant Interaction", (Ed. H.R. Schaffer), Academic Press, London and New York.

KELLEY, H.H. (1972). Attribution in social interaction. *In* "Attribution: Perceiving the Causes of Behavior", (Ed. E.E. Jones), General Learning Press, Morristown, N.J.

KELLEY, H.H. (1979). "Personal Relationships: Their Structures and Processes", Lawrence Erlbaum Association, N.J.

KELLEY, H.H. and THIBAUT, J.W. (1978). "Interpersonal Relations: A Theory of Interdependence", Wiley, New York.

KELVIN, P. (1977). Predictability, power and vulnerability in interpersonal attraction. *In* "Theory and Practice in Interpersonal Attraction", (Ed. S.W. Duck), Academic Press, London and New York.

KENDON, A. (1979). "Some theoretical and methodological aspects of the use of film in the study of social interaction". *In* "Emerging Strategies in Social Psychological Research", (Ed. G.P. Ginsburg), Wiley, New York.

KENNELL, J.H., TRAUSE, M.A. and KLAUS, M.H. (1975). Evidence for a sensitive period in the human mother. *In* "Parent — Infant Interaction", CIBA Symposium No. 33. (Ed. M.A. Hoffer), Associated Scientific Publishers, Amsterdam.

KEPHART, W.M. (1967). Some correlates of romantic love. *J. Marriage Family* **29**, 470-474.

KEPHART, W.M. (1970). The "dysfunctional" theory of romantic love: a research report. *J. Comparative Family Studies* **1**, 26-36.

KERCKHOFF, A.C. (1974). The social context of interpersonal attraction. *In* "Foundations of Interpersonal Attraction", (Ed. T.L. Huston), Academic Press, New York and London.

KERCKHOFF, A.C. (1977). More of the same. *Contemporary Psychol.* **22**, 189-190.

KERCKHOFF, A.C. and DAVIS, K.E. (1962). Value consensus and need complementarity in mate selection. *Am. Sociolog. Rev.* **27**, 295-303.

KIMMEL, D.C. (1979). Relationship initiation and development: A life-span developmental approach. *In* "Social Exchange in Developing Relationships", (Eds R.L. Burgess and T.L. Huston), Academic Press, New York and London.

KLAUS, M.H., TRAUSE, M.A. and KENNELL, J.H. (1975). Does human maternal behaviour after delivery show a characteristic pattern? *In* "Parent — Infant Interaction", *CIBA Foundation Symposium, 33.* (Ed. M.A. Hoffer), Associated Scientific Publishers, Amsterdam.

KLEIN, D.M., JORGENSEN, S.R. and MILLER, B.C. (1978). Research methods and developmental reciprocity in families. *In* "Child Influences on Marital and Family Interaction", (Eds R.M. Lerner and G.B. Spanier), Academic Press, New York and London.

KLEINKE, C.L. (1979). Effects of personal evaluation. *In* "Self-Disclosure", Chelune, G.J. *et al* (eds.). Jossey-Bass, San Francisco.

KLINGER, E. (1977). "Meaning and Void : Inner Experience and the Incentives in People's Lives", University of Minnesota Press, Minneapolis, Minnesota.

KNOX, D.H. and SPORAKOWSKI, M.J. (1968). Attitudes of college students toward love. *J. Marriage Family* **30**, 638-642.

KOHLBERG, L. (1969). Stage and sequence: the cognitive-developmental approach in socialization. *In* "Handbook of Socialization Theory and Research", (Ed. D. Goslin), Rand McNally, Chicago.

KOLB, W.L. (1950). Family sociology, marriage education, and the romantic love complex. *Social Forces* **29**, 65-72.

KOMAROVSKY, M. (1976). "Dilemmas of Masculinity: A Study of College Youth", Norton, New York.

KON, I.S. (1978). Psychology of adolescent homosexuality. *In* "Diagnosis, Treatment and Prevention of Sexual Disturbances", The Works of Moscow Scientific Research Institute of Psychiatry, **81**, 54-64 (Russian).

KON, I.S. (1979a). "The Adolescent Psychology", Moscow (Russian).

KON, I.S. (1979b). "Freundschaft", Rowholt, Hamburg.

KON, I.S. and LOSENKOV, V.A. (1978). Friendship in adolescence: Values and behavior. *J. Marriage Family* **40**, 143–155.

KONDRATJEVA, S.V. (1975). Age and sex differences in the school-children understanding of their age-mates. *In* "Theoretical and Applied Problems of Psychology of Anthropognostics", Krasnodar. (Russian).

KONNER, M. (1975). Relations among infants and juveniles in comparative perspective. *In* "Friendship and Peer Relations", (Eds M. Lewis and L.A. Rosenblum), Wiley, New York.

KRASNOR, L.R. and RUBIN, K.H. (1978). Preschoolers' verbal and behavioral solutions to social problems. Paper read at meeting of the Canadian Psychological Association, Ottawa, Ontario.

KREISMAN, D. (1970). Social interaction and intimacy in pre-schizophrenic adolescents. *In* "The Psychopathology of Adolescence", (Eds J. Zubin and A.M. Freedman), Grune and Stratton, New York and London.

KREUTZ, H. (1964). Jugend: Gruppenbild und Objektwahl. Dissertation.

KUHLEN, R.G. and HOULIHAN, N.B. (1965). Adolescent heterosexual interests in 1942 and 1963. *Child Dev.* **36**, 1049–1052.

KUHN, D. (1978). Mechanisms of cognitive and social development: One psychology or two? *Human Dev.* **21**, 92–118.

LABOV, W. and FANSHEL, D. (1977). "Therapeutic Discourse — Psychotherapy as Conversation", Academic Press, New York and London.

LA GAIPA, J.J. (1977a). Testing a multidimensional approach to friendship. *In* "Theory and Practice in Interpersonal Attraction", (Ed. S.W. Duck), Academic Press, London and New York.

LA GAIPA, J.J. (1977b). Interpersonal attraction and social exchange. *In* "Theory and Practice in Interpersonal Attraction", (Ed. S.W. Duck), Academic Press, London and New York.

LA GAIPA, J.J. (1979). A developmental study of the meaning of friendship in adolescence. *J. Adolescence* **2**, 201–213.

LA GAIPA, J.J. (1981). A systems approach to personal relationships. *In* "Personal Relationships", (Eds S.W. Duck and R. Gilmour), Academic Press, London and New York.

LA GAIPA, J.J. and BIGELOW, B.J. (1972). The development of childhood friendship expectations. Paper read at meeting of the Canadian Psychological Association, Montreal.

LA GAIPA, J.J. and WOOD, H.D. (1973). The perception of friendship by socially accepted and rejected children. Paper read at meeting of the Eastern Psychological Association, Washington, D.C.

LA GAIPA, J.J. and WOOD, H.D. (1976). The development and validation of the Children's Friendship Expectancy Inventory. Unpublished MS.

LA GAIPA, J.J. and WOOD, H.D. (1981). Friendship in disturbed adolescents. *In* "Personal Relationships. 3: Personal Relationships in Disorder", (Eds R. Gilmour and S.W. Duck), Academic Press, London and New York.

LAMB, M.E. (1979). The effects of the social context on dyadic social interaction. *In* "Social Interaction Analysis : Methodological Issues", (Eds M.E. Lamb, S.J. Suomi and G.R. Stephenson), University of Wisconsin Press, Madison, Wisconsin.

LAMB, M.E., SUOMI, S.J. and STEPHENSON, G.R. (Eds), (1979). "Social Interaction Analysis : Methodological Issues", University of Wisconsin Press, Wisconsin.

LAMBERT, W.E., YACKLEY, A. and HEIN, R.N. (1971). Child training values of English Canadian and French Canadian parents. *Canad. J. Behavioral Sci.* **3**, 217–236.

LANGFORD, M. (1962). "Community Aspects of Housing for the Aged", Cornell University Center for Housing and Environmental Studies, Ithaca, New York.

LAOSA, L.M. and BROPHY, J.E. (1972). Effects of sex and birth order on sex-role development and intelligence among kindergarten children. *Dev. Psychol.* **6**, 409–415.

LASSWELL, T.E. and LASSWELL, M.E. (1976). I love you but I'm not in love with you. *J. Marriage Family Counselling* **38**, 211–224.

LAUMANN, E.O. (1973). "Bonds of Pluralism: The Form and Substance of Urban Social Networks", Wiley, New York.

LAWTON, M.P. (1977). Environmental and health influences on aging and behavior. *In* "Handbook of the Psychology of Aging", (Eds J.E. Birren and K.W. Schaie), Van Nostrand Reinhold, New York.

LAWTON, M.P. and SIMON, B.B. (1968). The ecology of social relationships in housing for the elderly. *Gerontologist* **8**, 108–115.

LEBO, D. (1953). Some factors said to make for happiness in old age. *J. Clin. Psychol.* **9**, 385–387.

LEE, J.A. (1974). The styles of loving. *Psychol. Today* **8**, 43–51.

LEE, J.A. (1977). A typology of styles of loving. *Personality Soc. Psychol. Bull.* **3**, 173–182.

LEHR, E. (1978). The relationship of quantity and quality of exposure to peers and children's success at role taking. Unpublished Doctoral Dissertation, University of Maryland.

LEIDERMAN, P.H. and SEASHORE, M.J. (1975). Mother — Infant separation: some delayed consequences. *In* "Parent — Infant Interaction", CIBA Symposium No. 33. (Ed. M.A. Hoffer), Associated Scientific Publishers, Amsterdam.

LEMON, B.W., BENGTSON, V.L. and PETERSON, J.A. (1972). An exploration of the activity theory of aging, activity types and life satisfaction among inmovers to a retirement community. *J. Gerontol.* **27**, 511–523.

LERNER, M.J., MILLER, D.T. and HOLMES, J.G. (1976). Deserving and the emergence of forms of justice. *In* "Advances in Experimental Social Psychology", Vol 9. (Eds L. Berkowitz, E. Walster), Academic Press, New York and London.

LERNER, R.M. (1979). A dynamic interactional concept of individual and social relationship development. *In* "Social Exchange in Developing Relationships", (Eds R.L. Burgess and T.L. Huston), Academic Press, New York and London.

LERNER, R.M. and SPANIER, G.B. (1978). "Child Influences on Marital and Family Interaction: A Life-span Perspective", Academic Press, New York and London.

LEVINGER, G. (1972). Little sandbox and big quarry: comment on Byrne's paradigmatic spade for research on interpersonal attraction. *Representative Res. Soc. Psychol.* **3**, 3–19.

LEVINGER, G. (1979). A social exchange view on the dissolution of pair relationships. *In* "Social Exchange in Developing Relationships", (Eds R.L. Burgess and T.L. Huston), Academic Press, New York and London.

LEVINGER, G., SENN, D.J. and JORGENSEN, B.W. (1970). Progress toward permanence in courtship: A test of the Kerckhoff — Davis hypothesis. *Sociometry* **33**, 427–433.

LEVINGER, G. and SNOEK, J.E. (1972). "Attraction in Relationships: A New Look at Interpersonal Attraction", General Learning Press, Morristown, N.J.

LEVINSON, D.J. (1978). "The Seasons of a Man's Life", Alfred A. Knopf, New York.

LEWIN, K. (1951). "Field Theory in Social Science", Harper Row, New York.

LEWIS, M. and ROSENBLUM, L. (Eds). (1979). "The Child and its Family", Plenum Press, New York.

LEWIS, R.A. (1972). A developmental framework for the analysis of premarital dyadic formation. *Family Process* 11, 17-48.

LEWIS, R.A. (1973). A longitudinal test of a developmental framework for premarital dyadic formation. *J. Marriage Family* 35, 16-25.

LEWIS, R.A. (1975). A reply to Rubin and Levinger's Critique of Lewis' test of the PDF developmental framework. *J. Marriage Family* 37, 9-11.

LEWIS, R.A. (1978). Emotional intimacy among men. *J. Soc. Issues* 34, 108-121.

LILAR, S. (1965). "Aspects of Love in Western Society", McGraw-Hill, New York.

LINDSEY, J.S.B. (1976). Balance Theory: possible consequences of number of family members. *Family Process* 15, 245-249.

LIVESLEY, W.J. and BROMLEY, D.B. (1973). "Person Perception in Childhood and Adolescence", Wiley, Chichester and New York.

LOEVINGER, J. and WESSLER, R. (1970). "Measuring Ego Development, I: Construction and Use of a Sentence Completion Test", Jossey-Bass, San Francisco.

LOTT, A.J. and LOTT, B.E. (1971). The power of liking: consequences of inter-personal attitudes derived from liberalized view of secondary reinforcement. *In* "Advances in Experimental Social Psychology", Vol 5. (Ed. L. Berkowitz), Academic Press, New York and London.

LOTT, A.J. and LOTT, B.E. (1974). The role of reward in the formation of positive interpersonal attitudes. *In* "Foundations of Interpersonal Attraction", (Ed. T.L. Huston), 171-189. Academic Press, New York and London.

LOWENTHAL, M.F. (1964). Social isolation and mental illness in old age. *Am. Sociolog. Rev.* 20, 54-70.

LOWENTHAL, M.F. and BOLER, D. (1965). Voluntary versus involuntary social withdrawal. *J. Gerontol.* 2, 363-371.

LOWENTHAL, M.F. and HAVEN, C. (1968). Interaction and adaptation: intimacy as a critical variable. *Am. Sociolog. Rev.* 33, 20-30.

LOWENTHAL, M.F., THURNHER, M., CHIRIBOGA, D. and Associates (1975). "Four Stages of Life: A Comparative Study of Women and Men Facing Transitions", Jossey-Bass, San Francisco.

LOWRIE, S.H. (1965). Early marriage: premarital pregnancy and associated factors. *J. Marriage Family* 27, 48-56.

LUGINBUHL, J.E. and CROWE, D.H. (1975). Causal attributions for success and failure. *J. Personality Soc. Psychol.* 31, 86-93.

LUTTE, G. (avec la collaboration de S. Sarti et G. Kempen), (1971). "Le Moi Idéal de l'Adolescent. Recherche Génétique, Differencielle et Culturelle dans Sept Pays d'Europe", Dessart, Bruxelles.

LYNCH, J.J. (1977). "The Broken Heart: the Medical Consequences of Loneliness", Basic Books, New York.

LYNCH, M.A. (1975). Ill health and child abuse. *Lancet* ii, 317-319.

LYNESS, J.F. (1978). Styles of relationships among unmarried men and women. *Sociolog. Abstracts* 26, 1249.

MAAS, H.S. (1968). Preadolescent peer relations and adult intimacy. *Psychiatry* 31, 161-172.

MACCOBY, E. and JACKLIN, C. (1974). "The Psychology of Sex Differences", Stanford University Press, Stanford.

MACFARLANE, A. (1975). Olfaction in the development of a social preference in the human neonate. *In* "Parent — Infant Interaction", CIBA Symposium No. 33. (Ed. M.A. Hoffer), Associated Scientific Publishers, Amsterdam.

MADDOX, G. (1965). Fact and artifact: evidence bearing on disengagement theory from the Duke geriatric project. *Human Dev.* **8**, 117–130.

MANNARINO, A.P. (1976). Friendship patterns and altruistic behavior in preadolescent males. *Dev. Psychol.* **12**, 555–556.

MARCIA, J.E. (1976). "Studies in Ego Identity", Simon Fraser University, Canada.

MARLOWE, R.A. (1973). Effects of environment on elderly state hospital relocatees. Paper delivered at annual meeting of the Pacific Sociological Association, Arizona, May, 1973.

MARNEY, J.D. (1975). "Aging in American Society", Institute of Gerontology, Ann Arbor, Michigan.

MASLOW, A.H. (1955). Deficiency motivation and growth motivation. *In* "Nebraska Symposium on Motivation", (Ed. M.R. Jones), University of Nebraska Press, Lincoln.

MATTESON, D.R. (1977). Exploration and commitment: Sex differences and methodological problems in the use of identity status categories. *J. Youth Adolescence* **6**, 353–374.

MAUDRY, M. and NEKULA, M. (1939). Social relations between children of the same age during the first two years of life. *J. Genetic Psychol.* **54**, 193–215.

MCCALL, G.J. (1970). The social organization of relationships. *In* "Social Relationships", (Ed. G.J. McCall), Aldine, Chicago.

MCCALL, G.J. and SIMMONS, J. (1977). "Identities and Interactions", (Rev. ed.). Free Press, New York.

MCCANDLESS, B.R. (1970). Socialization. *In* "Experimental Child Psychology", (Eds H.W. Reese and L.P. Lipsitt), Academic Press, New York and London.

MCCARTHY, B. (1981). Studying Personal Relationship. *In* "Personal Relationships. 1: Studying Personal Relationships", (Eds S.W. Duck and R. Gilmour), Academic Press, London and New York.

MCGOVERN, J.S. (1975). Psychological approaches to loving: A.H. Maslow's levels of maturation in dyadic attachment orientation. Unpublished Doctoral Dissertation, Harvard University.

MCKENNA, H.V., HOFSTAETTER, P.R. and O'CONNOR, J.P. (1956). The concepts of the ideal self and of the friend. *J. Personality* **24**, 262–271.

MCKINNEY, J.P. (1968). The development of choice stability in children and adolescents. *J. Genetic Psychol.* **113**, 78–83.

MENNINGER, K. (1963). "The Vital Balance", Viking, New York.

MESSER, M. (1967). The possibility of an age-concentrated environment becoming a normative system. *Gerontologist* **7**, 247–251.

MIELL, D.E., DUCK, S.W. and LA GAIPA, J.J. (1979). Interactive effects of sex and timing of self disclosure. *Br. J. Soc. Clin. Psychol.* **18**, 355–362.

MILLAR, F.E. and ROGERS, L.E. (1976). A relational approach to interpersonal communication. *In* "Explorations in Interpersonal Communication", (Ed. G.R. Miller), Sage, Beverly Hills, CA.

MILLER, G.R. (1976). Foreword. *In* "Explorations in Interpersonal Communication", (Ed. G.R. Miller), Sage, Beverly Hills, CA.

MILLER, W.R. and ARKOWITZ, H. (1977). Anxiety and perceived causation in social success and failure experiences: disconfirmation of an attribution hypothesis in two experiments. *J. Abnormal Psychol.* **86**, 665–668.

MISCHEL, W. (1973). Toward a cognitive social learning reconceptualization of personality. *Psycholog. Rev.* **80**, 252–283.

MITCHELL, W.L. (1972). Lay observations on retirement. *In* "Retirement", (Ed. F.M. Carp), Behavioral Publications, New York.

MONTAIGNE, M.E. DE (1952). *In* "Great Books of the Western World", Vol 25. (Ed. R.M. Hutchins), Encyclopaedia Britannica, Chicago.

MORTON, T.L. (1978). Intimacy and reciprocity of exchange: a comparison of spouses and stranger. *J. Personality Social Psychol.* **36**, 72–81.

MORTON, T.L., ALEXANDER, J.F. and ALTMAN, I. (1976). Communication and relationship definition. *In* "Explorations in Interpersonal Communication", (Ed. G.R. Miller), Sage, Beverley Hills, CA.

MUDRIK, A.V. (1975). Age and sex differences in the meaning of the word "understanding" in school-children. *In* "Theoretical and Applied Problems of the Psychology of Anthropognostics", Krasnodar (Russian).

MUNNICHS, H. (1964). Loneliness, isolation and social relations in old age: a pilot survey. *Vita Humana* **7**, 228–238.

MUNRO, B. and ADAMS, G.R. (1978). Correlates of romantic love revisited. *J. Psychol.* **98**, 211–214.

MURSTEIN, B.I. (1970). Stimulus-Value-Role: a theory of marital choice. *J. Marriage Family* **32**, 465–481.

MURSTEIN, B.I. (1971). A theory of marital choice and its applicability to marriage adjustment. *In* "Theories of Attraction and Love", (Ed. B.I. Murstein), 100–151. Springer, New York.

MURSTEIN, B.I. (1974a). "Love, Sex, and Marriage through the Ages", Springer, New York.

MURSTEIN, B.I. (1974b). Clarification of obfuscation on conjugation: a reply to criticism of the SVR theory of marital choice. *J. Marriage Family* **36**, 231–234.

MURSTEIN, B.I. (1976). "Whom Will Marry Whom? Theories and Research in Marital Choice", Springer, New York.

MURSTEIN, B.I. (1977). The Stimulus-Value-Role (SVR) Theory of Dyadic Relationships. *In* "Theory and Practice in Interpersonal Attraction", (Ed. S.W. Duck), Academic Press, London and New York.

MURSTEIN, B.I. and SPITZ, L.T. (1973–1974). Aristotle and friendship: a factor-analytic study. *Interpersonal Dev.* **4, 1**, 21–34.

MUSGRAVE, P.W. and REID, G.R.B. (1971). Some measures of children's values. *Soc. Sci. Information* **10**, 137–153.

MUSSEN, P.H., CONGER, J.J. and KAGAN, J. (1969). "Child Development and Personality", Harper and Row, New York.

NAHEMOW, L. and LAWTON, M.P. (1975). Similarity and propinquity in friendship formation. *J. Personality Soc. Psychol.* **32**, 205–213.

NEISWENDER, M., BIRREN, J.E. and SCHAIE, K.W. (1975). Age and the experience of love in adulthood. Paper presented at American Psychological Association Convention.

NELSON, K. (1973). Structure and strategy in learning to talk. *Monographs of the Society for Research in Child Development* No. 149.

NEUBAUER, P.B. and FLAPAN, D.F. (1976). Developmental groupings in latency children. *J. Acad. Child Psychol.* **15, 4**, 646–664.

NEUGARTEN, B.L. (Ed.), (1968). "Middle Age and Aging: a Reader in Social Psychology", University of Chicago Press, Chicago.

NEUGARTEN, B.L. and DATAN, N. (1974). The middle years. *In* "American Handbook of Psychiatry", Vol 1. (Ed. S. Arieti), Basic Books, New York.

NEWCOMB, M.D. (1981). Heterosexual cohabitation relationships. *In* "Personal Relationships. 1: Studying Personal Relationships", (Eds S.W. Duck and R. Gilmour) Academic Press, London and New York.

NEWCOMB, T.M. (1968). Interpersonal balance. *In* "Theories of Cognitive Consistency: A Source Book", (Eds R.P. Abelson), Rand/McNally, Chicago.

NEWMAN, B.M. and NEWMAN, P.R. (1975). *Development through Life: A Psychosocial Approach.* Dorsey Press, Homewood, Illinois.

NEWSON, J. (1977). An intersubjective approach to the systematic description of mother — infant interaction. *In* "Studies in Mother — Infant Interaction", (Ed. H.R. Schaffer), Academic Press, London and New York.

NEWSON, J. (1979). Intentional behaviour in the young infant. *In* "The First Year of Life", (Eds D. Shaffer and J. Dunn), Wiley, Chichester.

NEWSON, J. and NEWSON, E. (1970). "Four Years Old in an Urban Community", Allen and Unwin, London.

NEWSON, J. and NEWSON, E. (1975). Intersubjectivity and the transmission of culture: on the social origins of symbolic functioning. *Bull. Br. Psychol. Soc.* **28**, 437-446.

NEWSON, J. and NEWSON, E. (1976). "Seven Years Old in the Home Environment", Allen and Unwin, London.

NEWSON, J. and NEWSON, E. (1978). "Seven Years Old in the Home Environment", Penguin, Harmondsworth, Middlesex, England.

NEWSON, J. and SHOTTER, J. (1974). How babies communicate. *New Society* **29**, No. 618, 345-347.

NIEBANCK, P.L. (1965). "The Elderly in Older Urban Areas", University of Pennsylvania Institute for Environmental Studies, Philadelphia, PA.

OAS, N.J. (1975). Romantic and rational love attitudes and their relationship to self-concept congruence. Unpublished Doctoral Dissertation, United States International University.

O'NEILL, N. and O'NEILL, G. (1972). "Open Marriage: A New Life Style for Couples", Evans, New York.

ORLOFSKY, J.L., MARCIA, J.E. and LESSER, I.M. (1973). Ego identity status and the intimacy versus isolation crisis of young adulthood. *J. Personality Soc. Psychol.* **27**, 211-219.

O'ROURKE, J.F. (1965). Field and Laboratory: the decision making behaviour of family groups in two experimental conditions. *Sociometry* **26**, 422-435.

OSOFSKY, J.D. (1971). Children's influences upon parental behaviour: An attempt to define the relationship with the use of laboratory tasks. *Genetic Psychology Monographs* **83**, 147-169.

PACKARD, V. (1972). "A Nation of Strangers", David McKay, New York.

PALMORE, E. and KIVETT, V. (1977). Change in life satisfaction: a longitudinal study of persons aged 46-70. *J. Gerontol.* **32**, 311-316.

PALMORE, E. and LUIKART, C. (1972). Health and social factors related to life satisfaction. *J. Health Soc. Behavior* **13**, 68-80.

PAM, A. (1970). A field study of psychological factors in college courtships. Unpublished Doctoral Dissertation, State University of New York at Buffalo.

PAM, A., PLUTCHIK, R. and CONTE, H. (1973). Love: a psychometric approach. *Proceedings of the 81st Annual Convention of the American Psychological Association*, **8**, 159-160.

PAPOUSEK, H. and PAPOUSEK, M. (1975). Cognitive aspects of preverbal social interactions between human infants and adults. *In* "Parent–Infant Interaction", (Ed. M.A. Hoffer), *CIBA Foundation Symposium, No. 33.* Associated Scientific Publishers, Amsterdam.

PAPOUSEK, H. and PAPOUSEK, M. (1977). Mothering and the cognitive headstart: psychobiological considerations. *In* "Studies in Mother–Infant Interaction", (Ed. H.R. Schaffer), Academic Press, London and New York.

PARKE, R.D. (1979). Emerging themes for social–emotional development. *Am. Psychol.* **34**, 930–931.

PARLEE, M.B. and the Editors of *Psychology Today* (1979). The friendship bond. *Psychology Today* **13**, 43–54.

PARSONS, T. and BALES, R.F. (1955). "Family, Socialization and Interaction Process", Free Press, Glencoe, Illinois.

PARSONS, T. and BALES, R.F. (1956). "Family, Socialization and Interaction Processes". Routledge/Kegan Paul, London.

PARTEN, M.B. (1932). Social participation among preschool children. *J. Abnormal Soc. Psychol.* **27**, 243–269.

PATAKI, F. (1970). The social world of secondary school students. *Hungarian Q.* **39**.

PATTERSON, G.R. (1977). Naturalistic observations in clinical assessment. *J. Abnormal Child Psychol.* **5**, 309–322.

PATTERSON, G.R. and MOORE, D. (1979). Interactive patterns as units of behavior. *In* "Social Interaction Analysis: Methodological Issues", (Eds M.E. Lamb, S.J. Suomi and G.R. Stephenson), University of Wisconsin Press, Madison, Wisconsin.

PAWLBY, S.J. (1977a). Imitative interaction. *In* "Studies in Mother–Infant Interaction", (Ed. H.R. Schaffer), Academic Press, London and New York.

PAWLBY, S.J. (1977b). A study of imitative interaction between mothers and their infants. Ph.D. Thesis, University of Notthingham.

PAWLBY, S.J. and HALL, F. (1980). Early interactions and later language development of children whose mothers come from disrupted families of origin. *In* "High-Risk Infants and Children: Disturbances and Interactions", (Ed. T. Field), Academic Press, London and New York.

PAYNE, S.L. (1953). The Cleveland survey of retired men. *Personnel Psychol.* **6**, 81–110.

PEEVERS, B.H. and SECORD, P.F. (1973). Developmental changes in attribution of descriptive concepts to persons. *J. Personality Soc. Psychol.* **27**, 120–128.

PEPLAU, L.A. (1979). Homosexual love relationships: a comparison of men and women. Presented at Pacific Sociological Association Convention, Anaheim.

PEPLAU, L.A. and COCHRAN, S.D. (1980). Value orientations in the intimate relationships of gay men. *J. Homosexuality* (in press).

PEPLAU, L.A., COCHRAN, S.D., ROOK, K. and PADESKY, C. (1978). Loving women: attachment and autonomy in lesbian relationships. *J. Soc. Issues* **34**, 7–27.

PEPLAU, L.A. and PERLMAN, D. (1979). 'Blueprint for a social psychological theory of loneliness'. *In* "Love and Attraction: an International Conference", (Eds M. Cook and G. Wilson), Pergamon, New York.

PEPLAU, L.A., RUBIN, Z. and HILL, C.T. (1977). Sexual intimacy in dating relationships. *J. Soc. Issues* **33**, 86–109.

PERLMAN, D., GERSON, A.C. and SPINNER, B. (1978). "Loneliness" among senior citizens: an empirical report. *Essence* **2**, 239–248.

PERLMAN, D. and PEPLAU, A.L. (1981). Loneliness. *In* "Personal Relationships. 3: Relationships in Disorder", (Eds R. Gilmour and S.W. Duck), Academic Press, London and New York.

PETERS, R.S. (1974). Personal understanding and personal relationships. *In* "Understanding Other Persons", (Ed. T. Mischel), Blackwell, Oxford.

PETROWSKY, M. (1976). Marital status, sex, and the social networks of the elderly. *J. Marriage Family* **38**, 749-756.

PFEIFFER, E. (1977). 'Psychopathology and social pathology'. *In* "Handbook of the Psychology of Aging", (Eds J.E. Birren and K.W. Schaie), Reinhold Van Nostrand, New York.

PHARES, E.J. (1976). "Locus of Control in Personality", General Learning Press, Morristown, NJ.

PHILBLAD, C.T. and ADAMS, D.L. (1972). Widowhood, social participation and life satisfaction. *Aging Human Dev.* **3**, 323-330.

PHILLIPS, D.L. (1969). Social class, social participation and happiness. A consideration of interaction opportunities and investment. *Sociol. Q.* **10**, 3-21.

PHILLIPS, G.M. and METZGER, N.J. (1976). "Intimate Communication." Allyn and Bacon, Boston, MA.

PIAGET, J. (1932). "The Moral Judgment of the Child", Free Press, New York.

PINEO, P.C. (1961). Disenchantment in the later years of marriage. *Marriage Family Living* **23**, 3-11.

POWERS, E.A. and BULTENA, G.L. (1976). Sex differences in intimate friendships of old age. *J. Marriage Family* **38**, 739-747.

PRICE, G.H., DABBS, J.M., CLOWER, B.J. and RESIN, R.P. (1974). At first glance: or, is physical attractiveness more than skin deep? Paper presented at Eastern Psychological Association Convention, Philadelphia.

PROVENCE, S. and LIPTON, R. (1962). "Infants in Institutions", International University Press, New York.

RAUSH, H.L., BARRY, W.A., HERTEL, R.K. and SWAIN, M.A. (1974). "Communication, Conflict, and Marriage", Jossey-Bass Publisher, San Francisco.

REEDY, M.N., BIRREN, J.E. and SCHAIE, K.W. (1976). Love in adulthood: Beliefs versus experience. Paper presented at American Psychological Association Convention, 1976.

REISMAN, J.M. (1979). "Anatomy of friendship", Irvington, New York.

REISMAN, J.M. and SHORR, S.E. (1978). Friendship claims and expectations among children and adults. *Child Dev.* **49**, 913-916.

REISS, I.L. (1964). Premarital sexual permissiveness among Negroes and whites. *Am. Sociolog. Rev.* **29**, 688-698.

RHEINGOLD, H.L. (1961). The Effect of environmental stimulation upon social and exploratory behaviour in the human infant. *In* "Determinants of Infant Behavior" Vol I (Ed. B. Foss), Wiley, New York.

RICHARDS, M.P.M. (1979). Effects on development of medical interventions and separation of newborns from their parents. *In* "The First Year of Life", (Eds D. Shaffer and J. Dunn), Wiley, Chichester.

RICHARDS, M.P.M. and ROBERTSON, N.R.C. (1978). Admission and discharge policies for special care units. *In* "Early Separation and Special Care Nurseries", (Eds F.S.W. Brimblecombe, M.P.M. Richards and N.R.C. Robertson), Clinics in Developmental Medicine, Heinemann.

RILEY, M.W. and FONER, A. (1968). "Aging and Society. Volume One: An Inventory of Research Findings", Russell Sage Foundation, New York.

RISKIN, J. and FAUNCE, E.G. (1972). An evaluative review of family interaction research. *Family Process*, **114**, 365-453.

ROBERTSON, J. and ROBERTSON, J. (1968). Young children in brief separation: III. John, aged seventeen months nine days in a residential nursery. Tavistock

Child Development Research Unit.

ROBSON, K.S. (1967). The role of eye-to-eye contact in maternal-infant attachment. *J. Child Psychol. Psychiatr.* **8**, 13–25.

ROGERS, C. (1978) The child's perception of other people. *In* "Issues in Childhood Social Development", (Ed. H. McGurk), Methuen, London.

ROSE, A.M. (1962). The subculture of the aging: a framework for research in social gerontology. In "Older Persons and their Social World", (Eds A.M. Rose and W.A. Paterson) F.A. Davis, Philadelphia.

ROSENBERG, G.S. (1970). "The Worker Grows Old", Jossey-Bass, San Francisco.

ROSENBLATT, P.C. (1967). Marital residence and the functions of romantic love. *Ethnology* **6**, 471–480.

ROSENBLATT, P.C. and COZBY, P.C. (1972). Courtship patterns associated with freedom of choice of spouse. *J. Marriage Family* **34**, 689–695.

ROSENBLUM, L.A., COE, C.L. and BROMLEY, L.J. (1975). Peer relations in monkeys: The influence of social structure, gender and familiarity. *In* "Friendship and Peer Relations", (Eds M. Lewis and L. Rosenblum), Wiley, New York.

ROSENMAYR, L. (1963). Familienbeziehungen und Freizeitgewohnheiten jugend-licher Arbeiter. Eine Untersuchung von 800 Lehrlinge in Wien und Niederoster-reich. Wien.

ROSOW, I. (1967). "Social Integration of the Aged", Free Press, New York.

ROSOW, I. (1968). Housing and local ties of the aged. *In* "Middle Age and Ageing", (Ed. B.L. Neugarten), University of Chicago Press, Chicago.

ROSOW, I. (1970). Old people: Their friends and neighbors. *Am. Behavioral Scientist* **14**, 59–69.

ROTTER, J.B. (1975). Some problems and misconceptions related to the construct of internal versus external control of reinforcement. *J. Consulting Clin. Psychol.* **43**, 56–67.

RUBENSTEIN, C., SHAVER, P. and PEPLAU, L.A. (1979). Loneliness. *Human Nature* (February) 58–65.

RUBIN, K.H. (1978). Role-taking in childhood: some methodological considerations. *Child Dev.* **49**, 428–433.

RUBIN, K.H. and MAIONI, T.L. (1975). Play preference and its relationship to ego-centrism, popularity, and classification skills in preschoolers. *Merrill-Palmer Q.* **21**, 171–179.

RUBIN, K.H. and PEPLER, D.J. (1980). The relationship of child's play to social-cognitive growth and development. *In* "Friendship and Social Relations in Children", (Eds H.C. Foot, A.J. Chapman, and J.R. Smith), Wiley, Chichester and New York.

RUBIN, L.R. (1976). "Worlds of Pain: Life in the Working Class Family" Basic Books, New York.

RUBIN, Z. (1970). Measurement of romantic love. *J. Personality Soc. Psychol.* **16**, 265–273.

RUBIN, Z. (1973). "Liking and Loving", Holt, Rinehart and Winston, New York.

RUBIN, Z. (1980). "Children's Friendships", Harvard University Press, Cambridge, MA.

RUBIN, Z., HILL, C.T., PEPLAU, L.A. and DUNKEL-SCHETTER, C. (in press). Self-disclosure in dating couples: sex roles and the ethic of openness. *J. Marriage Family.*

RUBIN, Z. and LEVINGER, G. (1974). Theory and data badly mated: a critique of Murstein's SVR and Lewis's PDF models of mate selection. *J. Marriage Family* **36**, 226–231.

RUBIN, Z., PEPLAU, L.A. and HILL, C.T. (1980). Loving and Leaving: sex differences in romantic attachments. *Sex Roles* (in press).

RUTTER, M. (1972). "Maternal Deprivation Reassessed", Penguin Books, Harmondsworth, Middlesex.

RUTTER, M. and MADGE, N. (1976). "Cycles of Disadvantage", Heinemann, London.

RYCHLAK, J. (1965). The similarity, compatibility, or incompatibility of needs in interpersonal selection. *J. Personality Soc. Psychol.* **2**, 334-340.

RYDER, R.G. (1970a). Dimensions of early marriage. *Family Process* **9**, 51-68.

RYDER, R.G. (1970b). A topography of early marriage. *Family Process* **9**, 385-402.

SACKS, H., SCHEGLOFF, E.A. and JEFFERSON, G. (1974). Simplest systematics for the organisation of turntaking for conversation. *Language* **50**, 696-735.

SCANZONI, J. (1979). Social exchange and behavioral interdependence. *In* "Social Exchange in Developing Relationships", (Eds R.L. Burgess and T.L. Huston), Academic Press, New York and London.

SCARLETT, H.H., PRESS, A.N. and CROCKETT, W.H. (1971). Children's descriptions of peers; a Wernerian development analysis. *Child Dev.* **42**, 439-453.

SCHAEFER, E.S. and BAYLEY, N. (1963). Maternal behaviour, child behaviour and their intercorrelation from infancy through adolescence. *Monographs of the Society for Research in Child Development*, (87), Vol. 28, (3).

SCHAEFER, E.S., BELL, R.Q. and BAYLEY, N. (1959). Development of a maternal behaviour research instrument. *J. Genetic Psychol.* **95**, 83-104.

SCHAFFER, H.R. (1971). "The Growth of Sociability", Penguin Books, Harmondsworth, Middlesex.

SCHAFFER, H.R.(1974). Early social behaviours and the study of reciprocity. *Bull. Br. Psychol. Soc.* 209-216.

SCHAFFER, H.R., COLLIS, G.M. and PARSONS, G. (1977). Vocal interchange and visual regard in verbal and pre-verbal children. *In* "Studies in Mother-Infant Interaction", (Ed. H.R. Schaffer), Academic Press, London and New York.

SCHAFFER, H.R. and EMERSON, P.E. (1964). The development of social attachments in infancy. *Monograph of Social Research into Child Development*, (29), No. 94.

SCHAFFER, H.R. and HARGREAVES, D. (1978). Young people in society: a research initiative by the SSRC. *Bull. Br. Psycholog. Soc.* **31**, 91-94.

SCHAIE, K.W. (1965). A general model for the study of developmental problems. *Psycholog. Bull.* **64**, 92-107.

SCHLAEGEL, J., SCHOOF-TAMS, K. and WOLCZAK L. (1975). Beziehungen zwischen Jungen und Mädchen. *Sexualmedizin* **4**, 205-218.

SCHLIEPER, A. (1975). Mother-child interaction at home. *Am. J. Orthopsychiatr.* **45**, 468-472.

SCHOOLER, K.K. (1975). Response of the elderly to environment: a stress theoretic perspective. *In* "Theory Development in Environment and Aging", (Eds P.G. Windley and G. Ernst), Gerontological Society, Washington, D.C.

SCOPERA, C.A., HORROCKS, J.E. and THOMPSON, G.G. (1963). A study of friendship fluctuations of college students. *J. Genetic Psychol.* **102**, 151-157.

SEAGOE, M.V. (1933). Factors influencing the selection of associates. *J. Educat. Res.* **27**, 32-40.

SEARS, R.R., MACCOBY, E.E. and LEVIN, H. (1957). "Patterns of Child Rearing", Row, Peterson, New York.

SELIGMAN, C.R. (1974). A test of three reward models of liking and loving. Unpublished Doctoral Dissertation, Northwestern University.

SELMAN, R.L. (1976) Toward a structural analysis of developing interpersonal relations concepts: research with normal and disturbed preadolescent boys. *In* "Minnesota Symposia on Child Psychology", Vol. 10, (Ed. A.D. Pick), The University of Minnesota Press, Minneapolis, Minnesota.

SELMAN, R.L. and JAQUETTE, D. (1977). Stability and oscillation in interpersonal awareness: A clinical-developmental analyses. *In* "Nebraska Symposium on Motivation", Vol. 25, (Ed. C.B. Keasey), University of Nebraska Press, Lincoln, Nebraska.

SELMAN, R.L. and SELMAN, A.P. (1979). Children's ideas about friendship: a new theory. *Psychology Today* 114, 71-80.

SEVERY, L.J. and DAVIS, K.E. (1971). Helping behavior among normal and retarded children. *Child Dev.* 42, 1017-1031.

SEYFRIED, B.A. (1977). Complementarity in interpersonal attraction. *In* "Theory and Practice in Interpersonal Attraction", (Ed. S.W. Duck), Academic Press, New York and London.

SHANTZ, C.U. (1975). The development of social cognition. *In* "Review of Child Development Theory and Research",Vol 5, (Ed. E.M. Hetherington), University of Chicago Press, Chicago.

SHEEHY, G. (1974) "Passages", E.P. Dutton, New York.

SHERMAN, S. (1975a). Mutual assistance and support in retirement housing. *J. Gerontol.* 30, 479-483.

SHERMAN, S. (1975b). Patterns of contacts for residents of age-segregated and age-integrated housing. *J. Gerontol.* 30, 103-107.

SHIELDS, M.M. (1978). Some communicational skills of young children. *In* "Recent Advances in the Psychology of Language", (Eds R.N. Campbell and P.T. Smith), Plenum Press, New York.

SHOTTER, J. and GREGORY, S. (1976). On First gaining the idea of oneself as a person. *In* "Life Sentences", (Ed. R. Harré) Wiley, Chichester.

SHULMAN, N. (1975). Life-cycle variations in patterns of close relationships. *J. Marriage Family* 37, 813-921.

SMITH, E.A. (1962). "American Youth Culture", Free Press, Glencoe, Illinois.

SMITH, P.K. and CONNOLLY, K. (1972). Patterns of play and social interaction in pre-school children. *In* "Ethological Studies of Child Behavior", (Ed. N. Blurton Jones), Cambridge University Press, Cambridge.

SMITH, W.M. (1954). Family plans for later years. *Marriage Family Living* 16, 36-40.

SNOW, C. (1972). Mother's speech to children learning language. *Child Dev.* 43, 549-565.

SNYDER, J.J. (1977). A reinforcement analysis of interaction in problem and non-problem children. *J. Abnormal Psychol.* 86, 528-535.

SOLOMON, D., ALI, F.A., KFIR, D., HOULIHAN, K.A. and YAEGER, J. (1972). The development of democratic values and behavior among Mexican-American children. *Child Dev.* 43, 625-638.

SPANIER, G.B. (1972). Romanticism and marital adjustment. *J. Marriage Family* 34, 481-487.

SPANIER, G.B. (1976). Use of recall data in survey research on human sexual behavior. *Soc. Biol.* 23, 244-253.

SPEIER, M. (1971). The everyday world of the child. *In* "Understanding Everyday Life", (Ed. J.D. Douglas), Routledge and Kegan Paul, London.

STEPHENS, J. (1975). Society of the alone. *J. Gerontol.* 30, 230-235.

STERN, D. (1971). A micro-analysis of mother-infant interaction behaviour regulating social contact between a mother and her three-and-a-half-month-old twins. *J. Am. Acad. Child Psychiatr.* **10**, 501–517.

STERN, D. (1974). Mother and infant at play: the dyadic interaction involving facial, vocal and gaze behaviours. *In* "The Effect of the Infant on its Caregiver", (Eds M. Lewis and L. Rosenblum), Wiley, New York.

STERN, D. (1977). "The First Relationship: Infant and Mother", Fontana/Open Books.

STERN, D., BEEBE, B., JAFFE, J. and BENNETT, S.L. (1977). The infant's stimulus world during social interaction. In "Studies in Mother — Infant Interaction", (Ed. H.R. Schaffer), Academic Press, London and New York.

STEVENS, L. and JONES, E.E. (1976). Defensive attribution and the Kelley cube. *J. Personality Soc. Psychol.* **34**, 809–920.

STRAUSS, E.S. (1974). Couples in love. Unpublished Doctoral Dissertation, University of Massachusetts.

STRAUSS, M.A. and BROWN, B.W. (1978). "Family Measurement Techniques", University of Minnesota Press, Minnesota.

STROEBE, W., INSKO, C.A., THOMPSON, V.D. and LAYTON, B.D. (1971). Effects of physical attractiveness, attitude similarity, and sex on various aspects of interpersonal attraction. *J. Personality Soc. Psychol.* **18**, 79–91.

STUEVE, C.A. and GERSON, K. (1977). Personal relations across the life-cycle. *In* "Networks and Places: Social Relations in the Urban Setting", (Ed. C.S. Fischer), Free Press, New York.

SUDMAN, S. and BRADBURN, N.M. (1974). "Response Effects in Surveys", Aldine, Chicago.

SULLIVAN, J.S. (1953). "The Interpersonal Theory of Psychiatry", Norton, New York.

SUOMI, S.J. (1977). Development of attachment and other social behaviors in rhesus monkeys. *In* "Attachment Behavior", (Eds T. Alloway, P. Pliner and L. Krames), Plenum Press, New York and London.

SURRA, C.A. (in prep.) Changes in dyadic and social network interaction from pre-marriage to marriage. MS in preparation.

SWENSEN, C.H. (1972). The behavior of love. *In* "Love Today: A New Exploration", (Ed. H.A. Otto), Association Press, New York.

SWENSEN, C.H. and GILNER, F. (1973). A scale for measuring the behavior and feelings of love. *In* "The 1973 Annual Handbook for Group Facilitators", (Eds J.W. Pfeiffer and J.E. Jones), University Associates, Iowa City.

TAGIURI, R. (1958). Social preference and its perception. *In* "Person Perception and Interpersonal Behavior", (Eds R. Tagiuri and L. Petrullo), 316–336. Stanford University Press, Stanford, California.

TAPLIN, P. and REID, J.B. (1977). Changes in parent consequence as a function of family intervention. *J. Consulting Clin. Psychol.* **45**, 973–981.

TAYLOR, D.A. (1979). Motivational bases. *In* "Self-Disclosure", (Eds G.J. Chelune *et al.*) Jossey-Bass, San Francisco.

TAYLOR, S.E. and KOIVUMAKI, J.H. (1976). The perception of self and others: Acquaintanceship, affect, and actor-observer differences. *J. Personality Soc. Psychol.* **33**, 403–408.

TENBRUCK, F. (1964). Freundschaft. Ein Beitrag zu einer Soziologie der persönlichen Beziehungen. *Kölner Zeitschrift für Soziologie und Sozialpsychologie* **16**, 431–456.

TESSER, A. and PAULHUS, D.L. (1976). Toward a causal model of love. *J. Person-*

ality and Soc. Psychol. **34**, 1095–1105.

THARP, R.G. (1963). Psychological patterning in marriage. *Psycholog. Bull.* **60**, 97–117.

THEODORSON, G.A. (1965). Romanticism and motivation to marry in the U.S., Singapore, Burma, and India. *Social Forces* **44**, 17–28.

THIBAUT, J.W. and KELLEY, H.H. (1959). "The Social Psychology of Groups", Wiley, New York.

THOMAN, E.B. (1975). How a rejecting baby affects mother–infant synchrony. *In* "Parent–Infant Interaction" CIBA Symposium No. 33. (Ed. M.A. Hoffer), Associated Scientific Publishers, Amsterdam.

THOMPSON, W.B. and NISHIMURA, R. (1952). Some determinants of friendship. *J. Personality* **20**, 305–314.

TIGER, L. (1969). "Men in Groups", Random House, New York.

TIZARD, B. and HODGE, J. (1978). The effect of early institutional rearing on the development of eight-year-old children. *J. Child Psychol. Psychiatr.* **19**, 99–118.

TIZARD, B. and REES, J. (1974). A comparison of the effects of adoption, restoration to the natural mother, and continued institutionalisation on the cognitive development of four year-old children. *Child Dev.* **45**, 92–99.

TIZARD, B. and REES, J. (1975). The effect of early institutional rearing on the behaviour problems and affectional relationships of four year-old children. *J. Child Psychol. Psychiatr.* **16**, 61–73.

TOFFLER, A. (1970). "Future Shock", Random House, New York.

TOMÉ, H.R. (1972). "Le Moi et l'Autre dans la Conscience de l'Adolescent", Delachoux et Niestlé, Neuchatel.

TOMÉ, H.R. (1973). A propos des personnes significatives dans l'entourage des adolescents. Etude différencielle. *L'Orientation scolaire et professionnelle* **2**.

TREAS, J. and VAN HILST, A. (1976). Marriage and remarriage rates among older Americans. *Gerontologist* **16**, 12–136.

TREVARTHEN, C. (1977). Descriptive analyses of infant communicative behaviour. *In* "Studies in Mother–Infant Interaction", (Ed. H.R. Schaffer), Academic Press, London and New York.

TREVARTHEN, C., HUBLEY, P. and SHEERAN, L. (1975). Les activités innées du nourrisson. *La Recherche* **6**, 447–458.

TRIGER, R.D. (1971). Psychological peculiarities of the young adolescent's interpersonal relations. Summary of a thesis. Moscow.

TUCKER, L.R. (1966). Learning theory and multivariate experiment: Illustration by determination of generalized learning curves. *In* "Handbook of Multivariate Experimental Psychology", (Ed. R.B. Cattell), Rand McNally, Chicago.

TURNER, R.H. (1970). "Family Interaction", Wiley, New York.

UDRY, J.R. (1971). "The Social Context of Marriage", (2nd edn), Lippincott, Philadelphia.

UDRY, J.R. (1974). "The Social Context of Marriage", (3rd end), Lippincott, Philadelphia.

VALLIANT, G.E. (1977). "Adaptation to Life", Little Brown, Boston, MA.

VALLIANT, G.E. (1978). Natural history of male psychological health: VI. Correlates of successful marriage and fatherhood. *Am. J. Psychiatr.* **135**, 653–659.

VANGGAARD, T. (1972). "Phallós: A Symbol and its History in the Male World", International University Press, New York.

VERBRUGGE, L.M. (1977). The structure of adult friendship choices. *Social Forces* **56**, 576–597.

WALDROP, M.F. and HALVERSON, C.F. (1975). Intensive and extensive peer behavior: longitudinal and cross-sectional analysis. *Child Dev.* **46**, 19–26.

WALLER, W. (1938). "The Family: A Dynamic Interpretation", Gordon, New York.

WALSTER, E. and WALSTER, G.W. (1978). "A New Look at Love", Addison-Wesley, Reading, MA.

WALSTER, E.H., WALSTER, G.W. and BERSCHEID, E. (1978). "Equity: Theory and Research", Allyn and Bacon, Boston, MA.

WATERMAN, C.R. and NEVID, J.S. (1977). Sex differences in the resolution of the identity crisis. *J. Youth Adolescence* **5**, 337–342.

WATZLAWICK, P., BEAVIN, J.H. and JACKSON, D.D. (1967). "Pragmatics of Human Communication", W.W. Norton, New York.

WEISS, R.L. and MARGOLIN, G. (1977). Assessment of marital conflict and accord. *In* "Handbook of Behavioral Assessment", (Eds A.R. Ciminero, K.J. Calhoun and H.E. Adams), Wiley, New York.

WELLS, G. (1979). Influences of the home on language development. *In* "Language and Learning at School and Home", (Ed. A. Davis), SSRC/Heineman, London.

WERNER, H. (1957). The concept of development from a comparative and organismic point of view. *In* "The Concept of Development", (Ed. D.B. Harris), University of Minnesota Press, Minneapolis, Minnesota.

WHITEBOURNE, S.K. and WATERMAN, A.S. (1979). Psychosocial development during the adult years: age and cohort comparisons. *Dev. Psychol.* **15**, 373–378.

WHITEN, A. (1977). Assessing the effects of perinatal events on the success of the mother–infant relationship. *In* "Studies in Mother–Infant Interaction", (Ed. H.R. Schaffer), Academic Press, London and New York.

WINCH, R.F. (1955). The theory of complementary needs in mate-selection: Final results on the test of the general hypothesis. *Am. Sociolog. Rev.* **20**, 552–555.

WINCH, R.F. (1958). "Mate Selection: A Study of Complementary Needs", Harper and Row, New York.

WINCH, R.F. (1974). Complementary needs and related notions about voluntary mate-selection. In "Selected Studies in Marriage and the Family", (Eds R.F. Winch and G.B. Spanier), Holt, Rinehart and Winston, New York.

WINCH, R.F., KTSANES, T. and KTSANES, V. (1954). The theory of complementary needs in mate-selection: an analytic and descriptive study. *Am. Sociolog. Rev.* **19**, 241–249.

WOLKIND, S.N., HALL, F. and PAWLBY, S.J. (1977). Individual differences in mothering behaviour: a combined epidemiological and observational approach. *In* "Epidemiological Approaches in Child Psychiatry", (Ed. P.J. Graham), Academic Press, London and New York.

WOOD, H.D. and LA GAIPA, J.J. (1978). Predicting behavioural types in preadolescent girls from psychosocial development and friendship values. Paper read at meeting of the Canadian Psychological Association, Toronto.

WOOD, V. and ROBERTSON, J.F. (1978). Friendship and kinship interaction: Differential effect on the morale of the elderly. *J. Marriage Family* **40**, 367–375.

WORTMAN, C.B., ADESMAN, P., HERMAN, E. and GREENBERG, R. (1976). Self disclosure: an attributional perspective. *J. Personality Soc. Psychol.* **33**, 184–191.

WRIGHT, H.J. and PAYNE, T.A.N. (1979). "An Evaluation of a School Psychological Service. The Portsmouth Pattern", Hampshire Education Department, England.

WRIGHT, P.H. (1978). Toward a theory of friendship based on a conception of self. *Human Commun. Res.* **4**, 196–207.

WRIGHT, P.H. (1979). Personal communication, 28 November, to John Reisman.

WURZBACHER, G. (1968). "Gesellungsformen der Jugend", Juventa, Munchen.

WYLIE, R.C. (1961). "The Self Concept: A Critical Survey of Pertinent Research Literature", University of Nebraska Press, Lincoln, Nebraska.

YANKELOVICH, D. (1972). "The Changing Values on Campus. Political and Personal Attitudes of Today's College Students", New York.

YARROW, L.J., GOODWIN, M.S., MANHEIMER, H. and MILON, I.D. (1974). Infant experiences and cognitive and personality development at ten years. *In* "The Competent Infant", (Eds L.J. Stone, H.T. Smith and L.B. Murphy), Tavistock Publications, London.

YARROW, M.R. and WAXLER, C.Z. (1979). Observing interaction: A confrontation with methodology. *In* "The Analysis of Social Interactions: Methods, Issues, and Illustrations", (Ed. R.B. Cairns), Lawrence Erlbaum, Hillsdale, N.J.

YARROW, M.Y., CAMPBELL, J.D. and BURTON, R.V. (1970). Recollections of childhood: a study of the retrospective method. *Monograph of the Society for Research in Child Development (138), Vol. 35, (5).*

YOON, G.H. (1978). The natural history of friendship: sex differences in best-friendship patterns. *Dissertation Abstracts* **39**, (3-B), 1553.

YOUNISS, J. (1978). The nature of social development: a conceptual discussion of cognition. *In* "Issues in Childhood Social Development", (Ed. H. McGurk), Methuen, London.

YOUNISS, J. (1980). "Parents and Peers in Social Development", University of Chicago Press, Chicago.

YOUNISS, J. and VOLPE, J. (1978). A relational analysis of children's friendships. *New Directions Child Dev.* **1**, 1–22.

ZAJONC, R.B. (1968). Attitudinal effects of mere exposure. *J. Personality Soc. Psychol.* **9**, 1–29.

ZAZZO, B. (1966). "Psychologie Différencielle de l'Adolescence", Presses Universitaires, Paris.

ZBOROWSKI, M. and EYDE, L.E. (1962). Aging and social participation. *J. Gerontol.* **17**, 424–430.

ZIMBARDO, P. (1977). "Shyness: What It Is, What To Do About It", Addison-Wesley, Reading, MA.

Author Index

277

Subject Index